Ranald S. Mackenzie on the Texas Frontier

RANALD SLIDELL MACKENZIE, 1863 OR 1864
(U. S. Signal Corps, Brady Collection, National Archives)

Ranald S. Mackenzie
on the
Texas Frontier

by
ERNEST WALLACE
Foreword by DAVID J. MURRAH

TEXAS A&M UNIVERSITY PRESS
COLLEGE STATION

Originally published in 1964 by the West Texas Museum Association, Lubbock

The paper used in this book meets the minimum requirements
of the American National Standard for Permanence
of Paper for Printed Library Materials, Z39.48-1984.
Binding materials have been chosen for durability.

Library of Congress Cataloging-in Publication Data

Wallace, Ernest.
    Ranald S. Mackenzie on the Texas frontier / by Ernest Wallace ;
foreword by David J. Murrah.
        p.   cm.
    Originally published: Lubbock : West Texas Museum Association,
1964. With new foreword.
    Includes index.
    ISBN 0-89096-487-4
    1. Mackenzie, Ranald Slidell, 1840–1889.   2. Soldiers–Texas–
Biography.   3. Comanche Indians–Wars.   4. Kiowa Indians–Wars.
5. Frontier and pioneer life–Texas.   6. Texas–History–1846–1950.
I. Title.
F391.M167W3   1993
976.4'06'092–dc20
[B]   92-29063
                                                         CIP

TO PATRICK EDWARD BARTON

Contents

Illustrations and Maps

Foreword to the 1993 Edition

Ernest Wallace did not consider *Ranald S. Mackenzie on the Texas Frontier* to be his best book, but there is no doubt that the action-filled narrative represents Ernest Wallace at his best. Painstakingly researched and highly detailed, this brief study of one phase of the life of the dashing cavalry officer not only documents Mackenzie's conquest of the Southern Plains but also provides a glimpse into the short, colorful, and unusual life of Ranald Slidell Mackenzie.

Born in New York City on July 27, 1840, Ranald Mackenzie enjoyed a splendid West Point career, finishing first of twenty-eight in the 1862 class. During the Civil War, young Mackenzie proved himself to be a valiant soldier, decorated after being wounded in both shoulders during his first battle, the Second Battle of Bull Run, in August, 1862. In March, 1863, he received the first of many rapid on-the-field promotions, including brevets of captain and major following the Battle of Gettysburg. In June, 1864, he obtained his first command as colonel of the 2nd Connecticut Volunteers Infantry Regiment. During the remainder of the war, Mackenzie was wounded five more times, but each time he quickly returned to service, and by the end he had been appointed brevet major general of U.S. Volunteers. He was only twenty-four years old.

After a short civilian life following the war, Mackenzie in

vii

February, 1866, resumed his military career and soon found himself in Texas as commander of the 41st Infantry Regiment serving on the Rio Grande. In February, 1871, he assumed command of the 4th Cavalry headquartered at Fort Concho, at present-day San Angelo, Texas. There he launched his career as an Indian fighter and during the next three years played the major role in subduing the Southern Plains Comanche, Kiowa, and Cheyenne, culminated by the Red River War of 1874.

After peace had returned to the Texas plains, the army used Mackenzie as a troubleshooter in the Black Hills following Custer's defeat. He then returned to the Texas Rio Grande before moving to Colorado to deal with the Utes, and later to Arizona to quell the Apaches. In 1882, Mackenzie was finally promoted to brigadier general, but by that time his physical and mental condition had strangely deteriorated, and in December, 1883, he was committed to a mental hospital. Three months later, Mackenzie was retired from the army. He did not recover from his illness and died January 19, 1889, at the age of forty-eight.

In a paper he presented at the 1982 meeting of the West Texas Historical Association, Charles Kenner, one of Wallace's brightest students, said that Mackenzie was "the most uniformly successful and least publicized Indian fighter of the 1870s, . . . almost the exact antithesis of the least successful and most publicized—George Custer." According to Kenner,

> They had one giant difference—the amount of grist left for the historian's mill. Whereas Custer specialized in penning lengthy, self-serving, and bombastic descriptions of his campaigns, Mackenzie was exasperatingly terse. As one critic noted, he was a modest, dedicated commander efficient in every respect except one—as a writer of reports. It was as though he considered that the time required for writing detailed memorandums could be better spent preparing for the next of his lightning moves against the Indians.

Furthermore, as Kenner noted, Mackenzie left no memoirs and little correspondence, and very few of his men wrote accounts of their service under him: "Scholars concentrated on the flamboyant and easy-to-research items . . . with Chivington and Custer playing the star roles. Meanwhile, the Mackenzies languished in relative obscurity." Fortunately for those of us who love the history of the American West, the dedicated Ernest Wallace discovered the dedicated Ranald Mackenzie and left for us this wonderfully written biography in spite of the paucity of sources.

The opportunity to become a college professor did not come easily to Ernest Wallace. A product of rural East Texas, he was born June 11, 1906, in Daingerfield, where his parents farmed. Educated in one- and two-room schools, Wallace read every book available so that, as he said in a 1980 speech, "by the time of the Treaty of Versailles, I had some knowledge of the geography and history of both the U.S. and Europe, enough that my mother kept telling me to become, like [Woodrow] Wilson, a historian and college president."

After graduating from Hughes Springs High School, Wallace entered East Texas State Teachers College at Commerce in 1924. After one year, however, his savings were exhausted and he sought work as a teacher. The situation drew him to the White Flat School in Nolan County east of Abilene and into West Texas, where he would ultimately spend his life teaching and researching the colorful history of the area. "That same school year [1925–26] two major events cemented my ties to West Texas," Wallace noted. "Texas Tech opened its doors to students and from the first seemed to cast a magnetic spell, and I married a charming West Texas girl [Ellen Kegans]."

But Texas Tech was to elude Wallace for ten years. In 1926, he returned to Commerce to continue his education. He also taught at Linden and Cornett, where he served for seven years as superintendent and "principal, coach, teacher, janitor, counselor, general flunky, and Sunday School teacher." In 1932, he completed his B.S. degree in mathematics at East Texas State.

Mathematcis? "Mathematics was easier and less time-consuming to teach," Wallace explained, "and it was almost impossible to obtain a high school math teacher. During my last summer of under-graduate study, however, I had a history course under Professor J. G. Smith . . . who extended me the honor of taking over his very large class part of the period. . . . I enjoyed every minute of it and concluded that the study of the past would be more interesting than impersonal figures."

In spite of the Great Depression, Wallace enrolled at Texas Tech in the summer of 1933, intending to pursue a Master's degree in math, education, and history, but by the time he completed his work, history had won the day. Meanwhile, he taught and coached the 1935–36 year at Tulia. When a vacancy in the History Department at Texas Tech occurred in September, 1936, Wallace was invited for an interview. "The president [Bradford Knapp], after I assured him I would get the Ph.D. as quickly as possible, said to the Dean, 'Dean, I believe there will be no harm in having one of our former students on the departmental faculty. Give him a contract,'" Wallace recalled. "I could have shouted for joy with more enthusiasm and sincerity than a repentant sinner in a Holy Roller summer camp meeting."

Wallace soon enrolled in the Ph.D. program at the University of Texas, attracted there by the eminent Walter Prescott Webb. Originally intending to minor in political science, Wallace changed his mind after W. C. Holden encouraged him to enroll in anthropology, because the discipline was a part of the History Department at Tech. "That decision was to change my future," Wallace recalled. By 1942, he had finished his dissertation, a biography of Charles DeMorse. The study of De-Morse, who was editor of the *Clarksville Standard*, Confederate veteran, and aggressive Reconstruction politician, gave Wallace a broad background for his future work in Texas history. The work became Wallace's first book, originally published in 1943

as *Charles DeMorse: Pioneer Editor and Statesman* by the fledgling
Texas Tech Press. The book was reprinted by the Wright Press
in 1985.

During his distinguished fifty-year career at Texas Tech University in Lubbock, Ernest Wallace produced eleven major
books. He is best remembered for his classic study, *The Comanches: Lords of the South Plains*, written with E. Adamson Hoebel
and published in 1952. Made possible in part by Wallace's decision to minor in anthropology, the book won many prestigious recognitions, including nomination for the Pulitzer Prize.
Now in its ninth printing from the University of Oklahoma Press,
The Comanches is still praised as a model study by both anthropologists and historians.

In a sense, *The Comanches* has always overshadowed the body
of other significant Wallace studies, including that of Ranald
Mackenzie. After the publication of *The Comanches*, Wallace
was chosen by the U.S. Department of Justice to serve as a consultant relative to land suits filed by the Kiowa, Comanche, and
Kiowa-Apache tribes. As a result, Wallace produced for the
government a major study entitled, "The Habitat and Range of
the Kiowa, Comanche, and Apache Indians before 1867." The
487-page manuscript, completed in 1959, remains unpublished.

Armed with the background of his previous studies, Wallace
then joined several of his colleagues at Texas Tech in producing the six-volume *Saga of Texas Series*, completed in 1965.
Wallace's contribution was a wonderful little book entitled
Texas in Turmoil, 1849–1875, and its chapters include an engrossing essay on the Texas frontier, which presents one of the best
available accounts of the tumultuous conflicts of the period.
Although considerable effort had been made to document the
closing of the frontier in West Texas, particularly through the
works of Rupert N. Richardson, Carl Coke Rister, and J. Evetts
Haley, none had sufficiently covered the story of the final Indian campaigns, and particularly of the Red River War of 1874.
But in the summer of 1961, Wallace spent three exhaustive

weeks in the National Archives in Washington compiling information on Mackenzie and the West Texas frontier. With this
he had ample material for *Texas in Turmoil.*

Wallace's work in the National Archives also led to an important and fortuitous discovery. There he met a young graduate
student from the University of New Mexico, Lessing Nohl,
who also was researching Mackenzie. By accident, Nohl had
found misplaced among the record series in the National Archives several reports, including one entitled "Memoranda of
the March of the First Column from Camp on the Fresh Fork
of the Brazos," which covered the events of September 20–29,
1874, which, of course, included the famous battle of Palo Duro
Canyon. "It was a rare discovery," Wallace noted in a 1980
speech, "for even the best informed authorities did not know
what had happened to them. Here was the base for a book that
hopefully would be a contribution to western historiography."

The discovery of the new materials gave Wallace the opportunity to apply to his research the methodology of the Von
Ranke school, as he noted in retrospect: "The official records
provided the major portion of the material, the writings of eye-
witnesses were used, but with caution, geography was checked
and rechecked from army and modern geological maps, and by
on-the-spot personal inspections, including Caprock inclines,
streams, lakes, and distances." Wallace also put his graduate
students to work on the topic. In 1963 Adrian Anderson, who
would later enjoy a long career at Lamar University, completed
his Master's thesis, which covered the crucial years of Mackenzie's 1873–74 activities. Anderson also served as Wallace's research assistant for the project.

Apparently, Wallace's original intention was to publish a full
biography of Mackenzie, but he soon fell to the temptation of
getting a part of the story in print before he had completed his
research. Invited by his mentor and colleague at Texas Tech,
W. C. Holden, to tell of Mackenzie's experiences in West
Texas for publication in the *Museum Journal* of the West Texas

Museum Association, Wallace agreed to write the history. But from Holden he secured a promise that the Museum Association would also issue the work as a hard-cover book.

The idea of a West Texas study also appealed to Wallace, because, as a champion of local history, he strongly felt that "a region should know and understand its own history." Here he saw the opportunity to tell the dramatic story played out on the plains and surrounding canyons of the Llano Estacado.

Wallace completed his manuscript in September, 1964, and the Mackenzie book appeared in the summer of 1965 — 958 copies in paper cover as a double volume of the *Museum Journal* and 525 copies in hard cover as a monograph. Stamped silver on a blue cover, the hard-bound issues proved to be a handsome, but very limited, edition, and the press run sold out quickly. Wallace later bound in green some of the original paper-cover issues of the *Museum Journal*.

Because the publisher had no national marketing plan, few individuals had the opportunity to review the book, but those who did were unanimous in their verdict. Lowell H. Harrison noted in the *Southwestern Historical Quarterly* that "Professor Wallace has been indefatigable in his research, particularly in the mass of War Department records in the National Archives. The result is an excellent volume which makes a distinct and welcome contribution to the history of the frontier." Robert Griffen in *The American West* praised Wallace for his "meticulous and careful research." And, Robert G. Athearn noted in the *New Mexico Historical Review*, ". . . the study is highly detailed and is the result of exhaustive examination of documentary sources in the National Archives. In addition, it is a well-organized, well-written account. Consequently, though its scope be somewhat limited, the work is of consequence and it will be required reading for any future student who attempts to understand or to write about the Southwest military-Indian frontier."

Wallace's work also caught the eye of an aging Hollywood actor who had just turned politician: "Today I received a letter from Ronald Reagan, the movie actor in California," wrote Mrs. B. Y. Peacock of Jacksboro in September, 1965. "He is a collector of cavalry history. I sent him brochures on your book and also the McConnell book. He sent for both and said he had long dreamed of playing the role of Mackenzie in the movies but now that he was in politics he would have to wait a while." Other commendations came through the years. Two college textbooks on creative writing cited passages from *Mackenzie* as excellent examples of historical narrative. Wallace, a meticulous writer who labored over every word, was particularly proud of the recognition.

Because of the excellent response to the book, Wallace quickly compiled his collection of Mackenzie's correspondence into two additional volumes for the *Museum Journal.* The first, Ranald S. Mackenzie's *Official Correspondence Relating to Texas, 1871–1873,* was published in 1967 as volume 9; the second, which covered 1873 to 1879, appeared the following year. The West Texas Museum Association published approximately five hundred copies of each of the volumes in book form.

In spite of the three volumes of work, Wallace was not through with Mackenzie and fully intended to expand the Texas study to an indepth account of Mackenzie's entire military career. He continued to collect information on Mackenzie and approached one major university press about the expanded study. But a massive heart attack in June, 1972, slowed his energetic pace and clouded his planned retirement activity. Although he recovered, other projects competed for his attention. In 1979 he completed *The Howling of the Coyotes: Reconstruction Efforts to Divide Texas,* published by Texas A&M University Press. Three years later, he finalized an extensive project for Texas A&M University Press, the editing of *Texas' Last Frontier: Fort Stockton and the Trans-Pecos, 1861–1895* by Clayton W. Williams, Sr. And, even though he had retired from Texas Tech University in 1976, he continued to teach part-time and to direct the dissertation of a recalcitrant graduate student, whose name appears below.

Wallace's writing and teaching career was only part of his academic life. He served Texas Tech in several capacities: director of the Summer School, assistant dean, graduate advisor, and chair of innumerable university committees. Among his many honors was his selection in 1967 by Texas Tech as one of the university's four original Horn Professors, a designation named for the school's first president and reserved for faculty members who have earned outstanding distinction. He also faithfully served his two favorite organizations, the Texas State Historical Association and the West Texas Historical Association, both of which honored him by electing him president.

Death claimed Ernest Wallace quickly and quietly on November 17, 1985, at the age of 79. Perhaps the only work he left uncompleted was his intended expansion of the Mackenzie book; however, the uncompromising thoroughness of his initial work ensures that *Ranald S. Mackenzie on the Texas Frontier* will remain an outstanding study of the colorful cavalry officer and an example of the exemplary work of Ernest Wallace.

—David J. Murrah

Preface

For a third of a century the Anglo-Americans had waged a
relentless struggle to drive the nomadic Comanche and Kiowa
Indians from their favorite hunting and camping grounds in
western Texas and to stop the Apaches and Mexican Kickapoos
from raiding along the Rio Grande border; the Indians just as
relentlessly had struck back against the sparsely populated
communities and isolated ranches along the frontier. Against
the wily warriors the whites had pitted many of their most
notable military officers — Jack Hayes, John S. ("Rip") Ford,
Joseph E. Johnston, Albert Sydney Johnston, John B. Hood,
Earl Van Dorn, and Robert E. Lee, but in 1871 the line of
settlement, which had reached Henrietta, Belknap, Brownwood, Bandera, and Uvalde, was slowly retreating. Four years
later the Indian barrier had been swept aside, and soon a surg-
ing wave of settlers had converted the western Texas wilderness into a land of cattle ranches, productive farms, and prosperous towns.

Colonel Ranald Slidell Mackenzie, a young cavalryman who
had achieved an amazing record during the Civil War, perhaps more than any other was responsible for the quick and
final subjugation of the Indians. Although his campaigns on
the hitherto unexplored Southern Plains and his raids across
the Rio Grande border won for him the respect and admiration

of his superiors and subordinates and the plaudits of the Texans of his day, within a single lifespan the "Fighting Colonel" had become hardly more than a legend. Neither the professional nor the lay historians have been able to piece together the story of his activities in Texas, possibly because the most important of his brief reports lay undiscovered in the National Archives. It is the purpose of this book to tell the long-overdue story of Mackenzie on the Texas frontier, a significant chapter in the history of the American West.

During the course of this study, I have become indebted to many people. The staffs at the National Archives and at The Southwest Collection at Texas Technological College were most cooperative in making material available. Dr. Benjamin Sacks of Baltimore at his own time and expense expedited the receipt of some important correspondence relating to Mackenzie's invasion of Mexico in 1878; Lessing H. Nohl, Jr., Albuquerque, New Mexico, made available a microfilm copy of Mackenzie's journal on the battle of Palo Duro Canyon; Mr. Ernest Lee of Wichita Falls and Dr. Earl Green of The Texas Technological College Museum staff drew the maps illustrating Mackenzie's scouts; and several of my graduate students prepared seminar papers on related topics. Most of all, I am indebted to Mr. Adrian N. Anderson who wrote his Master's thesis on Mackenzie's 1873–1874 activities in Texas and served as research assistant on this project, and to Mrs. Kay Irwin who edited and typed the manuscript through its several editions; the merits of the book, if any, are to a great extent the result of their meticulous and conscientious endeavor. Grants from Texas Technological College research funds sped the completion of the work. To all those who have lent a helping hand, including my wife, who so patiently tolerated a pounding typewriter night after night into the early hours of the newborn day, I wish to add a sincere "Thank you."

Texas Technological College   ERNEST WALLACE
September 19, 1964

Ranald S. Mackenzie on the Texas Frontier

CHAPTER I

The Genesis of an Indian Fighter

READERS FAMILIAR with events on the Texas frontier during the preceding fifteen years found in the Tuesday, December 18, 1883, issue of the *San Antonio Light* a short bit of heart-warming gossip:

It is rumored that General R. S. Mackenzie of this department will on Tuesday next be married to Mrs. [Florida] Sharpe, daughter of Mrs. F. P. Tunstall.

Two days later, however, the same paper painfully reported that the beloved Indian fighter was tragically ill:

It was a topic of almost universal conversation yesterday concerning the aberration of mind under which General McKenzie [sic], commanding this department, now suffers. ... He is a gallant gentleman, chivalrous in everything, manly and noble in every attribute which endows his life and record as a civilian. He is remembered with gratitude by the citizens of Texas, and especially those exposed on the frontier, because he was always prompt in the saddle and never tangled his spurs in the maze of endless red tape when it became necessary to rally a few years ago into Mexico. There will be one universal and harmonious prayer that General McKenzie [sic] may speedily be himself again.

But General Mackenzie never recovered from his sudden illness; the hero of the Texas frontier had become hopelessly insane. A few days after the notice appeared he was rushed to

Bloomingdale Asylum in New York City, where on March 5, 1884, an army retiring board pronounced the General, who had won the distinction of being one of the nation's two greatest Indian fighters, permanently unfit for further military duty and recommended that he be placed on the retired list.[1]

Less than five years later, on January 21, 1889, a brief notice in the obituary column of the *New York Times* read:

[Died] Mackenzie — At New Brighton, Staten Island, on the 19th January, Brig.-Gen. Ranald Slidell Mackenzie, United States Army, in the 48th year of his age.

This was all the publicity given to the death of a devoted military leader whom U. S. Grant had regarded "as the most promising young officer in the Army," and to whom the Texas legislature in special session had expressed "the *Grateful Thanks* of the people of the State, and particularly the citizens of our frontier" for "gallant conduct" against the Indians.[2] There was no editorial appraisal, not even a news item. Surely the public would have appreciated a reminder that Mackenzie in less than three years after graduation from West Point had received seven brevets for gallantry in action, six severe wounds, and a major general's cavalry command, that in three years of campaigning he had cleared West Texas of Comanche and Kiowa Indians, that he had brought quiet to the turbulent Rio Grande border and order to the Comanche-Kiowa Reservation, that in three months he had defeated one group of the Indians who had massacred George Custer on the Little Big Horn, that he had forced the defiant Utes in Colorado to go to a reservation and by a bold stroke ended the Apache uprising in Arizona, and that in appreciation of his having quieted the restless Navajoes and rebellious Apaches, New Mexico Republicans had included a plank in their 1882 platform calling for his promotion to the rank of brigadier general. But public recognition of his services did not come until a generation later when the grateful citizens of the young town of Lubbock, Texas, named a park in his honor.

Ranald Slidell Mackenzie, born to Alexander Slidell and Catherine Alexander Mackenzie in New York City on July 27, 1840,[3] was destined by heritage for high achievement. His naval commander father, Alexander Slidell, who in 1837 at the wish of a maternal uncle had taken his wife's family name, was the popular author of several books, including *A Year in Spain* and biographies of John Paul Jones and Oliver H. Perry,[4] whose brother Matthew C. Perry, opener of Japan to the West in 1853, was married to the elder Mackenzie's sister Jane Slidell. Two years after Ranald was born, Commander Mackenzie gained front-page publicity when aboard the brig *Somers* off the coast of Africa on December 1, 1842, he hanged without trial Midshipman Philip Spencer, the son of Secretary of War John C. Spencer, and two others for plotting mutiny; he faced court-martial because of these expeditious executions, but was acquitted.[5] This stern insistence on absolute loyalty and performance of duty Ranald acquired from his father.

Commander Mackenzie's brother, John Slidell, was one of two Confederate commissioners taken off the British steamer *Trent* by a United States naval officer in 1861, an action almost precipitating a war between the United States and Great Britain. Ranald's mother, the daughter of Morris Robinson of New York, was the granddaughter of Lady Catherine Alexander and William Duer of Revolutionary War fame, who afterwards was involved in some shady deals in the disposition of the federal domain and was an assistant secretary of the treasury under Alexander Hamilton.[6]

The military character of the family was inherited also by Ranald's two younger brothers. Alexander Slidell Mackenzie, Jr., two years younger than Ranald, entered the navy in 1857 as a midshipman, served in the Civil War, and attained the rank of lieutenant commander before he was killed in 1867 while leading a charge against Formosan natives.[7] Morris Robinson Slidell Mackenzie, who graduated from the Naval Academy in 1866, became a rear admiral before his death in 1915. The spinster sister Harriet lived with Ranald during his last months of service at Sante Fe and San Antonio, and cared for him after he became hopelessly ill.[8]

A few weeks after Ranald's birth the Mackenzies moved to a farm on the Hudson River between Tarrytown and Sing Sing, where they were still living when a short time after his return from the Mexican War in the spring of 1848, Commander Mackenzie died of a heart attack. Faced with financial hardships, the widow soon afterwards sold the farm on the Hudson and moved her family to or near the home of relatives in Morristown, New Jersey.[9]

Ranald, who had not been robust since the age of three when he had suffered a slight sunstroke which doctors later thought might have contributed to his insanity, quietly acquiesced in an uncle's suggestion that he prepare for the law profession. Thus, after attending Maurice's School at Sing Sing, the frail, shy youth at the age of fifteen entered Williams College, where he became known as a good fellow and joined Kappa Alpha fraternity, but failed to demonstrate any intellectual brilliance.[10]

To relieve his family of the financial burden of his education, Ranald during his junior year asked his mother's consent to and aid in securing an appointment to the Military Academy at West Point. Having decided that he wanted to prepare for an army career, young Mackenzie displayed his avid interest in and acute knowledge of tactics, upon which his later success in Indian warfare depended, almost at once; he was scheduled to give an oration he had written on "Military Tactics" at the Junior Rhetorical Exhibition on June 1, 1858, one month prior to entering the Military Academy. Williams College later conferred upon him two degrees, the A. B. in 1863 and the A. M. in 1873.[11]

Neither his family nor his friends were optimistic about his chances of success at the Military Academy. The family clergyman, upon being informed that young Mackenzie stood second in his class at the end of his second year at West Point, expressed his amazement to Mrs. Mackenzie: "No, it is not possible; Madam, . . . I had ventured to hint to my wife in strict confidence my certainty of the disappointment in store for you."[12]

Despite the feeling among his relatives and friends that he was doomed to fail at West Point, Mackenzie at the end of his first year stood fifth in his class and was popular with the cadets. Although the general excitement over the outbreak of the Civil War caused him to drop from second place in 1860 to twelfth in his junior year, at the time of his graduation on June 17, 1862, although serving as Acting Assistant Professor of Mathematics during his last year, he stood first in a class of twenty-eight.[13]

With his diploma, Mackenzie, not quite twenty-two, received an appointment as Second Lieutenant of Engineers and was assigned to General Ambrose E. Burnside's corps of the Army of the Potomac. By the time Second Lieutenant Mackenzie was ready for active duty, General George B. McClellan, commanding the Army of the Potomac, had been decisively defeated in the Seven Days Battle and had been recalled to the Potomac, and General Henry W. Halleck made general-in-chief. Halleck replaced McClellan with General John Pope, who had been his subordinate in the West, with orders to move from Washington directly toward Richmond. Along the route, the numerous streams had to be bridged ahead of the advancing army. This was the task to which Second Lieutenant Mackenzie was first assigned. One set of his instructions was for preparing locations for and constructing pontoon bridges; another directed the young engineer "to select at Banks and Fords good positions for batteries to cover crossings at those places . . . in the woods, if possible." [14]

Lee with the close cooperation of "Stonewall" Jackson boldly maneuvered Pope's Army of the Potomac into the spot he wanted, and on August 29–30 routed it in the Second Battle of Bull Run (Manassas). In this battle, his first, Mackenzie received a brevet for "gallant and meritorious service" and suffered a wound through both shoulders. About twenty hours later he was picked up where he had fallen and carried to an emergency hospital in Washington. When his mother visited him the next day, the proud young soldier hastened to explain that "I am wounded in the back, but I was not running away." [45]

Returning to his command on October 19, Mackenzie served with the Engineers Battalion in the Army of the Potomac until June, 1864. He was an assistant to the Chief Engineer when General Burnside, who had been placed in command of the Army of the Potomac, proved his incompetence at Fredericksburg on December 13, 1862, in one of the bloodiest and most disastrous Union defeats. In March, 1863, Mackenzie was promoted to first lieutenant. On May 3 at Chancellorsville, where "Fighting Joe" Hooker was as decisively defeated as his predecessor Burnside had been, and on July 4 at Gettysburg, where General George G. Meade, who had succeeded Hooker, checked Lee's advance, Mackenzie won brevets of captain and major. Promoted to the regular rank of captain in November, he commanded a company of engineers preparing the way as the new supreme commander, General U. S. Grant, riding side by side with Meade, tried in vain to beat back Lee in May and early June, 1864, in the battles of the Wilderness, Spotsylvania, and Cold Harbor. [16]

Although he performed his duties as an engineer zealously and well, Mackenzie considered a pontoon a "bore," and he longed for an opportunity to command fighting troops. The opportunity came on June 10, 1864, when General Meade appointed him colonel of the 2nd Connecticut Volunteers, Heavy Artillery (serving as infantry), in the 6th Army Corps, to fill the vacancy created by the death of its commanding officer in the slaughter at Cold Harbor. [17] Considering the few months remaining in the war, Mackenzie's subsequent advancement was phenomenal.

For several days the opposing armies faced each other across thousands of wounded, dying unattended, and corpses rotting on the ground. Then Grant changed his base to the James and on June 15 threw his forces against Petersburg in an effort to cut Lee's supply line. For "gallant and meritorious service" while commanding his regiment during the battle on the 18th, Mackenzie was brevetted a lieutenant colonel in the regular army, and four days later while still engaged in the siege of Petersburg, he had two fingers of his right hand shot off,[18] a disfigurement that later inspired the Indians to call him "Bad Hand."

Compelled to take a disability leave, he reported for duty on July 9, and on the next day was officially commissioned as colonel of his new regiment. A few days later, when Lee sent General Jubal Early on a diversionary movement against Washington, Mackenzie's regiment was among the troops sent to defend the capital, and afterwards was transferred to General Philip H. Sheridan's army for the offensive against Early in the Shenandoah Valley in the autumn of 1864.

Finding the 2nd Connecticut Regiment an easy-going group, not unusual among volunteer organizations where men and officers had known each other in civilian life, Mackenzie determined to make it into a well-disciplined and efficient fighting unit. His adjutant later wrote that "By the time we had reached the Shenandoah Valley he had so far developed as to be a greater terror to both officers and men than Early's grape and canister."[19] Unhappy with such a stern taskmaster, some of the men plotted to dispose of him during the next battle. When the time came, however, at the Battle of Winchester on September 29, the plot collapsed in the face of Mackenzie's audacious display of courage. Receiving a slight wound in the leg, but from the Confederates rather than from his own men, he tied a handkerchief around it and refused to go to the rear, even at the request of Sheridan, who was quite impressed with his young officer's movements and gallantry.[20]

Again Mackenzie was wounded — twice — on October 19 in

Early's defeat at Cedar Creek, for which action he was brevetted a colonel. On the same day he was appointed Brigadier
General, U. S. Volunteers, for "gallant and meritorious services" in the battles of Opaquan, Fisher's Hill, and Middleton,
Virginia, during the Valley campaign, but his wounds kept him
from taking command of his brigade until he returned to duty
on November 13.[21]

Mackenzie did not receive his official letter of appointment
as brigadier general, dated November 30, until December 28,
a delay which he hoped would not affect his pay raise.[22] In regard to this promotion, he later questioned the relative ranks
of himself and two brevet brigadiers appointed on the same
date but senior to him as colonels. "It seems to me," he wrote,
"that the full Commission should rank the Brevet appointments
of the same date," but his superiors disagreed.[23]

Soon after Mackenzie returned to duty, as commander of
the 2nd Brigade, 1st Division, 6th Army Corps, Sheridan, having driven Early from the Shenandoah Valley, sent his young
general across Virginia to rejoin Grant, who had maintained
his dreary siege of Petersburg ever since June. Although relatively inactive during the next few weeks, Mackenzie did
what he could "to try and justify General Sheridan's opinion
of having him promoted." Both Grant and Sheridan were
highly pleased with their young field commander — enough so
to promote him on March 13, 1865, to the rank of brigadier
general in the regular army, and four days later to the rank
of Brevet Major General, U. S. Volunteers, in anticipation of
taking the offensive against Lee.[24] At that time the twenty-
four-year-old major general, according to one of his biogra-
phers,

was a spare, slim young man of medium height. His youth was
accentuated by a clean-shaven face, in a day of heavily-bearded
men, except for long sideburns to the curve of his jaws. He had an
ascetic, hawk-like face and the air of a crusading Norman bishop,
who carried a mace into battle so as to kill without spilling blood.

His personal resemblance to Ralph Waldo Emerson was striking, if one can imagine that humanitarian philosopher exposed to shot and shell, blood and carnage, instead of the quiet optimism of Boston and Concord transcendentalism.[25]

By now Lee was in a precarious position; if he did not evacuate Petersburg, Grant, who with Sheridan's arrival had more than twice as many men, would envelop him; if he abandoned Petersburg, Richmond would fall. Lee decided to make an assault on the Union forces. Sheridan's cavalry, including Major General Mackenzie's division, drove back Lee's right on April 1 in the Battle of Five Forks, and on the next night Lee began his retreat along the railway line toward Danville. In his official report of the battle, Sheridan stated that Mackenzie had executed his orders "with a courage and skill, . . ." that merited "the thanks of the country and the reward of the government." [26]

Mackenzie continued active along the road to Appomattox and in the formalities of Lee's surrender. When Lee's troops on April 12 marched into an open field to lay down their arms and receive their parole, Mackenzie was there, at Grant's request, to take charge of Confederate property.[27] After taking possession of surrendered property in the vicinity of Appomattox, commanding the cavalry in the Department of Virginia from April 20 to August 11, 1865, and awaiting orders for several months — at least part of the time in New York City — Mackenzie was mustered out of service on January 15, 1866, as Brigadier General, U. S. Volunteers.[28] Although he had not entered until the second year of the war, Mackenzie in three years had collected seven brevets and six severe wounds, and had risen to higher rank than any other man in his West Point class.[29]

After being mustered out as brigadier general, Mackenzie resumed his permanent rank as Captain of Engineers in the regular army on February 28, 1866, and for the next fourteen months assisted in the construction of defenses for Portsmouth

Harbor, New Hampshire. He still preferred, however, to command fighting men, and hoped that in the reorganization of the army he would be commissioned a major in the line. Thus, when offered the command of the 41st Infantry Regiment on March 11, 1867, he welcomed the opportunity, although several officers had declined appointment to an inexperienced Negro unit. In acknowledging on April 26 his orders to report to his new command, Mackenzie agreed to proceed without delay, as soon as he could "make the necessary arrangements for my change in station and rank." On May 26 he assumed command at Baton Rouge, Louisiana, "free from all bodily and mental infirmity." [30]

Less than a month after reaching Baton Rouge, Mackenzie with his command was sent to Texas, and until 1870 was stationed along the lower Rio Grande. Until February 5, 1868, he commanded both the post of Fort Brown and the Sub-District of the Rio Grande. Afterwards, he was at Fort Clark for a year, and then moved his headquarters to Fort McKavett. When a reduction of the army was made in 1869, the 38th and 41st Infantry regiments were merged into the 24th Infantry, and by an order of March 15 Mackenzie assumed command of the new unit. Actually, the only change as far as Mackenzie was concerned was the regimental number. [31]

Although somewhat disappointed over the regiment assigned to him, Mackenzie, upon assuming command of the ignorant ex-slave field hands, had determined to make them into a good organization. As a first step, he had the regimental recruiting station moved from the South to the North and recruited only intelligent men. Then with the aid of his highly competent lieutenant colonel, William R. Shafter, he transformed his new outfit into one of the best Negro regiments in the service. Within a year it had the lowest desertion rate of any regiment, but Mackenzie, with no opportunity to test his infantry in the field nor to make use of his own special capabilities of commanding men in combat, was dissatisfied. Although the tempo of Indian raids on the Rio Grande border, Comanches from the north and Kickapoos from Mexico, increased significantly after 1867, the lackadaisical scouts against the raiders were always by detachments of the 4th, 6th, and 9th Cavalry. Except for one insignificant scout in the early summer of 1869, Mackenzie had to content himself with administration, garrison duty, repair and construction at the various posts, and several months at San Antonio on court martial duty, all to him boring and distasteful — all except his stay while in San Antonio at the boarding home of F. P. Tunstall, who had a lovely eighteen-year-old daughter.[32]

For another year and a half, however, the second youngest colonel in the service had to abide his fate. Since his regiment was practically inactive, he took an extended leave of absence from April to October, 1870, spending the time in the East. Two weeks after resuming his duties at McKavett, he received a wire from General J. J. Reynolds, commander of the Department of Texas, ordering him to proceed to Washington to serve on a Special Military Board. He started on the same day, but "delayed six days in Texas by high waters, in rivers . . . and one day by the grounding of mail steamer in Berwick's Bay," he did not reach the capital until November 1.[33] His service on the Board, which had convened before he arrived, continued until January 3, 1871; during its session, Mackenzie was informed that as of December 15 he was being transferred to the command of the 4th Cavalry, an appointment evidently desired by President Grant.[34]

Although he left no record testifying as much, Mackenzie was no doubt elated over his assignment, because his new regiment, though not the best, had a relatively good reputation. Organized as the 1st Cavalry in 1855 at Leavenworth, Kansas, by Secretary of War Jefferson Davis, the regiment numbered among its former officers several distinguished men, including Colonels Edwin V. Sumner and John Sedgwick, Lieutenant Colonels Joseph E. Johnston and W. H. Emory, and Captains

George B. McClellan and J. E. B. Stuart. It had its initiation
into Indian fighting in 1857 on the Solomon River against the
Cheyennes, and in the same year it had the ticklish job of main-
taining peace in turbulent Kansas. Reorganized as the 4th Cavalry Regiment in August, 1861, it participated in seventy-six
engagements against Confederate forces during the Civil War.
It helped keep Missouri in the Union, and later served in Ken-
tucky, Tennessee, and Georgia. After the close of the war, the
regiment was sent to Texas where it had been scattered, from
time to time, among no less than nine posts, extending from
Brown to Concho.[35]

The officers above the rank of second lieutenant, all veterans
of the Civil War, had little incentive for proficiency because
advancement, as in Mackenzie's case, seemed unlikely. To alleviate their frustration, they squandered their time at card
playing and hunting, instead of studying their profession. Many
of the enlisted men were war veterans who, unable to return
to a successful business life, found solace — so far as possible
on pay of thirteen dollars per month — in drink. Pay day, an
irregular affair on the frontier, often ended with ten per cent
of the enlisted men in the guardhouse, and desertion was common. But in the field the men were splendid soldiers.[36] This
was the 4th Cavalry when Mackenzie assumed command at
Fort Concho on February 25, 1871. In a letter home at the
time, he wrote that "I intend that it shall not be on account of
any laziness of mine if it falls below any other."[37]

All the officers and most of the men of the 4th Cavalry were
familiar with the record and reputation of their new commander; if not already impressed, they soon were. When Mackenzie
rode into Concho in February, he was an erect and relatively
slim man, thirty years of age, five feet nine inches in height,
and weighed but 145 pounds. His smooth-shaven face prom-
inently displayed its sensitive, ascetic features. Beneath a heavy
mop of straight brown hair, cold steel-gray eyes unblinkingly
gazed at those whom he directed or with whom he talked, re-

vealing a lack of humor and a determination that tolerated no compromise or foolishness in the performance of duty. Although he seldom laughed or had time for animated conversation, the Colonel had a faint smile that reflected his deep sense of human understanding and his friendliness toward those who pleased him with their best performance.

During the next few years, both men and officers were to learn that he was often fretful, irritable, and irascible, the result of a combination of his serious purpose and his suffering from old wounds and inability to relax; that he worked hard and late, slept little, ate moderately, and drank no intoxicants; that he had an indomitable will, unbelievable endurance, and unsurpassed courage. They were to learn also that although he was impatient and impulsive, imperious and impetuous, he could also be chivalrous and courteous, modest and dignified, and that he was at all times loyal and fair, gallant and bold.[38] Such was the new commander of the 4th Cavalry who at once ordered the officers to lay aside their hunting of wild game and began assiduously preparing to hunt more dangerous game — the Comanche and Kiowa Indians who were ravaging the Texas frontier. After a month of bustle and intensive training, Mackenzie with the headquarters and five companies of his cavalry left Concho for Fort Richardson, 230 miles nearer the Comanche-Kiowa reservation. He was again to have an opportunity to command a major expedition but in a new kind of war.

FOOTNOTES — CHAPTER I

[1] Report of Retiring Board, Bloomingdale Asylum, New York City, March 5, 1884. Records of the War Department (WD), 1282 Appointment, Commission, and Personal File (ACP) 1884 (filed with 3877 ACP 1873), Adjutant General's Office (AGO), Letters Rec'd, Record Group (RG) 94, National Archives. Unless otherwise indicated, all source materials hereafter identified as "AGO, RG 94," "DT, Army Commands, RG 98," or "ACP, AGO, RG 94" are located under "Letters Received" in the Records of the War Department of the National Archives.

[2] U.S. Grant, *Personal Memoirs of U.S. Grant* (2 vols.; New York, 1886), II, 541; "Joint Resolution of the Legislature of the State of Texas," quoted in

R. G. Carter, *On the Border with Mackenzie* (New York, 1961), 463–464 (hereafter cited as Carter, *On the Border*). Robert G. Carter, whose writings will be used extensively throughout this study, joined Mackenzie in the spring of 1871 as a second lieutenant in the 4th Cavalry. For "most distinguished gallantry" in the battle against the Comanches near the mouth of Blanco Canyon on October 10, 1871, Carter was brevetted first lieutenant and awarded the Congressional Medal of Honor. He was brevetted captain for "gallant service in action" during the Mackenzie raid into Mexico in 1873, and was promoted to first lieutenant in 1875. After his retirement in 1876, as a result of a leg wound received in the fight with the Comanches, Carter spent most of the next sixty years writing about his experiences with Mackenzie and the 4th Cavalry.

[3] Joseph H. Dorst, "Ranald Slidell Mackenzie," in *Twentieth Annual Reunion of the Association Graduates of the United States Military at West Point, New York*, June 12, 1889 (East Saginaw, Michigan, 1889), App., 1 (hereafter cited as Dorst, "Mackenzie," *20th Reunion*); Ranald S. Mackenzie to Brig. Gen. L. Thomas, June 29 and September 20, 1865, 673 M 1865 and 1219 M 1865 (both filed with 3877 ACP 1873), AGO, RG 94.

[4] "Ranald S. Mackenzie," in *Army and Navy Journal*, January 26, 1889, reprinted in *20th Reunion*, 73.

[5] Edward S. Wallace, "General Ranald Slidell Mackenzie, Indian Fighting Cavalryman," in *The Southwestern Historical Quarterly*, LVI (January, 1953), 379 (hereafter cited as Wallace, "Mackenzie," in *SWHQ*).

[6] Dorst, "Mackenzie," *20th Reunion*, App., 1; *Dictionary of American Biography* (22 vols.; New York, 1928), XII, 90–91 and V, 485–486.

[7] Dorst, "Mackenzie," *20th Reunion*, 73–74; Wallace, "Mackenzie," in *SWHQ*, LVI, 379.

[8] *Dictionary of American Biography*, XII, 90–91; *Who Was Who in America* (3 vols.; Chicago, 1960), I, 763; also various correspondence in Mackenzie's ACP, AGO file.

[9] Dorst, "Mackenzie," *20th Reunion*, App., 2.

[10] *Ibid.*; Wallace, "Mackenzie," in *SWHQ*, LVI, 380; Leverett Wilson Spring, *A History of Williams College* (Boston, 1917), 205.

[11] Wallace, "Mackenzie," in *SWHQ*, LVI, 380–381. Wallace quotes E. B. Parsons, Secretary, *Class of Fifty-Nine, Williams College* (Syracuse, 1884), 55–56.

[12] Quoted in Dorst, "Mackenzie," *20th Reunion*, App., 2–3.

[13] Dorst, "Mackenzie," *20th Reunion*, App., 2–4; Adjutant General R. C. Drumm, March 3, 1884, "Official War Department Record of Service of Ranald S. Mackenzie," 1149 AGO 1884, RG 94 (hereafter cited as "Mackenzie's Record of Service").

[14] *War of the Rebellion, Official Records of the Union and the Confederate Armies* (130 vols.; Washington, 1881–1901), Series I, Vol. LI, pt. I, p. 952 (hereafter cited as *War of Rebellion Records*).

[15] Dorst, "Mackenzie," *20th Reunion*, App., 4; Medical Certificate, 1122 M 1862 (filed with 3877 ACP 1873), AGO, RG 94; "Mackenzie's Record of Service," as cited.

[16] *Ibid.*; Carter, *On the Border*, 538; Mackenzie, acceptance of appointments, July 26, 1863, and January 20, 1864, M 984 D 1863 and 53 M 1865

(both filed with 3877 ACP 1873), AGO, RG 94; Dorst, "Mackenzie," *20th Reunion*, App., 5.

[17] "Mackenzie's Record of Service," as cited; Mackenzie, undated, relative to clarification of rank, 26 M 1865 (filed with 3877 ACP 1873), AGO, RG 94; Dorst, "Mackenzie," *20th Reunion*, App., 5; Carter, *On the Border*, 538.

[18] "Mackenzie's Record of Service," as cited; Mackenzie, undated, relative to clarification of rank, as cited; Dorst, "Mackenzie," *20th Reunion*, App., 6.

[19] Lieutenant T. F. Vaill as quoted in *ibid.*

[20] Wallace, "Mackenzie," in *SWHQ*, LVI, 382–383; Dorst, "Mackenzie," *20th Reunion*, App., 6–7.

[21] "Mackenzie's Record of Service," as cited; Mackenzie to Col. George D. Ruggles, Asst. Adj. Gen., Army of the Potomac, February 24, 1865, 157 M 1865 (filed with 3877 ACP 1873), AGO, RG 94; Mackenzie, "Certificate of Volunteer Organizations during Civil War," 684 ACP 1872, in *ibid.*; Dorst, "Mackenzie," *20th Reunion*, App., 5–6.

[22] Mackenzie, undated, relative to clarification of rank, as cited.

[23] Mackenzie to Ruggles, February 24, 1865, as cited.

[24] "Mackenzie's Record of Service," as cited; Mackenzie to Thomas, June 29, 1865, as cited; Francis B. Heitman, *Historical Register and Dictionary of the U.S. Army* (2 vols.; Washington, 1903), I, 672 (hereafter cited as Heitman, *Historical Register*).

[25] Wallace, "Mackenzie," in *SWHQ*, LVI, 383–384.

[26] *War of Rebellion Records*, Series I, Vol. XLVI, pt. I, p. 1109.

[27] *Ibid.*, 1152, 58.

[28] "Mackenzie's Record of Service," as cited; Mackenzie to Thomas, October 15 and November 6, 1865, 1105 M 1865 and 2246 M 1865 (both filed with 3877 ACP 1873), AGO, RG 94.

[29] "Mackenzie's Record of Service," as cited; Wallace, "Mackenzie," in *SWHQ*, LVI, 378; Dorst, "Mackenzie," *20th Reunion*, App., 16.

[30] "Mackenzie's Record of Service," as cited; Mackenzie to Thomas, March 11, 1867, 268 M 1867 (filed with 3877 ACP 1873), AGO, RG 94; Medical Certificate, March 13, 1867, B 429 C. B. 1867, in *ibid.*; Mackenzie to E. D. Townsend, Asst. Adj. Gen., April 26, 1867, 434 M 1876 (filed with 3877 ACP 1873), AGO, RG 94.

[31] "Mackenzie's Record of Service," as cited; G. W. Cullum, *Biographical Register of Officers and Graduates United States Military Academy* (Boston 1891), II, 841, 843; Secretary of War, "Report," 1870, 41 Cong., 2 Sess., *House Exec. Doc.* I, pt. 2 (Washington, 1870), pp. 25–28, 34–35, 143–150, 170–171; Richard Marcum, "Fort Brown, Texas: The History of a Border Post" (Ph.D. dissertation, Texas Technological College, Lubbock, 1964), 179–185.

[32] Dorst, "Mackenzie," *20th Reunion*, App., 9; Wallace, "Mackenzie," in *SWHQ*, LVI, 384; Edward S. Wallace "Border Warrior," in *American Heritage*, IX (June, 1958), 22–25; Cullum, *Biographical Register*, II, 843; Secretary of War, "Report," 1870, as cited; Secretary of War, "Report," 1869, 40 Cong., 3 Sess., *House Exec. Doc.* I, pt. 1 (Washington, 1869), pp. 704–769; AGO, *Chronological List of Actions etc. with Indians, from January 1, 1866 to January, 1891* (Washington, 1891).

[33] Mackenzie to Maj. Gen. Winfield S. Hancock, November 1, 1870, 3469 ACP 1871 (filed with 3877 ACP 1873), AGO, RG 94.

[34] "Mackenzie's Record of Service," as cited; Wallace, "Mackenzie," in *SWHQ*, LVI, 384; Dorst, "Mackenzie," *20th Reunion*, App., 9; Heitman, *Historical Register*, I, 672.

[35] *Ibid.*, 70; John K. Herr and Edward S. Wallace, *The Story of the U. S. Cavalry* (Boston, 1953), 75–82, 138–141; James Parker, *The Old Army: Memories, 1872–1918* (Philadelphia, 1929), 20–21; *War of Rebellion Records*, Series III, Vol. I, p. 403; also the pertinent annual reports of the Secretary of War.

[36] Parker, *The Old Army*, 16–17. Parker joined the 4th Cavalry as a second lieutenant in 1876.

[37] Dorst, "Mackenzie," *20th Reunion*, App., 9.

[38] *Ibid.*; Carter, *On the Border*, xxii–xxiii, 536–540; J. Evetts Haley, *Fort Concho and the Texas Frontier* (San Angelo, Texas, 1952), 159–160 (hereafter cited as Haley, *Fort Concho*); Charles A. P. Hatfield in *Motor Travel*, XXII (January, 1931), 19, 22; Sergeant John B. Charlton in R. G. Carter, *The Old Sergeant's Story* (New York, 1926), passim. Hatfield was a lieutenant and Charlton a sergeant in the 4th Cavalry.

CHAPTER II

The Texas Frontier

MACKENZIE'S NEW ASSIGNMENT was no sinecure. For a third of a century the Anglo-Americans had been waging a relentless struggle to drive the nomadic Comanche and Kiowa Indians from their favorite Texas hunting grounds; the Indians just as relentlessly had struck back with barbaric cruelty. Against their wily warriors the whites had pitted many of their most notable military officers — Jack Hayes, John S. ("Rip") Ford, Henry McCulloch, Joseph E. Johnston, Albert Sydney Johnston, Robert E. Lee, George Thomas, Earl Van Dorn, Randolph B. Marcy, John B. Hood, and others — but the line of settlement when Mackenzie established the headquarters of the 4th Cavalry at Jacksboro in 1871 did not extend as far west as it had a decade earlier.

At the end of the Mexican War when the United States assumed the responsibility of defending the Texas frontier, the western limit of white settlement was marked by the newly established towns of Sherman, Farmersville, Dallas, Waxahachie, Ennis, and Fredericksburg, all along the eastern edge of the Comanche-Kiowa country. Between December, 1848, and July, 1849, the United States established a line of military posts to deter the Indians from passing into the settlements. From south to north the forts forming this line were Duncan, on the

Rio Grande at Eagle Pass; Inge, near Uvalde; Lincoln, on the
Seco River, fifty-five miles west of San Antonio; Martin Scott,
at Fredericksburg; Croghan, just south of present Burnet;
Gates, on the Leon River near present Gatesville; Graham, on
the Brazos River about fourteen miles west of Hillsboro;
Worth, at present Fort Worth; and Washita, 120 miles north
of Fort Worth in Indian Territory. The inability of the militia
at the posts to provide protection, the demand to open new
lands for settlement along the western Cross Timbers, the pressure to safeguard the California roads, and the obligation to prevent its Indians from raiding in Mexico led the federal government in 1851 to move its posts westward to more strategic locations.

Consequently, the new sites were not in a straight line. By
November, 1852, seven new forts had been established, generally more than a hundred miles west of the 1849 line. From
north to south they were Belknap, on the Brazos at the present
town of Newcastle; Phantom Hill, fourteen miles north of
present Abilene on the Clear Fork of the Brazos; Chadbourne,
on Oak Creek in Coke County; McKavett, on the upper San
Saba River about twenty-four miles above Menard; Terrett, on
the North Llano River halfway between present Junction and
Sonora; Mason, at the present town by that name; and Clark,
at the present town of Brackettville.

As soon as the new posts had been established, there was a
rush of settlers into the intervening lands. Within two years
settlements had been made at McKinney, Cleburne, Stephen-
ville, Gatesville, San Saba, and Bandera. When the new line of
posts, often under-manned with foot-soldiers, failed to deter
the mounted warlike Indians determined to keep the settlers
off their hunting grounds, the Texans fitted out Ranger or
Minutemen companies to drive the Indians from the borders of
their state. By 1861 the aggressive Texans, aided by the military,
had cleared the Indians from the region of the western Cross
Timbers and built their log cabins as far westward as Henrietta,

Archer City, Belknap, Palo Pinto, Comanche, Brownwood, Llano, Kerrville, and Uvalde. The reservation Indians had been driven from the state in 1859, and it seemed that the hostile Comanches and Kiowas must either perish or accept the will of the white men and remain on a small out-of-the-way reservation. The outbreak of the Civil War, however, relieved the pressure by the settlers, and the final contest had to await the conclusion of the great struggle between the white men of the North and South.

During the Civil War Texas had to provide for its own frontier defense. Even before the federal troops had departed, the state sent Ranger forces to the frontier and in addition provided for the organization of companies of minutemen in each of the thirty-seven frontier counties. Although the Texas and Confederate governments succeeded early in 1861 in negotiating treaties of peace with a part of the Comanches,[1] the Texans took no risks. In December, 1861, the legislature provided for ten companies of Rangers, known as the Frontier Regiment, to guard the frontier. During the following spring the Frontier Regiment established sixteen camps between the Red River and the Rio Grande along a relatively straight line extending from Archer County southward by Belknap, Breckenridge, Hubbard's Creek, just west of Brownwood, Richland Creek in San Saba County, Kerrville, the head of the Seco River in Bandera County, and Uvalde to Eagle Pass. Fifty to sixty men were maintained at each camp and the entire line between the posts was patrolled every other day, but the Comanches outwitted the Rangers by crossing just behind the patrols.[2] In 1863 the commanding officer replaced the regular patrols with intermittent scouting expeditions in hope of surprising raiding parties. Although the new system was more effective in encountering Indians, raiding parties became more numerous. Cooke, Denton, Montague, Wise, Parker, and Hood counties were pillaged. By the end of the year the Indians had driven off more than ten thousand head of cattle.

In December, the legislature, faced with increased Confederate pressure for men, reorganized its frontier defense system. All men in a tier of counties from the Red River to the Rio Grande were enrolled into companies, at least one-fourth of the men, approximately 1,066, to be in the field at all times. The continued drain of these men into Confederate service and the declining morale, however, left the western frontier without any effective defense.[3]

Fortunately, there was only one severe Indian attack after 1863. In 1864 the Comanches and Kiowas moved away temporarily from the Texas frontier to join the Cheyennes and Arapahoes in a war against the United States, but in October two hundred or more of their warriors made a formidable attack on a Confederate outpost near "Fort" Murrah, about twelve miles north of Fort Belknap in Young County. The raiders killed five troopers and then struck the Elm Creek settlement, sixteen miles west of Belknap, where they killed eleven whites and carried off seven women and children.[4] The state defense system continued to provide some protection for a few months after the collapse of the Confederacy, but it gradually fizzled out, and by the spring of 1866 when the Indians renewed their war against the Texans all pretense of organization was gone.

To the north of Texas, J. H. Leavenworth, the United States agent to the Southern Plains tribes, persuaded officials in Washington that more could be accomplished by treaty than by war. Accordingly, on October 15, 1865, United States commissioners signed the Treaty of the Little Arkansas with the Kiowas and a party of the Comanches. The treaty provided that these Indians would relinquish their claim to Texas lands east and south of a line connecting the southeast corner of New Mexico and the junction of the North and South forks of the Red River in return for specified annuity payments.[5] The treaty was defective because some of the most war-like Comanche bands were not present and because the commissioners had no authority to assign any of the lands of Texas since they were reserved to the state.

Neither the federal government nor the Indians kept the treaty for very long. By the next summer, the Indians, unhappy with the quality of goods they were receiving, were again raiding the Texas frontier.[6] The Kiowas, left without a strong leader after the death of Chief Dohason, were divided among several ambitious war chiefs who sought to gain increased tribal prestige; and the powerful Kwahadi Comanches, who inhabited the headstreams of the Colorado, Brazos, and Red rivers along the eastern edge of the Llano Estacado, had developed a lucrative market in stolen Texas livestock with the *Comancheros* (New Mexican traders). Under such conditions the isolated and undefended settlements, in a country they still regarded as their own, provided a temptation too great for restless warriors to resist.

The Comanches and Kiowas again entered the settlements in droves. A Waco newspaper in April claimed that not more than one-fifth of the ranches in that vicinity were still occupied, and Governor James W. Throckmorton in August stated that the "frontier many hundred miles in extent" was being desolated. He was soon besieged with deplorable reports and petitions for help. The citizens from Denton and surrounding counties in a mass meeting agreed to abandon their homes unless help had arrived by October 20. The population of Wise County dropped from 3,160 in 1860 to 1,450 in 1870, but in 1880, five years after the end of the Indian problem, it had swelled to 16,601.[7]

There were similar stories from all along the frontier. Governor Throckmorton sent the reports and petitions to the military commander with a recommendation that a new post be established at Jacksboro and that other companies of troops be located at strategic points on the northern frontier. Although the legislature authorized the organization of one thousand state troops, General Sheridan, commanding in Texas, vetoed

the use of state forces, even under the command of federal officers, but sent an inspector to investigate conditions along the
frontier and authorized the sending of troops if they were
needed.

As a result of the inspection, the 4th Cavalry in December
reoccupied forts Mason, Inge, Clark, and Camp Verde to cover
the line between the Colorado River and the Rio Grande, and
on January 4, 1867, six companies of the 6th Cavalry arrived
at Jacksboro. Nevertheless, the Indian raids grew worse. In his
final report on August 5, 1867, Governor Throckmorton stated
that from May, 1865, to July, 1867, the Indians had killed 162
persons, wounded 24, and carried 43 into captivity, not including those of Wise and Young counties, two of the hardest hit.[8]

Even with cavalry troops again present, defense against the
Comanches and Kiowas on the northwestern frontier was practically negligible. The 6th Cavalry, under command of Colonel
S. H. Starr, a New Yorker, abandoned Jacksboro in April,
1867, for what was hoped were more desirable sites. Starr selected Belknap for his headquarters and sent two companies to
Buffalo Springs, about twenty miles north of Jacksboro. Composed primarily of inexperienced Negro troops, the 6th Cavalry was not an efficient frontier fighting force. In July, 1867,
when word arrived at Buffalo Springs that a party of about 250
Indians was depredating in the vicinity, Major B. O. Hutchins,
the post commander, set out with a company of men, but instead of going into the settlement where the Indians were reported to be, he turned west to Fort Belknap, played poker for
two days, and then returned to Buffalo Springs. Meanwhile,
the Indians had gathered up all the horses for some distance,
and on their way home had besieged for two days the sixty men
left at the post.[9] Such incidents poignantly contrast the 6th
Cavalry's lackadaisical attitude with the later performance of
the relentless Mackenzie and the 4th Cavalry.

The slowness of the military in establishing permanent posts
was partially due to a new effort to obtain peace by treaty-

making – if the Indians could be induced to keep the peace, forts and war would be unnecessary. Although officials in Washington did not realize the extent of the depredations, they were aware that affairs in the Indian territory were not satisfactory, and in June, 1867, Congress authorized a commission to secure a lasting peace. At Medicine Lodge Creek, seventy-five miles south of the Great Bend of the Arkansas, the commissioners, accompanied by a military escort, met the Southern Plains tribes in what seems to have been the most colorful council ever held between Indians and whites in the American West.

When the Council opened, Satanta, leader of the Kiowa raids into Texas, scorned the suggestion of houses or schools or labor, and insisted that all the land south of the Arkansas, including western Texas, belonged to the Kiowas and Comanches and that he did not want to give any of it away. Ten Bears, a Yamparika Comanche chief, spoke for the Comanches. Having seen the numbers and wealth and power of the white men on his visit to Washington two years before, he realized that the proposals represented an alternative to utter destruction, but he blamed the Texans for taking his country and pled that his people might be allowed to continue their nomadic life.[10] The treaty signed on October 21, 1867, the last ever made with the Comanches and Kiowas, provided that these Indians should accept an agency, schools, and farms – none of which they wanted – and a reservation in present southwestern Oklahoma north and east of the Red River and its North Fork, south of the Washita River, and west of the ninety-eighth meridian. This area of almost three million acres was small indeed compared to the vast Comanchería of old, but in return the United States promised annuities. The Lords of the Southern Plains were about to become the wards of the federal government.[11]

Washington, however, was slow to activate the treaty, and meanwhile the Comanche and Kiowa raids into Texas continued with increasing fury. When Agent Lawrie Tatum arrived on July 1, 1869, the powerful Kwahadi and Kotsoteka bands, approximately 1,500 of an estimated 2,416 Comanches, refused to move onto the reservation; they were joined from time to time by other Indians who disliked an idle, monotonous life on the reservation. Agent Tatum, who began his work at the Kiowa-Commanche agency with a blind faith in the Quaker Peace Policy which President Grant had adopted in the spring of 1869, found from the very first that without the presence of troops, the reservation became a sanctuary for marauders who slipped away to raid in Texas. As long as game was plentiful and arms and ammunition were available from the traders, the Indians could not be kept on the reservation except by force.

Fortunately, the War Department had reestablished its defense line across western Texas. In the spring of 1867 additional posts on the western frontier were put "in proper order for the reception of troops." On May 25, 1867, Fort Chadbourne was reoccupied by Co. G, 4th Cavalry, and within a few days Lieutenant Peter M. Boehm with a detachment of fifty men was sent to establish a camp on the Middle Concho, to scout the vicinity for depredating Indians, and to "protect the trains and droves of cattle" moving over the trail Charles Goodnight had blazed the preceding year from the Palo Pinto region to New Mexico. Boehm established his "permanent camp" on the Middle Concho, eighteen miles above the junction of the North and South Concho. By the end of June, when Captain Eugene B. Beaumont arrived from Fort Mason to take command, the Chadbourne garrison had 331 men. In July, the command of the post changed again when Captain George G. Huntt with his troops from Camp Verde took over the post, bringing its strength up to 423 men.[12]

Because the water was bad and in short supply and the timber in their vicinities was inadequate, Chadbourne, Belknap, and Buffalo Springs were abandoned as permanent posts. During a hot, dry spell there was not nearly enough water at Buffalo Springs to meet the needs of the post; at Belknap, not even the horses would drink from the saline Brazos, and the well dug there furnished little water; and the Quartermaster General for Texas recommended the removal of Chadbourne to "a more favorable and convenient locality," because of the "insufficiency and unhealthy quality of the water . . . together with the distance of the post from the most frequented routes of travel." [13] On July 21, 1867, Lieutenant Colonel S. D. Sturgis with four companies of the 6th Cavalry from Fort Belknap established Camp Wilson on the south side of the Clear Fork of the Brazos, about fifteen miles north of present Albany, where there was an abundance of timber and good water. Upon the recommendation of Sheridan's inspection board late that year, Camp Wilson was designated a permanent post and renamed Fort Griffin. [14]

After inspecting Buffalo Springs, the Board recommended Jacksboro as a more suitable location. The move began immediately. On November 19, one company left to establish Fort Richardson, built to accommodate ten full companies, on Lost Creek on the southwest edge of Jacksboro, and the final evacuation occurred on March 1, 1868. [15]

The inspection board likewise condemned Chadbourne and selected a site on the Concho River as suitable for a permanent post. Leaving Chadbourne on November 23 with an escort, and with detachments of Cos. M and H trailing only a few days behind, Captain Huntt on December 4, established his headquarters at the newly selected site, which he designated Camp Hatch in honor of Major John P. Hatch, a member of the location board and later commander of the post. Before the end of the year the post on the Concho had a total garrison of 16 commissioned officers and 372 enlisted men. In deference to the wishes of Major Hatch, the name of the post was changed to Camp Kelley in memory of a recently deceased officer of the 4th Cavalry, and then on February 6, 1868, permanently to Fort Concho. [16]

Fort McKavett, a mass of ruins with only one habitable building, was reoccupied on April 1, 1868, by Colonel Mackenzie's infantry troops. A year later Mackenzie made it his headquarters and built it into the finest post on the Texas frontier. Fort Duncan was reoccupied about the same time as McKavett, and Stockton in July, 1867. In the fall of 1869 there were 129 officers and men stationed at Fort Concho, 234 at Griffin, and 218 at Richardson, the three key posts guarding the Texas frontier against the hostile Comanches and Kiowas; the average distance between all the frontier posts was about eighty-five miles.

Meanwhile, under the Quaker Peace Policy the reservation became a sanctuary for Indians marauding in Texas, who found little difficulty in slipping by the widely scattered posts. In the fall of 1870 the Kiowas killed a man who lived at Henrietta and took to Fort Sill as captives the other six members of the family. During the winter other war parties repeatedly ravaged the Texas border. In January, 1871, a band of Kiowas led by Mamanti and Quitan killed and scalped four Negroes, including Brit Johnson, the man who had secured the release of the captives taken during the Elm Creek raid in 1864, on the Butterfield Trail two miles south of Flat Top Mountain. When overtaken by a few soldiers of the 6th Cavalry, the Indians wounded the commanding officer and drove the troops back to their post.[17] By April the Indians were boldly attacking within three miles of Fort Richardson. The area between forts Richardson and Griffin, particularly Salt Creek prairie near present Graham, bore the brunt of the attacks. Altogether fourteen persons were killed by the Indians during the spring of 1871. Governor Edmund J. Davis complained that "the atrocities recently committed by the Indians" were even beyond "all previous experience of their murderous doings." General Sheridan, now commander of the Division of the Missouri, and General William Tecumseh Sherman, General of the Army, confronted with a storm of protests and numerous reports of atrocities, concluded that something had to be done. The 6th Cavalry, which had never won any plaudits for its service on the frontier, was sent to Kansas; Colonel Mackenzie, Grant's "most promising young officer," was ordered to move his headquarters to Fort Richardson and to assume responsibility for the defense of that sector of the Texas frontier. Furthermore, Sherman decided to make a personal inspection of the entire frontier from San Antonio to Kansas to determine for himself whether the settlers' constant clamor for protection was justified and if so, to determine the remedy. The Quakers and Colonel Benjamin H. Grierson, commanding at Fort Sill, were insisting that the agency Indians were peaceful and that the Texans, besides highly exaggerating their accounts, were themselves to blame for whatever trouble had occurred.

General Sherman, accompanied by Inspector General Randolph B. Marcy, a veteran of the northwestern Texas frontier, two staff members, and fifteen cavalrymen, on May 2 headed north from San Antonio by way of forts Mason, McKavett, Concho, and Griffin to Fort Richardson. Along the way he saw isolated settlers' cabins, but no Indians, and remained skeptical of the Texans' reports. "They expose women and children singly on the road and in cabins far off from others," he wrote, "as though they were safe in Illinois. Of course I have heard other stories, but such actions are more significant than words. If the Comanches don't steal horses it is because they cannot be tempted." [18]

Marcy, who had spent much time in the area before the Civil War, differed with Sherman. Noting at Belknap and beyond the ghostly chimneys that marked burned cabins, the hastily abandoned fields and the graves at unexpected locations, he recorded in his journal that "This rich and beautiful section does not contain today so many white people as it did when I visited it eighteen years ago, and if the Indian marauders are not punished, the whole country seems to be in a fair way of becoming totally depopulated." [19]

As the party on May 18 made its way across Salt Creek prairie, a dangerous spot on the road for several years, it miraculously escaped being annihilated by a band of about 150 Kiowa Indians who from their hiding place on a nearby hill quietly watched it pass because Mamanti (Touching-the-Sky or Sky-Walker), the medicine leader who had made medicine on the evening before, had instructed his followers that two parties would pass along the Richardson-Belknap road the next day; the first must not be attacked, but an attack on the second would be successful.[20]

Sherman arrived at Richardson at sunset and the party camped in tents near Mackenzie's crude quarters. That evening, after greeting the officers of the post and listening politely but skeptically to a delegation of citizens who complained about the seriousness of the Indian depredations in the area, the weary General promised to investigate and retired for the night.

Later that night Thomas Brazeal, who had been shot in the foot, limped into the post and told Sherman a pitiful story. He was a teamster, he said, for a wagon train owned by Henry Warren, a government freighting contractor, hauling shelled corn to Fort Griffin. The train, consisting of ten wagons and twelve men, had been attacked the previous afternoon on the Salt Creek prairie two or three miles from Cox Mountain. Seven of the men were killed, one being chained to a wagon wheel and burned; the others, including Brazeal, had escaped in the nearby woods while the Kiowas were intent upon mutilating the bodies of the dead teamsters, plundering the train, and taking possession of forty-one mules.[21] The General, not aware, of course, that his life had been spared as a result of the uncanny suggestion of an Indian medicine man, but realizing, no doubt, that it could as well have been his mutilated body bloating in the hot sun on Salt Creek prairie, quickly decided that the Texans' complaints were fully justified and that drastic military action was necessary. Fortunately, he had at hand the able and energetic Mackenzie and a contingent of his tough 4th Cavalry. He at once ordered the Colonel to take his available cavalry, investigate the report and, if found true, to pursue the raiders, even to the reservation.[22] Mackenzie and his cavalry hit their saddles and left in a blinding rain. A new era in the history of the Texas frontier had begun.

FOOTNOTES — CHAPTER II

[1] *War of Rebellion Records*, Series IV, I, pp. 542–554.

[2] W. C. Holden, "Frontier Defense in Texas during the Civil War," in West Texas Historical Association *Year Book*, IV (1928), 19–21.

[3] *Ibid.*, 27–28; Claude Elliott, *Leathercoat, The Life of James W. Throckmorton* (San Antonio, 1938), 80–90.

[4] C. C. Rister, *Fort Griffin on the Texas Frontier* (Norman, 1956), 48 (hereafter cited as Rister, *Fort Griffin*).

[5] "Journal of treaties," Commission meetings, October 5–24, 1865, Item 6, Treaty File No. 341, Office of Indian Affairs, RG 75, National Archives; Charles J. Kappler (ed.), *Indian Affairs, Laws and Treaties* (3 vols.; Washington, 1904), II, 892–895.

[6] "Proceedings of a Council held at the Big Bend of the Arkansas river in the State of Kansas, with the Indians of the Upper Arkansas, November 26, 1866," Treaties and Council files, Office of Indian Affairs, National Archives.

[7] *Texas Almanac* (Dallas, 1947), 132.

[8] R. N. Richardson, *The Comanche Barrier to South Plains Settlement* (Glendale, Calif., 1933), 293 (hereafter cited as Richardson, *Comanche Barrier*.)

[9] Theronne Thompson, "Fort Buffalo Springs, Texas Border Post," in West Texas Historical Association *Year Book*, XXXVI (1960), 169–170 (hereafter cited as Thompson, "Fort Buffalo Springs"); H. H. McConnell, *Five Years a Cavalryman* (Jacksboro, Texas, 1889), 99–100.

[10] "Record Copy of the Proceedings of the Indian Peace Commission Appointed under the Act of Congress Approved July 20, 1867," MS, Office of Indian Affairs, National Archives; Avonlee English, "United States-Southern Plains Indian Relations, 1865–1868" (M. A. thesis, Texas Technological College, Lubbock, 1962), 92–116.

[11] Ernest Wallace and E. A. Hoebel, *The Comanches, Lords of the South Plains* (Norman, 1952), 308–309; English, "United States-Southern Plains Indian Relations, 1865–1868," 116–127.

[12] Haley, *Fort Concho*, 122–125.

[13] *Ibid.*, 127.

[14] Rister, *Fort Griffin*, 64–65.

[15] Thompson, "Fort Buffalo Springs," 156, 172–173, as cited; Donald W. Whisenhunt, "Fort Richardson. Frontier Post in Northwest Texas, 1867–1878" (M. A. thesis, Texas Technological College, Lubbock, 1962), 17–19.

[16] Haley, *Fort Concho*, 126–131.

[17] W. S. Nye, *Carbine and Lance, The Story of Old Fort Sill* (Norman, 1937), 123.

[18] Quoted in *ibid.*, 124.

[19] R. B. Marcy, May 17, 1871, "Journal," in W. T. Sherman's Official Papers, I, February 11, 1866-February 8, 1878 (MS, Library of Congress, Washington); copy of "Journal" entry in Rister Papers, The Southwest Collection, Texas Technological College, Lubbock.

[20] The Indian account in Nye, *Carbine and Lance*, 126-127.

[21] "Tabular Statement of Expeditions and Scouts against Indians, made in Department of Texas, during the year ending September 30, 1871," 3719 AGO 1871, RG 94 (hereafter cited as "Tabular Statement of Expeditions" followed by appropriate date).

[22] Sherman to Mackenzie, May 19, 1871, 1894 AGO 1871, RG 94.

CHAPTER III

Initiation into Plains Indian Warfare

PACKING RATIONS for thirty days, Mackenzie with four of his cavalry companies, A, B, D, E, consisting of 9 officers, 193 enlisted men, 16 Indian scouts, and 2 post guides, Henry W. Strong and Jim Dozier, on May 19 headed west along the old Butterfield Road in a heavy rainstorm for Salt Creek prairie.[1] Reaching the scene of the massacre shortly before night, Mackenzie had a gruesome and sickening introduction to Plains Indian warfare. The naked, bloated bodies of the seven murdered teamsters, riddled with bullets and arrows, their skulls crushed, their scalps removed, were horribly mutilated. One of the bodies, its tongue cut out, was chained to a burned wagon; some of the men had been beheaded, their fingers, toes, and privates cut off and stuck into their mouths. The corpses were placed in one of the wagon beds and buried beside the road.[2]

Sending couriers off to Richardson to confirm the tragedy and others to Griffin with Sherman's orders directing Major W. H. Wood at that post to cooperate with the Colonel by scouting the country to the head of the Little Wichita,[3] Mackenzie then headed north after the Kiowa raiders, slowly following the trail almost obliterated by the flood. On the next day, when Mackenzie reached the Little Wichita, where he had to wait for the swollen stream to subside, the raiders were farther north, crossing the Big Wichita. Lieutenant Boehm and twenty-five men of the 4th Cavalry, who were scouting the area, surprised four Kiowas who had lingered behind to kill some buffalo before crossing the river, and killed one raider but at a cost of one trooper and two horses wounded.[4] Without waiting to ascertain the intention of the cavalrymen, the Kiowas, crossing between Vernon and Electra, hurried to the north side of the Red River, where they felt safe, and then moved leisurely to their village west of Fort Sill. Mackenzie, who had started the pursuit a full day behind, lost the trail south of the Red River, and then scoured the country for several days in heavy rains in search of the Kiowa village.[5] Unable to find any further sign of Indians south of Red River, Mackenzie gave up the search and on June 4 rode into Fort Sill, where he found his quarry under arrest in the post guardhouse.

Meanwhile, General Sherman, riding in a Dougherty ambulance, had left Fort Richardson with a small infantry escort on May 20, crossed Red River late the next day, and arrived at Fort Sill on May 23. At once he called upon the conscientious Quaker agent, Lawrie Tatum, informing him of the Salt Creek prairie massacre and inquiring if any Indians had recently left the reservation. The horrified Tatum replied that he had heard that Satanta's band was away; he would find out in a few days when the Indians came in for their rations. Strangely enough, Tatum, who already had lost his faith in the Peace Policy, had just written to his superior, Enoch Hoag, head of the Central Superintendency at Lawrence, Kansas, asking permission to arrest Indian murderers and depredators and to turn them over to civil authorities for trial in conformity with white man's law. Sherman agreed with the proposal, and Hoag's rejection was too late to save the leaders of the Salt Creek prairie raid. When on Saturday, May 27, the principal Kiowa chiefs, including Satanta, Big Tree, Kicking Bird, and Lone Wolf, came to the agency to draw their rations and were questioned about the Salt Creek prairie raid, Satanta arrogantly and contemptuously

described it and boastfully claimed sole credit for leading it.⁶
Tatum, thoroughly disillusioned, requested Sherman to arrest
the guilty chiefs and send them to Jacksboro for trial.

Since the military had no authority on the agency premises,
General Sherman called for a council of the chiefs on the front
porch of the home of Colonel Grierson, commander at Fort
Sill of the 10th Cavalry. There, with armed soldiers concealed
in the house and others strategically placed and carefully instructed, Sherman asked the Indians about the recent raid.
When Satanta proudly reaffirmed both his story to Tatum and
the account sent by Mackenzie, Sherman informed the Indians
that Satanta, Satank, Big Tree, and Eagle Heart were under
arrest and would be sent to Texas to stand trial for murder and
that the tribe would have to surrender forty-one good mules to
reimburse the owner of the wagon train.

Although Satanta immediately changed his story, claiming
that he had merely gone along as an observer, and Kicking Bird,
a friendly chief, offered to exchange the mules for the chiefs,
Sherman would not yield. For a moment a bloody fight seemed
inevitable, but the shutters banged open, revealing the armed
soldiers just in time. In the melée one warrior was killed and
Eagle Heart escaped. The other three arrested chiefs, man-
acled hand and foot, were sent to the post guardhouse to brood
over their unfortunate fate. After waiting on Mackenzie until
Tuesday, May 30, Sherman issued orders for him to carry the
prisoners to the civil authorities at Jacksboro for trial, and left
for Fort Gibson.

When Mackenzie, irritated over his failure to find the Indians, rode into Fort Sill on June 4, he was highly pleased with
his new orders. On the morning of June 8 Lieutenant William
A. Thompson, 4th Cavalry, loaded the three prisoners, hand-
cuffed and hobbled in iron chains, into two wagons, forcing
the defiant Satank into the front wagon, the others clambering
into the second; two guards were placed in each wagon and
mounted troops on all sides.

As the caravan pulled out of the fort, Satanta asked a Caddo scout to tell his people to return the stolen mules and not to raid any more. The humiliated Satank, a member of the Kait-senko war society whose number was limited to the ten bravest warriors in the tribe, began to chant his death song. Fortu-nately, the post interpreter understood its meaning and warned the corporal of the guard of impending trouble. As the wagons rumbled down the hill toward a ford on the creek, Satank called to his fellow prisoners that he would be dead before he reached a large tree about a mile down the road, and then asked the Caddo scout to "Tell my people I died beside the road. My bones will be found there. Tell my people to gather them up and carry them away."[7] Old Satank then covered his head with his blanket and continued his death song. Approximately at the place he had indicated, Satank suddenly stripped his handcuffs from his wrists, threw the blanket from his shoulders, pulled a knife concealed in his breechclout, and stabbed one of the guards.[8] In the ensuing struggle, both guards jumped from the wagon, leaving the old chief in possession of a Spencer carbine, but before he could work its mechanism Corporal John B. Charlton, who was riding in the wagon with Satanta and Big Tree, fired two .50 caliber bullets into his body.[9] Just as the commotion ended, Mackenzie, who had lingered with Colonel Grierson for a few minutes after the column started, rode up and listened to the explanations; without either commending or reprimanding any of his men, including Corporal Charlton, he ordered the guards to dump the mortally wounded old war-rior, who preferred death to dishonor, beside the road approxi-mately where he had sent word to his people to pick up his body.

During the remainder of the trip, Mackenzie took precau-tions to prevent the Kiowas from surprising the command and retrieving their captive chiefs. At night strong pickets and "sleeping parties," small detachments who slept on their wea-pons in strategic locations, were placed around the command,

and the prisoners were spread out on the ground with their arms and legs bound to stakes, helpless, suffering victims of swarms of bloodthirsty mosquitoes, particularly through the Wichita River bottoms. On June 15, a clear, warm day, Mackenzie and his weary sun-tanned troopers rode into Richardson to be greeted by the garrison band and the entire population of Jacksboro, anxious to get a look at the celebrated prisoners, particularly at the immense Satanta, the "Orator of the Plains," who glared back with proud disdain. The two prisoners were lodged in the guardhouse to await trial with two reliefs of guards, about twenty men each, assigned to prevent them from escaping and to protect them from being mobbed. They were later moved to the post morgue for better safety.

Three weeks later in a highly dramatic and significant departure from previous treatment of Indian prisoners, Satanta and Big Tree were brought to trial for the murder of the Texans on Salt Creek prairie. The grand jury indicted them on July 5, and Big Tree's trial began the same afternoon in Judge Charles Soward's Thirteenth District Court in a room overflowing with spectators, most of whom were armed. Prosecuting attorney S. W. T. Lanham, later governor of Texas, presented the case for the state, using as witnesses Brazeal, the wounded teamster, Tatum, and Mackenzie. During the course of his argument to the jury, Lanham denounced the government's Peace Policy and praised Sherman and Mackenzie, saying that if the defense of the frontier were left to the distinguished Colonel, the Indian problem would soon be eliminated.

Thomas Ball and J. A. Wolfork, court-appointed attorneys, made an able defense of the prisoners, but without any influence upon the cowboy jury. After only short deliberations, the jury, the same in both trials, returned verdicts of guilty, and Judge Soward sentenced both prisoners to be hanged. The Judge saw that the prisoners had a fair trial in accordance with Texas law, but any other verdict likely would have led to mob violence.[10]

By the time the trial was over, supporters of the Quaker Peace Policy across the nation were raising a storm of protest. The execution of the chiefs would be murder, they insisted, and would completely thwart their work. Superintendent Hoag wrote President Grant that their execution would precipitate an Indian war, and even Judge Soward and Agent Tatum advised Governor Davis that life confinement would be a more severe punishment than death and a more effective restraint on the Kiowas. On August 2 the Governor commuted the sentences to life imprisonment, and on September 12 Satanta and Big Tree were sent to the state penitentiary at Huntsville.

While returning the prisoners to Texas, Mackenzie gave a great deal of thought to the Indian problem and to the opinions of Tatum and Sherman, and as soon as he reached Fort Richardson he wrote Sherman his recommendations: the garrisons of the frontier posts should be concentrated for a campaign against the marauders, who were all coming from either the eastern edge of the Staked Plains or the Fort Sill reservation. Tatum would not be able "to elevate" the Kiowas and Comanches, he thought, until they had been dismounted, disarmed, and made to raise corn. "The Kiowas and Comanches are entirely beyond any control and have been for a long time. Mr. Tatum . . . is anxious that the Kiowas and Comanches now out of control be brought under. This can be accomplished only by the Army . . . Either these Indians must be punished or they must be allowed to murder and rob at their own discretion." [11]

On the same day, Mackenzie reported to Reynolds, advising an immediate expedition against the Kiowas and another in the autumn unless these Indians and the Comanches off the reservation had returned. Without waiting for the recommendations, Reynolds, in anticipation of their nature, on June 17 ordered the 9th Cavalry to relieve the 4th Cavalry at several posts so that Mackenzie could concentrate his troops for the campaign.[12] After the receipt of Mackenzie's recommendations, Reynolds on July 6 informed him that his proposed immediate expedition against the Indians had been approved, but that approval of the fall expedition would have to await the decision of the War Department.[13]

Mackenzie on June 29 began assembling additional companies of his cavalry at Richardson. Company C from Laredo, L from Brownsville, and K from McKavett arrived on July 16 and 17 and went into camp along Lost Creek; G and I from Concho and D and H from Griffin arrived on July 28 and 29. Not since the Civil War had so many companies of the 4th Cavalry been congregated at one point, the largest concentration of troops in Texas.[14] About the same time Mackenzie fortunately secured as his Quartermaster First Lieutenant Henry W. Lawton, a Civil War veteran and an administrative and logistical genius who, no doubt, deserves a great deal of the credit for Mackenzie's later success not only in western Texas but also in Montana against Chief Dull Knife and elsewhere. Six-feet-four in height and unequalled in energy, Lawton may have owed part of his ability to cope with any emergency to his supreme contempt for army manuals and red tape.[15]

Meanwhile, Mackenzie had sent Cos. B, E, and F of the 4th Cavalry and one of the 11th Infantry to Gilbert's Creek, a small tributary of the Red River, to establish a base from which to scout for the Kiowas.[16] He also made arrangements to obtain for the troops in the field large amounts of forage and grain from Whaley's ranch at the mouth of the Big Wichita River.

In the routine of making preparations, Mackenzie violated regulations, either through an oversight in his eagerness to get the campaign underway, or because he felt it necessary for the success of the expedition and that with Sherman's backing he need not be hampered by army red tape. On July 1 he invoiced forty-six pack mules to the officers of four companies instead of to the quartermaster as prescribed by regulations, and then he submitted a requisition for $50,000 worth of ordnance equip-

ment to Colonel Reynolds. The infuriated Reynolds reported
Mackenzie to higher authorities and ordered him to abide by
regulations. Mackenzie corrected his "culpable oversight," and
Reynolds thereupon provided some of the requested ordnance.[17] This was only one of the incidents that led to a rupture in relations between Mackenzie and his immediate superior; Mackenzie had already fired off letters on June 28 and 30
to the commander of the Division of the South, charging Reynolds with fraud and corruption in connection with the purchase of forage for military use.

After delaying his scout long enough to appear as a witness
in a court martial at Fort Concho,[18] Mackenzie upon his return
sent ahead to the Little Wichita Captain N. B. McLaughlin, a
former brevet brigadier general, with six companies of the 4th
Cavalry, A, C, D, G, I, and H, with instructions to have a
bridge on that stream ready for the wagon train. Then, starting the remaining company, L, a few hours ahead, Mackenzie,
neglecting to report his departure time to the departmental
commander,[19] and Lieutenant Boehm, wearing a white, wide-
brimmed hat by special permission, and his Tonkawa scouts
rode out of Fort Richardson on August 2 under a bright moon
as far as the West Fork of the Trinity, where with the tired
troopers of Co. L they were soon fast asleep.[20] Mackenzie's
first campaign against the Comanches and Kiowas was underway.

From the West Fork, the command followed the road across
a parched and waterless stretch of country that had been black-
ened by a prairie fire to Buffalo Springs. The last rain had been
on May 19, the day Mackenzie inspected the massacre on the
Salt Creek prairie. Finding the waterholes at Buffalo Springs
choked with dead and dying cattle, the command rode on
across the burned-over prairie to Camp Wichita, an abandoned 6th Cavalry post, where some very bad water "was better than nothing." On August 4, after passing through Henrietta, where nothing was left by the Indians but "two or three

old broken-down, partly burned ranches," it joined McLaughlin on the Little Wichita, and a day later, when McLaughlin
had finished constructing the bridge, the wagons were pulled
across by hand, the horses and mules swimming the river.[21]

Beyond the Little Wichita the country became rougher and
travel slower. At the Big Wichita, the cavalrymen rested in
their tents during a heavy rain while Quartermaster Lawton
and his detail prepared a ford. The next morning, the last of
the twenty-five wagons in the train and its supporting infantry
company having crossed the river, the command marched for
Gilbert's Creek, north of present Wichita Falls, where it joined
Cos. B, E, and F shortly after noon.[22]

At Gilbert's Creek Mackenzie organized the ten companies
of the 4th Cavalry into five battalions, issued enough provisions
for the cavalrymen to load the ninety "green" pack mules, assigned the two infantry companies to guard the wagons, and
about 6:00 a.m. on August 7 headed for the crossing on the
Red River and Indian Territory. During the long, hot march
the pack mules gave trouble, at one time scattering provisions
over the prairie. The first night beyond Gilbert's Creek, while
camped on the south bank of Red River, the command had a
narrow escape when the dry cane brakes suddenly burst into
flame. With great difficulty the wagons were hauled into the
dry bed of the Red River in time to save them. Expecting to
be attacked at any moment, the troops struggled through the
sand dunes bordering the river and then continued over rolling
prairies, covered with verdant grass and many buffalo, ante-
lope, prairie dogs, and rattlesnakes, for fourteen miles beyond
Red River before camping for the night of August 8 on West
Cache Creek, west of the present town of Walters. From here
the column travelled northwest over a prairie abounding with
buffalo and prairie dogs to Otter Creek, near old Camp Radi-
ziminski, where Colonel Grierson with most of his 10th Cavalry was waiting to join Mackenzie in the campaign against
the Kiowas. Mackenzie's wagon train, after halting several

times to load up with buffalo meat, pulled into the Otter Creek camp several hours behind the cavalry.[23]

Here, after holding several conferences and inspecting the vicinity, Mackenzie and Grierson established a rendezvous or supply camp, and then with their pack trains and cavalry set out to find Kicking Bird's camp, Grierson into the country between the Wichita Mountains and the North Fork and Mackenzie into the badlands between the North Fork and the Salt Fork of Red River, where Matthew Leeper, the agency interpreter who had joined Mackenzie's command on Otter Creek, thought the Kiowas might be.[24]

Starting on August 16, Mackenzie crossed the North Fork of the Red River three miles from the supply camp and began working his way up the west side of that stream through shinnery and sand hills and at times over a sun-parched, burned-off prairie. On the next day, while still struggling through this inhospitable region adjacent to the North Fork, a courier overtook the command with dispatches for the Colonel. Upon reading one of the messages, Mackenzie's behavior suddenly changed; thereafter on the campaign the Colonel became increasingly nervous and irritable and less eager to find any Indians, but he made no explanation to his puzzled staff, and Lieutenant Carter, his adjutant who later did considerable research in the military records, apparently never learned the nature of the message.[25]

Actually, the dispatch that disturbed Mackenzie was a copy of a letter from General Sherman to the adjutant general, copies of which had also been sent to the Secretary of War and to Colonel Reynolds. After acknowledging receipt of a number of letters, including one from Mackenzie, Sherman stated that Mackenzie, in his opinion, "should abide by Reynolds' order of July 5 not to cross the boundary of Texas into the Indian country unless called upon by General Grierson," as the latter had ample force to deal with the Kiowas, and that the hanging of Satanta and Big Tree would have a salutary effect upon their tribesmen. He had already authorized Mackenzie to make an expedition in the autumn into the country "west of Double Mountain." Reynolds informed Sherman that his instructions had granted Mackenzie "no authority to enter the reservations unless in actual pursuit." [26] Obviously, until this moment Mackenzie had considered that his expedition was in "pursuit" of Kicking Bird, but to be doubly safe he had decided to search west of the North Fork of the Red, outside the limits of the reservation.

Meanwhile, the Kiowas, who had fled from the vicinity of the agency when their chiefs were arrested, had camped for a few days west of present Granite, Oklahoma, and then had moved westward to Sweetwater Creek near present Mobeetie, Texas. When Grierson, who had been campaigning quite leisurely, learned that Kicking Bird had delivered the required forty-one mules to Agent Tatum on August 11, he sent the Fort Sill interpreter to warn him to move his band onto the reservation to be safe from attack by Mackenzie. Leaving four companies at Otter Creek, Grierson returned to Fort Sill and reported directly to Sherman, voicing the opinion that the campaign would have a good effect upon the Indians and criticizing Mackenzie for not scouting the country south of the South Fork of the Red, although he was aware that the Kiowas were not in that area.[27]

Mackenzie, certain only that he should not fight Indians outside of Texas, moved northwest through the rough, sun-parched region between the North Fork and the Elm Fork of the Red, where the warm gypsum water thoroughly impregnated with buffalo excrement left the men nauseated and weakened with diarrhea until they could hardly stay on their horses. To prevent heat strokes, the Colonel required every man to place a wet sponge in his hat and to carry an extra canteen of water to keep it moist. As he floundered over the wasteland belt and the men and horses grew weaker, Mackenzie slept very little and became more irritable and exacting, snapping the stumps of his amputated fingers with "more than usual vigor." [28]

After striking good water at Sweetwater Creek and ascending that stream unwittingly to within nine miles of Kicking Bird's camp, Mackenzie turned back on August 28 and worked his way by short marches toward the supply train on Otter Creek. Men and horses suffered greatly; ten horses and two mules were abandoned on the Salt Fork on August 31, but the next day the command rode into its Otter Creek camp, where it found the companies left in the field by Grierson living in relative luxury. Here Mackenzie found a copy of Tatum's letter to Grierson stating that Kicking Bird had delivered the required number of mules and had decided to cease fighting and to remain on the reservation. [29]

Since there was no reason to remain in Indian Territory, Mackenzie decided to send his command to Richardson and Griffin and to prepare for a campaign against the Comanches in Texas, where the Indian Bureau and Grierson had no authority. Consequently, after forage and supplies from Fort Sill had arrived and the men and horses had recuperated, on September 6, he broke camp on Otter Creek, taking companies C, E, and I of the 4th Cavalry and the infantry company to Fort Richardson and sending all the remainder under the command of Captain Clarence Mauck to Fort Griffin with directions to begin preparations. Mackenzie's detachment returned by its outgoing route, crossing the Little Wichita on the previously constructed ramshackle bridge. After a miserable experience with vicious ants in camp near the river, Mackenzie left the troops in command of McLaughlin to follow at a more leisurely pace and accompanied by the post guide and Adjutant Carter covered the remaining forty miles to Fort Richardson, arriving just before dark on September 13 in a drenching thunderstorm, two days ahead of the troopers. After allowing it a short rest, Mackenzie sent Co. I to Fort Concho, its home post. [30] The expedition had been a failure, except for the knowledge of the geography and the experience in campaigning against Plains Indians, and the fighting commander was unable to hide the chagrin and disappointment "which seemed to possess his soul and disturb his peace of mind."

The imprisonment of Satanta and Big Tree and the campaign in Indian Territory had a quieting effect upon the Kiowas, but many incorrigible Comanches, particularly the bands of Mow-way (Handshaker) and Para-o-coom (He Bear), were still at large and were actively engaged in plundering the Texas frontier. These two chiefs had repeatedly told Tatum that not until the "blue coats" had invaded their country and whipped them would they move onto the reservation and "walk on the white man's road." They scorned the government's annuities, for they could acquire white man's goods from the *Comancheros* who periodically crossed the Llano Estacado with their loaded carts to meet them on the Canadian in the Texas Panhandle, at Quitaque springs, in the Mucha-que valley between present Gail and Snyder, at Laguna Sabinas, about fifteen miles northwest of present Lamesa, and in Cañon del Rescate, Yellowhouse Canyon, at present Lubbock. Impressed with the success of the military in quieting the Kiowas, Agent Tatum in his letter informing Grierson that Kicking Bird had restored the mules wrote that "I would be very glad if thee and General Mackenzie could get that little captive [Clinton Smith of Boerne, who with his younger brother had been captured in 1869] and induce Mow-way and his band to come into the reservation and behave." [31]

Unhampered in Texas by the Quaker Peace Policy and with Sherman's authorization for an autumn expedition in hand,[32] Mackenzie as soon as he returned to Richardson began preparations to find Mow-way. On September 24 he started Co. K, commanded by Captain Edward M. Heyl, and one company of the 11th Infantry from Richardson for the rendezvous camp on the Clear Fork of the Brazos, a day ahead of his own departure.[33] He had selected the site of old Camp Cooper, five miles north of Fort Griffin and on the north side of the Clear Fork of the Brazos, as his point of concentration for departure.

Pending his arrival, Mackenzie had placed Captain Wirt Davis, commander of Co. F, in command of the camp. By September 25 eight companies of the 4th Cavalry (A, B, D, F, G, H, K, and L), two companies of the 11th Infantry, twenty Tonkawa scouts and about one hundred pack mules had reached the rendezvous. On that night a party of Indians in an effort to create a diversion ran off 120 cattle and 13 horses from Murphy's ranch, about twenty miles from the camp. The angry settlers demanded that the cavalry take up the trail, but Captain Davis refused to pursue because he had orders to remain in camp resting his men and horses.

Five days later Mackenzie sent Carter with a detachment of eight cavalrymen and five Tonkawa scouts to find a practicable road for the wagon train. When Carter returned on October 3, the entire command, consisting of about six hundred men and nearly one hundred pack mules, rode out of its "bivouac on the beautiful bend of the Clear Fork," the troopers merrily singing their old regimental song, "Come home, John, don't stay long; Come home soon to your own Chick-a-biddy!" Carter rode at the head of the column, following the road he had selected. Lieutenant Boehm and his Tonkawa scouts were far out in advance, combing the vicinity of the route for fresh signs of Indians, and as a further precaution against a surprise attack Mackenzie had a small detachment of cavalry between the scouts and the column. Quartermaster Lawton, trailing the troopers with his wagon train, had difficulty in keeping up, particularly when crossing California and Paint creeks, both quicksand streams with steep banks.[34]

Moving from the rendezvous camp by way of the military road to the south side of the Clear Fork near Fort Griffin, the command marched west-northwest, recrossing the Clear Fork about three or four miles upstream from the common southern corner of Throckmorton and Haskell counties. Continuing in the same direction, it crossed California Creek in the northwest corner of Jones County just below the Haskell County line, crossed the south fork of Oteys or Paint Creek near its intersection with the Jones-Haskell County line, passed through the northern edge of the present city of Stamford, then travelled approximately along the thirty-third parallel to its next night's camp in plain sight of the Double Mountains. Starting early the next morning, the column veered more to the northwest, crossed the Double Mountain Fork of the Brazos at the bend in southeastern Stonewall County, about twenty miles above its confluence with the Salt Fork and due north of the present town of Hamlin, and camped at night near Cottonwood Springs, between Double Mountain and the present town of Aspermont, where it had "the vilest of water" but plenty of fresh buffalo meat for food and excellent grazing for the animals.

All day he had travelled in the midst of an immense herd of buffalo, and knowing that wherever buffalo were in number the Indians were not likely to be far away, Mackenzie took extra precautions for safety, including a special guard with the horses and mules, "sleeping parties," the regular camp guards, and picket outposts. Indians, however, were not the problem. Shortly after midnight, Lieutenant Carter, who was in charge of the guard that night, heard the thunderous noise of stampeding buffalo coming directly toward the camp, inadvertently placed across the trail to their watering place. Carter's first instinct was to order the guards to fire directly into the leading animals but, since Mackenzie had ordered that no weapon be fired unless absolutely essential, he had them dash toward the animals, yelling and waving their blankets. The scheme worked, and the loping brown mass careened off to the left of the camp just in time to save the horse herd and a disaster.

Starting early the next morning, the column splashed across the shallow water of the Salt Fork of the Brazos at the bend in western Stonewall County, about four or five miles south-west of the present town of Peacock, and, continuing in the same direction across rolling prairie, populated with prairie dogs and buffalo as far as the eye could see, struck the Salt Fork again about three miles southwest of present Jayton, and then travelled up that stream a few miles before making camp for the night on Duck Creek near the present town of Spur, where Lawton was to establish his supply base.[35] During the day's march, Carter noticed a number of abandoned *Coman-chero* "trading stations," half dug-outs supported by a frame-work of poles in the banks or bluffs.[36]

That night, October 7, Mackenzie sent the Tonkawa scouts out to search for the Kwahadi Comanche village. At dark on the following evening, after a detachment of cavalry had scouted toward the headwaters of Duck Creek without seeing any signs of either the Comanches or the Tonkawa scouts, Mac-kenzie, leaving the two infantry companies to guard the supply camp, set out with his cavalry and about ninety pack mules to make a surprise attack on the Comanche village without wait-ing for the scouts to report its location.[37]. He expected to find the Kwahadi band of Quanah Parker, the half-breed son of Peta Nocona and Cynthia Ann Parker, a white captive, camped near where Blanco Canyon cuts through the Caprock to form the Freshwater Fork of the Brazos.

After much confusion and many tribulations and bruises, and with both horses and men extremely weary, Mackenzie found himself about midnight in a small box canyon with a towering, rocky wall too steep to scale at the projection of the Caprock, west of present Dickens. Hopelessly entrapped and unable to find his way out in the inky blackness of a cloudy night, he quietly bivouacked without fire. As soon as there was enough light to see, he led the troops by a flanking movement out of the pocket, skirted the bluffs, and at mid-morning on October 9 the tired and weary troopers unsaddled their horses,

built fires, and ate breakfast at the Freshwater Fork of the Brazos (White River) between present Crosbyton and Spur.[38]

While most of the troopers rested from their harrowing experience of the preceding night, Mackenzie sent Captain Heyl
with a small detachment on a short reconnaissance. About mid-
afternoon the exhausted and famished Tonkawas, who had had
very little food or sleep since leaving the Duck Creek base, rejoined the command. Just before their arrival, the Tonks had
discovered four Comanches observing both Captain Heyl and
the troopers' camp, but the hostiles had made their escape. The
Tonks also reported that they had found a fresh trail which
they believed led to the Kwahadi village upstream in Blanco
Canyon.[39]

Mackenzie promptly moved out, Captain Davis with Co. F
in the lead and the pack mules strung out behind. When the
column was about two miles from camp, a trooper accidentally
discharged his carbine, causing considerable confusion and delay. Without finding the village, Mackenzie camped for the
night where the water of White River rushed from the deep cut
in the eastern edge of the Llano Estacado to form the Freshwater Fork of the Brazos. Fearing that the Comanches might
try to stampede his horses, Mackenzie had the men to "cross
sideline" them by tying a hindfoot to the opposite front foot,
and to tie these side-line ropes to picket pins driven into the
ground. A horse thus secured could move about and graze
without getting entangled in the lariat, but he could not run.
Even so, Mackenzie, as yet inexperienced in Comanche warfare, unfortunately did not take adequate precaution. He failed
to ring the horseherd and the camp with "sleeping parties" and
to throw out adequate sentinel outposts. He would eventually
learn, but only after two humiliating experiences.

About 1:00 a.m., just as the moon had gone down, the stillness suddenly erupted into pandemonium. A band of Comanches, led by the young Quanah Parker, raced through the
camp, yelling, firing guns, ringing cowbells, and dragging raw-

hides. The troopers, rudely aroused from their sleep, fired wildly at the elusive forms only dimly seen in the darkness, while the terrified animals struggled at the end of their lariats. Realizing the tragedy of being set afoot in wild Comanche country, Mackenzie loudly ordered "Every man to his lariat," but not in time, for as the men floundered for their mounts amidst the tangled ropes and flying stake pins, part of the herd thundered off into the darkness.

It required quite a while in the darkness and confusion for the men to find, quiet, and saddle their mounts. By the time they had succeeded, a new day was dawning and the chagrined command could tally its loss — sixty-six horses, including the fine gray pacer of Colonel Mackenzie.[40]

Two detachments of cavalry commanded by Captain Heyl and Lieutenant W. C. Hemphill set out at once to search for the missing horses. When alerted Comanche scouts galloped to their village not far up the canyon, shouting a warning that the soldiers were coming, Chief Para-o-coom, a huge man with curly hair who "always wanted to kill somebody," immediately made a pep talk, boasting of his own bravery and exhorting the warriors to be brave and fight the bluecoats. After the chief had finished his talk, the warriors got their war shields, tied sheets about their waists, tied up their horses' tails, and had a parade.[41]

East of the river and three miles from the bivouac, Heyl's cavalry, mostly raw recruits, spied a small group of Indians driving off a bunch of horses and gave chase. Upon going over a hill in the ragged edge of the canyon, the troops ran head on into a much stronger force of painted, yelling Comanches. Drawing rein to survey the situation, Captain Heyl, turning to Lieutenant Carter who had joined in the chase, exclaimed: "Heavens, but we are in a nest! Just look at the Indians." [42] The situation for a moment was indeed perilous. The soldiers quickly dismounted and fell back to a ravine, firing as they retreated. A Comanche informant stated that the sound of the soldiers' bullets was like the roar of a sling whirling through the air. "Some of the soldiers were dismounted, some mounted. They were about 250 yards away. None of us got hit. Our medicine man must have been very powerful." [43]

Suddenly, Heyl and seven recruits dashed for safety. Unlocking the magazines of their big Spencer carbines, Carter, who received a Congressional Medal of Honor for his action during the fight, and the five men with him checked the Comanches with a rapid fire and then rode for an arroyo. During the retreat, Private Seander Gregg, whose horse gave out and stumbled, was shot by the Comanche war chief, whom Carter believed to be Quanah Parker. In telling the story of the battle, a Comanche informant stated: "One of the soldiers got behind. We killed and scalped him. The scalp was no good, but we had a big celebration over it anyway." [44]

At that moment the detachment was saved by the approach of Mackenzie with the entire cavalry force, Lieutenant Boehm and the Tonkawa scouts in the van. The Comanches fled up the canyon into the bluffs and boulders along its walls, sniping at the troopers for awhile, and then gradually disappeared over the rim onto the Llano Estacado. His horses too weak to keep up with the fleeing Indians, Mackenzie led his men back down the valley and, after burying Private Gregg at the southeast corner of the butte where he had fallen, went into temporary bivouac until the scouts could report on the trail left by the fleeing Comanches. [45]

About mid-afternoon the scouts came in saying that they had discovered a fresh trail which they believed led up the canyon to the village. Mackenzie soon had the trumpeter sound "boots and saddles" and the entire command moved out, the pack train and the dismounted troopers bringing up the rear. The fagged men and horses were able to make only a short distance before stopping for the night. This time Mackenzie not only had the horses cross-sidelined and staked, but placed "sleeping parties" among them as well. On the next morning,

Mackenzie sent the dismounted troopers back to the supply camp on Duck Creek, nearly forty miles in the rear, and then again took up the march along the bank of the beautiful, clear White River, lined with grass, that flowed at the bottom of Blanco Canyon. Late in the afternoon he came upon the site of the long-sought village, the signs indicating that it had been hastily abandoned only a short time before. By crossing and recrossing their trails, the villagers succeeded in confusing the Tonkawa scouts, and Mackenzie had to bivouac for the night in the canyon, not far from the site of the abandoned village. But soon after the men had started on the following morning, October 12, the Tonkawas signaled from the eastern rim of the canyon that they had found the trail. After a considerable effort, the cavalry finally made its way up the steep ascent to the scouts, where "as far as the eye could reach, not a bush, or tree, or a twig or stone, not an object of any kind or a living thing was in sight."

The troopers followed the traces left by dragging lodge poles and horses' hooves, scarcely discernible on the hard ground covered by buffalo grass, until about noon, when the trail suddenly turned and they again found themselves at the bottom of the canyon. In a few minutes, however, the Tonks signaled from the western rim that they had again located the trail. Ascending the canyon wall for the second time that day, the command found broad and plain tracks made by lodge poles and an estimated two to three thousand horses, pointing west by northwest into the fathomless "desert" of the Llano Estacado.

Concluding that cavalry could overtake an entire village on the move, Mackenzie set out in pursuit. Along the route numerous *Comanchero* cart trails crossed the plains. As the chase continued, the troopers noted an increasing number of items discarded by the villagers in their haste to stay ahead of their pursuers — lodge poles and skins, stone hammers, wood, and puppies. Some of the warriors could be seen from time to time dogging the rear and sides of the column, endeavoring to delay the advance. To prevent them from stampeding the pack mules, Mackenzie closed up the formation and completely boxed in the train with detachments of cavalry. Late that afternoon, dark clouds rolled in, and soon a drizzle had turned to sleet and snow. Suddenly topping a ridge, the troopers saw dimly in front of them hundreds of moving forms, identified by the Tonks as the stampeding Comanche village.[46]

Just then the wind became stronger and the sleet and snow storm blinding. With the band at his mercy, Mackenzie for some reason halted the column and dismounted, perhaps out of mercy for the Indian women and children, but more likely out of fear that the storm might destroy his fagged men and horses. Besides, his supply base was, he estimated, one hundred miles away. A band of warriors charged, fired into the command, and then disappeared into early darkness. Mackenzie sent Captain Davis with a detachment in pursuit, but the men could see nothing in the snow and darkness and found their way back to the command only by yells from the Tonkawa scouts.

To keep the men, clad in summer uniforms, from freezing, tarpaulins, robes, and blankets were unpacked to provide shelter and covering during that long, dreadful night. Mackenzie asked no special favors for his own comfort, but finally someone wrapped a buffalo robe around his almost frozen body.[47]

The morning of October 13 dawned clear and beautiful, and without breakfast Mackenzie took up the trail again, but the spirit of the column had taken a sharp drop, the animals were showing signs of giving out, water was very scarce, there was no wood for fires, and the signs indicated that the Indians had kept travelling during the night. Consequently, Mackenzie, after having followed the Indians an estimated forty miles (almost to present Plainview, Carter many years later thought), turned back on the trail, camping that night where the command had weathered out the storm. During the next day's march the men gathered up the dry fourteen-foot cedar lodge poles dropped by the fleeing Indians along the trail to use as fuel when camp was made that evening.[48]

On the 15th, as the relaxed troopers quite leisurely descended the wall of Blanco Canyon, the Tonkawa scouts, who were in the lead, spotted two Comanches inspecting the outward trail of the column. The scouts gave chase, forcing the Comanches to take cover in a bushy ravine along the wall of the canyon. Mackenzie ordered Lieutenant Boehm to take fifteen dismounted men and drive the Indians from cover. When Boehm moved up slowly and cautiously, Mackenzie impatiently rode to the front to direct the skirmish. As he did, one of the Indians sent a barbed arrow to the bone in the middle front of his right thigh. As soldiers helped their wounded commander to the rear where Surgeon Rufus Choate cut out the arrow and dressed the wound, a rattle of rifle fire dispatched the two Indians, but not before they had wounded one other trooper. For some unknown reason, possibly embarrassment or pride, Mackenzie in his official report of the campaign never mentioned that he had been wounded, stating only that "one soldier was wounded." [49]

As it was getting late in the day, the command went into camp near where Mackenzie had been wounded. From there it continued unhurriedly to the mouth of the canyon where it was met by Lawton with forage and rations. Here Mackenzie allowed the men and horses to rest for a few days.

However, he was not yet ready to abandon the campaign; he felt that Quanah Parker would return to his favorite camping ground at the headwaters of the Pease River near the eastern edge of the Llano Estacado. Thus on October 24, after starting the disabled and dismounted men and weak animals to the Supply Camp on Duck Creek, Mackenzie at the head of the remainder of the command headed for the headwaters of the Pease.

The Colonel's leg, however, became so bad that he left Cap-

tain Mauck in command and on October 29 rejoined the others
on Duck Creek, "so irritable" and "onery" that no one wanted
to go near him, but he stuck to his job. Finally, Doctor Greg-
ory, the surgeon at the camp, attempted a ruse to improve his
disposition. After examining the leg, he informed the Colonel
that the wound was worse and that unless he kept quiet and
calm, it might have to be amputated. The ruse fell flat, for at
the mention of amputation Mackenzie flew into a rage and
tried to use his crutch on the doctor, who quickly left the tent,
to his chagrin and to the amusement of the troopers who were
in on the trick.[50]

Mackenzie then issued orders preparatory to breaking up
the expedition. Lieutenant Thompson, a jolly and mischievous
but efficient and fearless fellow, was directed to start at once
for Richardson with eleven mounted and twenty-one dismounted men; Lawton was sent with his supply train to Griffin
for a half load of corn for the final march; and Carter was directed to take the remaining dismounted and disabled men and
the incapacitated horses to Cottonwood Springs, near Double
Mountain, to avoid delay when Mauck returned from scouting the headwaters of the Pease. After making these arrangements, Mackenzie climbed into an ambulance and, escorted by
a lieutenant and four privates, arrived at Fort Richardson on
November 8, a day ahead of Thompson and his command. His
wound was healing satisfactorily, although it was ugly and
still disposed to open.[51] Captain Mauck had reached the Duck
Creek camp on November 6 in the midst of a heavy snowstorm, five inches having fallen during the preceding night.
He had not found any Comanches, but he had lost a number of
horses that had died at the end of their picket lines, and many
of the survivors were thin and jaded. Lawton's wagons rumbled
in the next day with the badly needed corn, and with great
suffering in the intense cold the column after a series of slow
marches rode into Fort Griffin on November 12 singing: "Come
home John, don't stay long; come home soon to your own

Mary Ann." The Fort Richardson contingent, Cos. B, F, K, and L, 4th Cavalry, and one company of the 11th Infantry, under the command of Captain Mauck struggled on through another sleet and snow storm to its home post, where it arrived on November 18, a beautiful autumn day.[52]

Mackenzie was well aware, of course that the campaign had failed to produce any noteworthy results. He had marched 509 miles with the loss of only one man, but he had lost many horses and had done no more than frighten one hostile band of Comanches. In his official report of the expedition on November 15, he neither claimed any creditable accomplishments nor attempted to justify his apparent failure. Nevertheless, the campaign had not been a failure. Mackenzie and his 4th Cavalry had penetrated the very heart of the hostile Indian country, even venturing onto the abysmal Llano Estacado in an area hitherto unexplored by the United States military. He had learned a great deal about Comanche customs and warfare, and concomitantly about the best ways of making war on these nomadic Lords of the South Plains — lessons that later helped him become one of the country's greatest Indian fighters.

FOOTNOTES — CHAPTER III

[1] "Tabular Statement of Expeditions," September 30, 1871, as cited; Carter, *On the Border*, 81; Henry W. Strong, *My Frontier Days and Indian Fights on the Plains of Texas* (n. p., 1924), 21 (hereafter cited as *My Indian Fights*).

[2] Carter, *On the Border*, 81; Nye, *Carbine and Lance*, 131. Nye quotes the eye-witness description by J. H. Patzki, Mackenzie's surgeon on the expedition, and also cites a personal interview with J. B. Terrell, who visited the scene a day or two after the massacre.

[3] Sherman to W. H. Wood, May 19, 1871, 1894 AGO 1871, RG 94.

[4] Nye, *Carbine and Lance*, 132.

[5] Sheridan to Adj. Gen., June 23, 1871, 2199 AGO 1871, RG 94; Sherman, Fort Sill, May 24, 1871, 2016 AGO 1871, RG 94; Major J. K. Mizner to departmental headquarters, San Antonio, June 11, 1871, 2294 AGO 1871, RG 94 and DT 1871, Army Commands, Letters Sent, Fort Richardson, Vol. 70, RG 98.

[6] Sheridan to Adj. Gen., June 23, 1871, 2199 AGO 1871, RG 94; Sherman to Adj. Gen., May 28, 1871, 1950 AGO 1871, RG 94; Lawrie Tatum to Jona Richards, May 30, 1871, copy in Rister Papers, as cited. Nye, in *Carbine and Lance*, 132–147, has covered this subject thoroughly from both the white and Indian accounts.

[7] Sherman, Ft. Leavenworth, to Adj. Gen., June 16, 1871, 2084 AGO 1871, RG 94; Sheridan to Adj. Gen., June 23, 1871, as cited; Nye, *Carbine and Lance*, 145, credits the Indians George Hunt, Hunting Horse, and Andrew Stumbling Bear with giving him this information.

[8] *Ibid.*, 146.

[9] Carter, *On the Border*, 91–94; Nye, *Carbine and Lance*, 145–146.

[10] "Minutes of the 43rd Judicial District of Texas" (typed copy in Rister Papers, as cited); McConnell, *Five Years a Cavalryman*, 284–287; I. L. Hucka-bay, *Ninety-four Years in Jack County* (Austin, 1949), 182–185; Carrie J. Crouch, *A History of Young County, Texas* (Austin, 1956), 50; C. C. Rister (comp.), "Texas 1867–1911, General W. T. Sherman, Satanta and Big Tree" (MS, Rister Papers, as cited); Carter, *On the Border*, 98–102.

[11] Mackenzie, Fort Richardson, to Sherman, June 16, 1871, DT, Army Commands, Fort Richardson, Letters Sent, Vol. 70, RG 98; also W. T. Sherman Papers, Library of Congress, quoted in Nye, *Carbine and Lance*, 148.

[12] Reynolds, Special Orders, No. 124, June 17, 1871, 471 DT 1871 (filed with 2477 AGO 1871), RG 94; also, AGO, Special Orders, Vol. 522, DT, RG 94.

[13] Reynolds to Mackenzie, July 6, 1871, 2477 AGO 1871, RG 94.

[14] Carter, *On the Border*, 105–114; "Tabular Statement of Expeditions," September 30, 1871, as cited.

[15] Carter, *On the Border*, 106–114.

[16] Mackenzie to Grierson, July 4, 1871, filed with 2441 AGO 1876, RG 94.

[17] Special Orders 153, Fort Richardson, July 1, 1871, DT 1871, Army Commands, RG 98; Reynolds to War Department, filed with 2441 AGO 1876, RG 94; Mackenzie to departmental headquarters, May 11, 1876, 3888 AGO 1876 (filed with 2441 AGO 1876), RG 94; Reynolds to Adj. Gen., July 6, 1871, 2477 AGO 1871, RG 94.

[18] Mackenzie to Grierson, July 4, 1871, as cited.

[19] "Charges and Specifications Preferred against Colonel Ranald S. Mackenzie," with Mackenzie to Grierson, July 4, 1871, 3888 AGO 1876 (filed with 2441 AGO 1876), RG 94.

[20] Carter, *On the Border*, 114.

[21] *Ibid.*, 116–117.

[22] *Ibid.*, 118–119.

[23] *Ibid.*, 120–122.

[24] *Ibid.*, 122–123.

[25] Carter claimed that many years later he was told by S. M. Woodward, Grierson's adjutant at the time of the expedition, that the supporters of the Quaker Peace Policy in Washington, fearing Mackenzie would precipitate an Indian war, got an order placing both columns while in Indian Territory under the command of Grierson, who was the senior officer and in sympathy with the Peace Policy. *Ibid.*, 122.

[26] Sherman to "Col. McCoy or the Adjutant General," July 29, 1871, 2682 AGO 1871 (filed with 2477 AGO 1871), RG 94; Reynolds to Adjutant General, August 3, 1871, 471 DT 1871 (filed with 2477 AGO 1871), RG 94. In the letter, referred to by Sherman, Mackenzie expressed his plan for dealing with the Kiowas. Needless to say, Mackenzie thereafter had no love for Grierson.

[27] Lawrie Tatum to Grierson (copy to Mackenzie), August 12, 1871, quoted

in Carter, *On the Border*, 144; Grierson, Fort Sill, to Sherman, September 5, 1871, cited in Nye, *Carbine and Lance*, 149.

[28] Carter, *On the Border*, 134, 137, 143.

[29] *Ibid.*, 142–144; Tatum to Grierson, August 12, 1871, as cited.

[30] Carter, *On the Border*, 145–147; "Tabular Statement of Expeditions," September 30, 1871, as cited; "Medical History of Posts, Vols. 236 & 238, Richardson, Texas," Vol. 236, p. 233, AGO, RG 94 (hereafter cited as "Medical History of Fort Richardson").

[31] Quoted in Richardson, *Comanche Barrier*, 345–346.

[32] Sherman to McCoy or the Adj. Gen., July 29, 1871, as cited.

[33] "Medical History of Fort Richardson," Vol. 236, p. 18, as cited.

[34] "Regimental Returns," September, 1871, 3719 AGO 1871, RG 94, and October 1871, 4099 AGO 1872, RG 94; Carter, *On the Border*, 158–159.

[35] See map of route, p. 66. Between the Salt Fork and the Supply Camp on the Freshwater Fork near the mouth of Blanco Canyon during the campaigns of 1872 and 1874, one branch of the road followed the river fairly closely and another took an almost direct short cut, passing through the present town of Spur. Carter, *On the Border*, 159–161, 531–535; Rister, Fort Griffin, 88–89; Major G. L. Gillespie, "Map of Portions of Texas, New Mexico and Indian Ty. including the Staked Plains (Llano Estacado), Showing the Trails of Expedition Commanded by Col. R. S. Mackenzie, 4th Cav., Col. Nelson Miles, 5th Inf. and Lt. Col. J. W. Davidson, 10th Cav." (hereafter cited as Gillespie, "Map of Expeditions"), 1876, in Cartographic Records Division, RG 75, National Archives.

[36] Carter, *On the Border*, 161.

[37] *Ibid.*, 162; Rister, *Fort Griffin*, 89.

[38] Carter, *On the Border*, 162–163; Rister, *Fort Griffin*, 89–90; Nye, *Carbine and Lance*, 151; "Tabular Statement of Expeditions," September 28, 1872, 4099 AGO 1872, RG 94.

[39] Carter, *On the Border*, 163.

[40] "Tabular Statement of Expeditions," September 28, 1872, as cited; Mackenzie to departmental headquarters, November 15, 1871, DT 1871, Army Commands, Fort Richardson, Letters Sent, Vol. 70, RG 98; Carter, *On the Border*, 165–168; General Wirt Davis, Co. F, 4th Cavalry, "To Whom It May Concern," December 6, 1904, in *ibid.*, 210–211; Haley, *Fort Concho*, 185–186; Rister, *Fort Griffin*, 90.

[41] Statement of Cohaya, a Comanche participant in the engagement, in Nye, *Carbine and Lance*, 151.

[42] "Tabular Statement of Expeditions," September 28, 1872, as cited; Carter, *On the Border*, 170.

[43] Quoted in Nye, *Carbine and Lance*, 151.

[44] Carter, *On the Border*, 172–176; statement of Cohaya, in Nye, *Carbine and Lance*, 151.

[45] Carter, *On the Border*, 178–182, 212–213; Mackenzie to departmental headquarters, November 15, 1871, as cited.

[46] Carter, *On the Border*, 184–192.

[47] *Ibid.*, 192–195; R. G. Carter, "General Ranald Mackenzie," in *Corral Dust* (Washington Westerners), II (March, 1957), 1–6.

[48] Mackenzie to departmental headquarters, November 15, 1871, as cited;

Carter, *On the Border*, 196–197; "Medical History of Fort Richardson," Vol. 236, p. 241, as cited.

[49] Mackenzie to departmental headquarters, November 15, 1871, as cited; Carter, *On the Border*, 197–198. Dorst, *20th Reunion*, App., 10, states that Mackenzie was wounded because of his concern for a young officer who had gone to the front. *Chronological List of Actions*, p. 27, lists Mackenzie among the wounded, but the information did not come from the official report.

[50] Carter, *On the Border*, 202–203.

[51] "Medical History of Fort Richardson," Vol. 236, p. 241, as cited; Carter, *On the Border*, 203–205.

[52] Carter, *On the Border*, 205–206; "Medical History of Fort Richardson," as cited; "Regimental Returns," November, 1871, as cited.

CHAPTER IV

Chasing Comancheros across the Staked Plains

THE LONG WINTER confinement at the isolated frontier post of Richardson was a greater strain on the morale of the 4th Cavalry than the strenuous but abortive campaigns of the previous summer had been. The post facilities were crude and inadequate, the health of the men was not so good as when they were in the field, and except for saloons there was very little recreation and entertainment to break the dull routine of camp life. Furthermore, both Mackenzie and his men, not yet at their peak toughness and efficiency but thoroughly disappointed with the results of their summer campaign and disgusted with Washington's pacifist policy, were involved in considerable disciplinary problems.

Most of the officers were housed quite uncomfortably during the cold weather in crude four-room wooden buildings, one and a half stories high, finished in cottage style with large windows and porches and heated by open fireplaces; nine of the twenty-seven officers at the post in April, 1872, were living in tents. The troops were housed in barrack buildings, approximately 85x20 feet, each warmed by two wood-burning stoves, a situation deplorable to the post surgeon. There were four men to the bunk, two to each bed, sleeping on bedsacks filled with hay. In the absence of bathrooms, the men bathed in the open and used outdoor toilets at the rear of the barracks.[1]

In November, some 55 of the 441 men at the post were taken ill. The post surgeon noted that "the cold and wet of the fall, the fatigue of field service, the almost total lack of fresh vegetables, the irregular supply of fresh meat and salt, and the bad water" had resulted in many cases of scurvy. Spring brought enough improvement in health conditions that at the inspection of April 30 Mackenzie pronounced the health of the command as "good." Of the 621 men then at the post, only 37 had been ill during the month.[2]

Combined with the deep-felt frustration over failure to capture Quanah Parker's village, the poor conditions led to a rash of disciplinary infractions and desertions. Although in trouble with his own departmental commander, Mackenzie maintained strict discipline among his men, generally through punitive and corrective measures within prescribed limitations rather than through court martials. Drunkards were subjected to a "dip" in a waterhole or confinement in the orderly room. Obstreperous violators of regulations and insubordinates were put in a "sweatbox," were forced to walk the beat carrying a thirty-pound log, or were spread-eagled on the spare wheel of a caisson.

Troop commanders on the frontier where detection was extremely difficult were often plagued with desertions, as Mackenzie was during the winter of 1871-72. When on November 29 ten men deserted en masse, the Colonel determined to put an end to such malefactions or else make the culprits pay dearly. He immediately dispatched Lieutenants Lawton and Carter with armed details to search every settlement and town even as far as New York, if necessary, and instructed them not to "come back until you have accomplished results." On December 8 Carter returned to the post with all ten of the deserters, captured near Cleburne.[3] In January, 1872, two details were sent in pursuit of deserters, and in April five and in May seven men left the post without authorization, but during June only twenty-seven were confined to the guardhouse, "mostly for trivial offenses," and the discipline was rated as "very good." [4] Mackenzie had successfully disciplined his men; sometimes he had been stern and even at times severe, but according to his men he was not a martinet.[5] A spirit of teamwork henceforth prevailed among his officers. He was ready for a new effort against the Comanches.

Meanwhile, Colonel Reynolds, angry and humiliated at Mackenzie's behavior towards him, had initiated court martial proceedings against the commander of the 4th Cavalry for "Disobedience of Orders; Contempt and Disrespect Towards His Commanding Officer; Conduct Unbecoming an Officer and Gentleman; and Conduct Prejudicial to Good Order and Military Discipline." [6] Reynolds probably would have ignored Mackenzie's negligence in making reports and issuing ordnance stores contrary to the manual, but a court martial seemed to be his only defense when he learned that his serious and honest young subordinate had charged him with fraudulent practice in connection with army contracts.

Mackenzie had not been in Texas long before he began to suspect that the contracting firm of Adams and Wickes of San Antonio, with the connivance of certain government officials, was not entirely honest in fulfilling its obligations. While at McKavett in 1869, his suspicions were further aroused when Reynolds, disregarding his protest, had paid Adams and Wickes the full contract price for corn that failed to meet specifications. He became fairly certain that Reynolds was implicated in the dealings when in January, 1871, he heard a rumor that Adams and Wickes had presented Reynolds with a house and lot in San Antonio.

Soon after moving to Richardson in March, 1871, Mackenzie had other evidence against Reynolds. Contracts to Adams and Wickes for forage and wood for Fort Richardson, in excess of requirements, were let without proper publicity, but the supplies were not delivered. Since his forthcoming campaign against the Kiowas had been authorized directly by General Sherman, who he felt would not tolerate situations that might interfere, Mackenzie ordered two thousand bushels of forage from another source. On June 28, however, Reynolds informed him that Adams and Wickes would supply his post and ordered him to cancel his contract. Mackenzie refused. On June 28 and 30 he informed the commander of the Division of the South, General Henry W. Halleck, of the whole matter and asked for an investigation. "I will not allow myself," he wrote, "to be quietly made an actor in what I consider to be a fraud." Mackenzie, aware that the success of his forthcoming expedition was to a great extent dependent upon the condition of his horses, did not intend complacently to risk failure, or even possibly to sacrifice the lives of his men, because of questionable practices in handling contracts for supplies.

When he learned of Mackenzie's letters to Halleck, Reynolds sent his demand for court martial proceedings against Mackenzie to General Sheridan, who in turn forwarded the papers to Secretary of War W. W. Belknap. Belknap, later to resign under charges of corruption, referred the charges to the Judge Advocate General, who ruled that it was "clearly not expedient to prosecute." Belknap concurred, and directed that Mackenzie merely be admonished about his conduct toward a superior officer. No doubt, the Judge Advocate had evidence that Reynolds' operations were questionable; Mackenzie, at least, had obtained a copy of a deed to a house and lot in San Antonio transferred to Reynolds by Adams and Wickes.[7]

Both Sherman and Sheridan, who were determined to solve the Comanche-Kiowa problem in Texas as quickly as possible, wanted Mackenzie for their field commander and had little regard for the politically ambitious Reynolds as an Indian fighter. They had the Department of Texas put in the Division of the Missouri, and as soon as Mackenzie had been exonerated, in January, 1872, they replaced Reynolds with Brigadier Gen-

eral C. C. Augur, a veteran campaigner on the Plains, who to
the limit of his instructions and ability would be willing to support Mackenzie. Upon assuming his new command on January
29, Augur issued an order that henceforth officers would be
expected to make a vigorous effort, even to the extent of priva-
tion, to overtake and punish marauders.[8] This was what Mackenzie wanted to hear.

When the grass turned green in the spring of 1872, the Comanches and Kiowas became bolder than ever, and conflict developed more rapidly than had been anticipated. While Mackenzie at Richardson was still diligently engaged in acquiring
recruits, horses, and supplies, and in drilling for the forthcoming campaign, Sergeant William H. Wilson with a detachment
of the 4th Cavalry from Fort Concho surprised a band of marauders, killing two and capturing one prisoner, Polonis Ortiz,
who confessed that he was one of fifteen from La Cuesta, New
Mexico, employed to steal Texas cattle; other New Mexicans,
he stated, were likewise engaged. According to Ortiz there was
a good wagon road across the Staked Plains with plenty of water and grass, and all the stolen cattle were driven over it to
New Mexico. Mow-way's Comanches, he claimed, generally
camped along Rescate and Blanco canyons; his party had met
the Comanches at Mucha-que Hill, four and a half miles southeast of present Gail.[9]

Upon receipt of this information, Augur ordered Major
John T. Hatch, commanding at Fort Concho, to investigate.
Captains McLaughlin and Joseph Rendlebrock with four officers, thirty-eight enlisted men, and prisoner Ortiz left Concho
on April 27; in the Mucha-que Valley (formed by present Bull,
Silver, and Willow creeks), between present Snyder and Gail,
the command found substantiating evidence. At least one thousand horses had been herded there only a few days before, and
a camp of 150 to 200 lodges had been abandoned not more than
twenty-four hours.[10]

Augur lost no time in forming his plan of operation to stop

the organized raiding. On May 20 he summoned Mackenzie to
San Antonio and, with Sheridan's authorization in hand, on
May 31 issued his orders. To break up the cattle stealing and
stop the incursions of hostile Indians along the northern frontier of Texas, Mackenzie was to establish his supply camp on
the headwaters of the Colorado or on the Freshwater Fork of
the Brazos, and from there to scout in such direction and manner as to give the most effective protection. He was to carry
from Richardson three companies of his cavalry (A, Captain
Beaumont; B, Captain Mauck; and L, Captain Theodore J.
Wint), twelve six-mule teams, and the cavalry pack mules, and
at Griffin to pick up Captain Davis' Co. F, one company of the
11th Infantry, Lieutenant Boehm and twenty of his Tonkawa
scouts, eight six-mule wagons, and the pack animals there.
Troops D and I of the 4th Cavalry, commanded at Concho by
Captains John Lee and McLaughlin, were to meet Mackenzie
at his supply base and to have with them prisoner Ortiz. From
McKavett Lieutenant Colonel Shafter, who had gained valuable experience the previous year in an expedition onto the
southern fringe of the Staked Plains, was ordered to bring
three companies of the 24th Infantry and five six-mule wagons,
some additional wagons from San Antonio, seven six-mule
teams from Concho, ambulances, and surgeons, and to meet
Mackenzie on July 1 on the Freshwater Fork. These additions
would give Mackenzie a total of six cavalry and four infantry
companies and more than thirty-two wagons. Company G under Captain Rendlebrock was left at Concho to escort cattle
herds en route to the Pecos;[11] and Captain Heyl, who had
sought safety in flight during the fight in Blanco Canyon, was
assigned with Co. K to guard a railroad surveying party.

Mackenzie started with the Fort Richardson contingent on
June 19, and on the evening of the next day arrived at Fort
Griffin. The two-day trip caused alarm from the frontier to
Washington. In some inexplicable manner a rumor was printed,
even by the *New York Times*, that Mackenzie, two of his offi-

cers, and ten enlisted men had been ambushed between Richardson and Belknap by sixty Indians and all but three of the group slain. Augur assured the anxious adjutant general in Washington that there was "Not one word of truth in it." [12]

While at Griffin, Mackenzie made known his intention to scout first the Freshwater-Blanco Fork of the Brazos, where he had been wounded in a fight with the Comanches the previous autumn, leaving his train with an infantry guard on Duck Creek and from there marching with his cavalry to Blanco Canyon. The *Galveston Daily News* announced the campaign with the sage prophecy, "Look out for stirring things to follow," [13] and the *San Antonio Herald* informed its readers that "General Mackenzie is a man who means business when he is ordered to perform any particular duty." [14]

Leaving Griffin on June 22, the troops in high spirits singing their old regimental song, "Come home, John, don't stay long; Come home soon to your own Chick-a-biddy," Mackenzie led the command along the road he had laid out in 1871 across California and Paint creeks. He cut the bend of the Brazos and on June 27 pulled to a halt on Duck Creek, where he was met by his two calvary companies from Concho. Next day, he ordered Major E. A. Latimer to take the two companies from Concho and proceed slowly up the Freshwater Fork. With the remaining cavalry, Mackenzie marched to the head of Duck Creek, crossed the tableland to Blanco Canyon and then proceeded down the Freshwater Fork until he met Latimer's command on July 1. When Mackenzie found that Shafter, who had been ordered to leave Concho, 170 miles distant, not later than June 25 and to reach the rendezvous by July 1, had not arrived, he was in a frenzy. He had hoped to catch the Indians between his three forces, but he had not even seen any fresh signs. [15]

While waiting for Shafter's arrival and for the wagons to go to Griffin for more supplies, including 19,200 rounds of cartridges, Mackenzie sent McLaughlin and Lee to scout the Mucha-que country. Starting on July 2, the captains marched

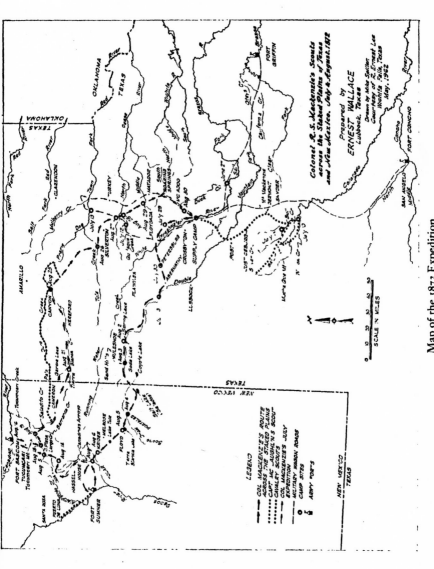

Map of the 1872 Expedition

south-southwest, keeping in sight the Caprock three to ten miles distant, crossed the Salt Fork of the Brazos twenty-three miles from their starting point, forded the Double Mountain Fork five miles farther in the vicinity of present Post, followed closely the base of the Caprock southward to within ten or twelve miles of present Snyder, and then turned sharply toward the southwest into the Mucha-que Valley. At the head of the valley the command on July 7 found and followed an Indian trail northward for twenty miles to a salt lake on the Staked Plains, but gave up and returned to the valley, the horses having gone thirty hours without water. After scouting the valley for two more days, the command back-tracked its trail to the Freshwater Fork camp where it arrived on July 14, having marched 294 miles in thirteen days.[16] While McLaughlin and Lee were searching the Mucha-que Valley on July 9, two hundred of the Indians they sought were capturing a herd of fifteen hundred cattle on the Pecos River twenty-three miles above Horsehead Crossing, almost two hundred miles to their southwest, and another group four days later stampeded a herd of 2,600 head only twelve miles from Fort Concho.[17]

While waiting for supplies to accumulate and for the detachment to return, Mackenzie with a larger force made a short scout northward to the Red River, first asking Sheridan to send an adequate amount of supplies to Camp Supply, Indian Territory, in case the two short scouts indicated a necessity to move northward beyond the accessibility of his own base. Sheridan complied immediately.[18] Leaving his Supply Camp on the afternoon of July 9 with the companies of Beaumont, Mauck, Davis, and Wint, totaling six officers and two hundred troopers, and Lieutenant Boehm and his Tonkawa scouts, Mackenzie marched up Blanco Canyon twenty miles before camping for the night. Starting at the break of day the next morning, he emerged from the canyon just south of present Floydada, turned northeast across the Staked Plains, and did not go into camp until dark. Although he had a long day, Mackenzie, as was his custom when campaigning, studied far into the night the reports of scouts and engineer officers, maps, and other available information. After travelling five miles on the Plains on the third day, he descended the Caprock on Quitaque Creek and camped three miles below it during a heavy rainstorm. On the next night, he camped on the south bank of the Red River after covering thirty-five miles through rough country on a very hot day, and on the following day crossed the Red River eight miles east of the Staked Plains and trudged a few miles beyond into the region south of present Clarendon. Having gone as far north as he intended and having found no fresh sign of Indians, here he turned back. Before sunrise on Sunday, July 14, the men were in their saddles, headed southwesterly for their Supply Camp on the Freshwater Fork of the Brazos.

The return route, several miles east of the out-going but still in sight of the Caprock, was approximately through the present towns of Turkey, Matador, Roaring Springs, and McAdoo. The command arrived at its Freshwater Fork camp on the morning of July 19, having marched 208 miles with but few indications of the recent presence of Indians in the area scouted.[19]

Mackenzie was now confident that the Comanches were either on the North Fork of Red River or on the Palo Duro, where Ortiz had told him that they always were. As soon as he had adequate forage and rations at his camp on the Freshwater and at Supply Camp in Indian Territory, he intended to scout the two spots. There was no country better adapted in winter to all the wants of the Indians, he wrote in his report, than the headstreams at the eastern base of the Staked Plains. His train had just pulled in from Fort Griffin with enough supplies to last until September 10 but not enough for the campaign he planned; therefore he was sending it again on the 23rd—twenty-one wagons to Concho and thirteen to Griffin (but in the future all wagons would go to Griffin because the road was better and the distance was less).[20] During Mackenzie's absence

Shafter, who had finally arrived on July 6, had ordered Lieutenant Wentz C. Miller to take fifty-five men, including one
Indian guide, and to make certain there were no Indians lurking south of Supply Camp at the foot of the Staked Plains along
the Main and Double Mountain forks of the Brazos. Miller had
reported after five days' scouting that the only Indian sign encountered was a two-day old trail made by six Indians.[21]

Before final preparations were completed for the expedition
to the North Fork of the Red, Ortiz and the scouts discovered
a wide and heavily travelled road leading out onto the Staked
Plains, its appearance indicating that large herds of cattle had
been driven over it.[22] Since the second part of Augur's general
order had been for Mackenzie to break up the cattle stealing,
he determined, very properly, according to Augur, to follow
it and possibly to recover some of the cattle. A Comanche chief,
who knew the country well, had told Francisco Amangual,
the leader of an 1808 Spanish military expedition from San
Antonio to Santa Fe, that not even a horse could cross the South
Plains from the vicinity of Mucha-que toward Santa Fe,[23] and
Randolph B. Marcy, one of the most successful explorers of
the vast area, had carefully avoided any such attempt.

For his daring venture across the Llano Estacado, Mackenzie
selected the companies of Captains Beaumont, Mauck, Lee,
Davis, and McLaughlin, consisting of 8 officers and 240 enlisted
men. In addition, he carried with him Quartermaster Lawton
with an undisclosed number of wagons and pack mules, Lieutenant Boehm and his Tonkawa scouts, Ortiz, and Captain J.
W. Clous, 24th Infantry, who served as the engineer officer.
Wint, who only recently had been promoted to the rank of
captain, with his Co. H was left behind to help the infantry
guard the Supply Camp.[24]

Mackenzie recorded very little about the expedition, even
less than usual; the entire correspondence amounted to three
short letters and a map of the route prepared by Captain
Clous.[25] Fortunately, however, it is possible to piece together

from these sources and others an account of the first official
United States expedition to cross the vast and unexplored area
of the Southern Plains, including its exact route. Clous' map
shows the location of Mackenzie's camp each night; at least
two other reliable army maps show Mackenzie's routes as
shown by Clous; [26] still another shows the route of Captain C.
D. Viele in 1875 from Supply Camp on the Freshwater Fork to
Portales Springs to be identical with that of Mackenzie, and
Shafter in his report for 1875 confirmed it. [27] The return route
was that identified by Ortiz. In the routes on this expedition,
as well as on all Mackenzie's movements in western Texas, the
longitude lines are several miles too far east, an error that was
not corrected by geographers until after the turn of the twentieth century; Lake Garcia, for example, which is east of the
103rd meridian in southwest Deaf Smith County, is shown on
the maps of the 1870's just west of the 103rd meridian in New
Mexico.

Mackenzie pulled out on July 28, stopping for the night on
the east side of the river at the mouth of Blanco Canyon about
six miles above his Supply Camp, a familiar campsite before
his campaigning in western Texas was finished. The next morning, he climbed the gradual slope to the Staked Plains east of
Blanco Canyon, camped for the night about five miles east of
the canyon and almost midway between present McAdoo and
Floydada, and on the following day rounded the head of Blanco
Canyon south of present Floydada, where he bent toward the
southwest across the head of Crawfish Creek, and made his
third camp at present Petersburg. On the 31st he struck the
Double Mountain Fork of the Brazos ten or fifteen miles northwest of present Abernathy and a short distance southeast of the
eastern tip of the Sand Hills, where he laid over a day for his
horses to recuperate on the luxuriant and nutritious grass before
proceeding up the Double Mountain Fork which skirts the
southern edge of the Sand Hills to the New Mexico line.

After camping for a night at a "Spring," Spring (Soda)

Lake, and at a "Waterhole" near present Muleshoe, the expedition on August 4 passed the western end of the Sand Hills, skirted the north side of "Salados" Lake just west of the Texas-New Mexico line, where settlers later obtained salt by the wagonload, and camped that evening at Portales Springs near where the town named for them now stands. From Portales Mackenzie turned sharply northwest to Tierra Blanca Lake, ten miles west. After passing Lake Tule, six and one-half miles southwest of the present village of Melrose, he pushed ahead of his wagon train to the upper Las Cañadinas Arroyo, about four miles north of present Tolar, where he waited for the remainder of the expedition.

From his camp on Las Cañadinas, Mackenzie on August 7 made his first report since leaving Supply Camp. He had reached the place the previous evening, having followed from the Freshwater Fork an old wagon trail which led to a plainer wagon road and a very large cattle trail from some point north of Mucha-que to Salado Lake. Very heavy rains had provided plenty of water along the route, but had made it impossible to tell the precise date of the tracks. It had not been his inclination to come into New Mexico, but the trail was so plain that he had concluded it should be followed. He was planning to return by the route Ortiz had described, which lay to his north.[28]

Sending Lawton to Fort Sumner to purchase forage and supplies, Mackenzie the next day followed the cattle trail to a fork at Alamogordo Creek, which enters the Pecos about a dozen miles above Fort Sumner, and then continued along one fork of the trail up the Pecos River to within four miles of the town of Puerta de Luna where it broke up. At Puerta de Luna he wished to arrest three men whom Ortiz had named as leaders or equippers of the raiding parties, but they had scattered, to escape a more fearful foe than the troops, he assumed; John Hittson, one of the largest cattle owners in Texas, with a force of ninety cowboys and gunmen had just recovered "between five or six thousand head of cattle . . . but at enormous expense,

nearly equal to the value of the property recovered," stolen
from his range in Coleman and Callahan counties.[29]

Foiled in his effort to catch the thieves, Mackenzie dropped
back to Fort Sumner to rest his horses, to replenish his supplies,
and to gather information. After three days in that vicinity, he
moved his command northward, passing the present villages of
House, Hassell, and Ima, then turned east and went into camp
at the head-springs of the Plaza Larga (Tucumcari) Creek at
the crossing of the Santa Fe-Fort Smith Road, about a dozen
miles southwest of Tucumcari Mountain. At his camp on the
Tucumcari Mackenzie wrote his second, and again brief, report. Colonel J. J. Gregg, 8th Cavalry, he wrote, had left Fort
Bascom on August 7 by way of the Fort Smith Road to scout
the vicinity of Adobe Walls and the headwaters of the Red
River. If possible, he would recross the Staked Plains between
his westward route and the road Gregg had taken eastward.[30]

Going to Fort Bascom on the Canadian River north of the
town of Tucumcari on August 16 to draw supplies for the return trip, Mackenzie was unable to leave before his troopers, to
the delight of the post sutler and the disgust of their commander, had exchanged their money and boredom for sizeable
quantities of whiskey and splitting headaches.[31] Two nights
later, however, Mackenzie had the column again camped on
Plaza Larga Creek, where lightning knocked one man senseless
and killed the prized horse of Lieutenant John A. McKinney.
Here final preparations were made for another daring venture
across the Staked Plains by an unknown route — unknown,
that is, except to the Indians and the *Comancheros*. But Mackenzie had Ortiz who had travelled it.

Starting his return on August 19, Mackenzie led his column
southeast across Plaza Larga and Barranca creeks, thence up
the Saladito Creek to its headsprings, between the present
towns of Norton and Cameron, where he intersected the *Comanchero* road leading eastward from Puerta de Luna. A short
distance beyond the springs of the Saladito, he entered the

Staked Plains, six miles northwest of the present town of Cameron, where Indians were seen moving eastward toward the head of Palo Duro Creek. The command started in pursuit, but the Tonkawa scouts, after forging ahead, reported that it was only a small party a long way from the village. Not taking any chances, Mackenzie sent a detachment of cavalry down the Palo Duro, while with the main command he returned to and followed the wagon road which Ortiz had described.[32]

The route continued southeast to the Tierra Blanca Creek south of Lake Garcia. From there Mackenzie followed the Tierra Blanca to its junction with the Palo Duro at the present city of Canyon, reuniting on August 23 with his detached cavalry unit. From that point the cavalry scouted the Palo Duro and Blanca Cita (Cita) canyons, rejoining the main command at the head of the Blanca Cita with geographical information that proved invaluable two years later. The command continued southeast along a well-marked road to the head of Tule Canyon, sixteen miles above its junction with the Red River, and thence on August 27 eastward and southward to descend the Caprock on Cottonwood Creek east of present Silverton. After lingering three days for the horses to graze along the head-streams of the Pease, the column moved southeastward to the present village of Roaring Springs, where it turned southwest along the tracks of its returning scout in July, ascended the Staked Plains near McAdoo, and on the night of August 31 reached the site of its No. 1 camp at the mouth of Blanco Canyon.

In a period of one month Mackenzie had crossed the Staked Plains not once but twice, and by different routes in an area never before penetrated by the military. His return route had permanent and excellent water at no point more than thirty miles distant. Both routes, he reported, were better than the Pecos Trail, and by his command could be made safe to legitimate cattle drovers. Fretting that he had travelled such a great distance without having accomplished anything very useful, he informed Augur that it would require possibly two weeks for his horses to recuperate before he could start for the headwaters of the Red River.[33]

In reality, Mackenize had made a highly significant contribution to the exploration and opening of the Great American West. He had found two routes across the treacherous Plains. The discovery of the roads and the good water would make it possible to keep the hostile Indians constantly on the run until they would surrender, or all be surprised and captured or killed. He had explored the Brazos and Mucha-que country to the south and southwest, and had travelled northward through the rough lands at the eastern base of the Staked Plains beyond Red River. In his annual report, prepared a few days after the expedition returned to its Freshwater Fork base, General Augur lauded his field commander's achievement: "This fact, that troops can be so moved, and the general knowledge of the country, and the specific knowledge of the routes and *modus operandi* of the cattle thieves, obtained by General Mackenzie I regard as very important, and well worth the summer's labor." [34]

But Mackenzie had not finished. On September 21, he headed for the North Fork of Red River, and just eight days later won a decisive victory over the Comanches, a happy climax to a summer of strenuous campaigning.

FOOTNOTES — CHAPTER IV

[1] "Medical History of Fort Richardson," Vol. 236, pp. 10 ff., as cited.
[2] *Ibid.*, pp. 235–265.
[3] *Ibid.*, pp. 242, 245; Carter, *On the Border*, 222–243.
[4] "Medical History of Fort Richardson," Vol. 236, pp. 265–270, as cited.
[5] Carter, *On the Border*, xiii, 538.
[6] This account of the Reynolds-Mackenzie controversy is taken from Mackenzie to Adjutant General, May 11, 1876, Mackenzie to departmental headquarters, July 11 and 19, 1871, a copy of "Charges and Specifications Preferred against Colonel Ranald S. Mackenzie," and sixty other documents, 3888 AGO 1876 (filed with 2441 AGO 1876), RG 94.
[7] *Ibid.*
[8] Brig. Gen. C. C. Augur, San Antonio, annual report, September 28, 1872, 4099 AGO 1872, RG 94.

[9] *Ibid.*; Mackenzie to departmental headquarters, May 3, 1872, 1339 DT 1872, Army Commands, RG 98; Major John T. Hatch, Fort Concho, to departmental headquarters, April 15, 1872, (no index no.) AGO 1872, RG 94; Statement of Polonis Ortiz, May 21, 1872, 1478 DT 1872, Army Commands, RG 98.

[10] Napoleon B. McLaughlin, Fort Concho, report of scout, May 15, 1872, 1385 DT 1872, Army Commands, RG 98.

[11] Augur, Special Orders, No. 102, DT, May 31, 1872, printed copy, AGO 1872, RG 94; "Tabular Statement of Expeditions," September 28, 1872, 4099 AGO 1872, RG 94; Augur, annual report, September 28, 1872, as cited.

[12] "Regimental Returns," June, 1872, as cited; *New York Times*, June 30, 1872; *Galveston Daily News*, June 28, 1872; Townsend, Adj. Gen., to Augur, July 1, 1872, 1915 DT 1872, Army Commands, RG 98; Augur to Townsend, July 1, 1872, 2642 AGO 1872, RG 94.

[13] *Galveston Daily News*, July 2, 1872.

[14] Quoted in the *Dallas Herald*, August 10, 1872.

[15] Mackenzie to departmental headquarters, June 20, 28, and July 5, 1872, 1870 DT 1872, 2091 DT 1872, and 2155 DT 1872, Army Commands, RG 98.

[16] McLaughlin, "Itinerary of March Made by a Scouting Party," July 2-14, 1872, enclosed with Mackenzie to departmental headquarters, July 18, 1872, 2312 DT 1872, Army Commands, RG 98.

[17] Hatch to departmental headquarters, July 15, 1872, 2144 DT 1872, Army Commands, RG 98.

[18] Mackenzie, Freshwater Fork of Brazos, to departmental headquarters, July 5, 1872, as cited; undated endorsement by Adj. Gen., Chicago, 2334 DT 1872, Army Commands, RG 98.

[19] Mackenzie, "Itinerary of a march made by a Scouting Expedition," July 9-19, 1872, 2312 DT 1872, Army Commands, RG 98; Mackenzie, Camp on Fresh Fork of Brazos, to departmental headquarters, July [22], 1872, 2312 DT 1872, Army Commands, RG 98; Lt. William Hoffman, "Map of a part of the territory scouted by Genl. McKenzie's [sic] Command during the summer of 1872," Map Files, Department of Engineers, Southern Department, Fort Sam Houston, Texas (photocopy in possession of author).

[20] Mackenzie to departmental headquarters, July [22], 1872, as cited.

[21] Lt. Wentz C. Miller, report of scout, July 17-21, 1872, forwarded by Mackenzie to departmental headquarters, September 2, 1872, 2658 DT 1872, Army Commands, RG 98. Miller had a map of his route accompanying his report.

[22] Mackenzie, Camp on Las Cañadinas, New Mexico, to departmental headquarters, August 7, 1872, 2506 DT 1872, Army Commands, RG 98.

[23] Francisco Amangual, "Diary of the Incidents and Operations Which Took Place in the Expedition Made from the Province of Texas to the (Province) of New Mexico in Compliance with Superior Orders" (trans., MS, 117 typed pp., dated March 30, 1808; property of H. Bailey Carroll, Austin, Texas).

[24] Promotions in 4th Cavalry, departmental headquarters, July 1, 1872, 1944 DT 1872, Army Commands, RG 98; "Regimental Returns," July and August, 1872, as cited.

[25] The original Clous map has disappeared, but a photograph of it made on November 23, 1885, in the Office of Engineers, Department of Texas,

exists in the Photographic Records Division, U.S. Signal Corps, National Archives.

²⁶ Lt. L. H. Orleman, "Map of Parts of Indian Territory, Texas, and New Mexico" (prepared by order of General J. W. Davidson), 1874, in Cartographic Records Division, RG 75, National Archives; Gillespie, "Map of Expeditions," as cited.

²⁷ Alex L. Lucas, "Map of the Country Scouted by Colonels McKenzie [sic] and Shafter, Capt. R. P. Wilson and Others in the Years 1874 & 1875" (drawn by order of Gen. Ord), 1875, 2832 AGO 1876, RG 94; Lt. Col. W. R. Shafter, Fort Duncan, to departmental headquarters, January 4, 1876, 4688 AGO 1876, RG 94.

²⁸ Mackenzie, Camp on Las Cañadinas, New Mexico, to departmental headquarters, August 7, 1872, as cited.

²⁹ Charles Kenner, "John Hittson: Cattle King of West Texas," in West Texas Historical Association *Year Book*, XXXVII (1961), 79. Kenner states that Hittson's family later claimed and collected compensation for 3,600 cattle stolen during 1872, which "according to one of his old trailhands, was not 'one-half of those he actually lost by Indian raids.'"

³⁰ Mackenzie, Camp at Fort Smith Crossing 25 miles from Fort Bascom, New Mexico, to departmental headquarters, August 15, 1872, 2570 DT 1872, Army Commands, RG 98.

³¹ Strong, *My Indian Fights*, 34.

³² Mackenzie, Camp on Fresh Water Fork of Brazos, to departmental headquarters, September 3, 1872, 3883 AGO 1872, RG 94; Statement of Ortiz, May 21, 1872, as cited.

³³ Mackenzie to departmental headquarters, September 3, 1872, as cited.

³⁴ Augur, annual report, September 28, 1872, as cited.

CHAPTER V

The Battle of the North Fork of Red River*

MACKENZIE COULD ill afford to quit without encountering the hostiles. The assault on the frontier had continued unabated all the way from Henrietta to the Pecos, and public sentiment, led by the frontier editors, was turning against the erstwhile hero. The Gainesville *Gazette* editorialized:

We had great faith that Colonel Mackenzie would teach the Indians a lesson they would not soon forget for all time to come, and have anxiously waited to hear a good report of his command but in vain. The Indians are committing more depredations in Texas today than when General Augur issued his order. We know nothing of the plan of the Indian campaign, but we do know that Colonel Mackenzie extends but little protection to the frontier people in either life or property.[1]

Well aware of the need to deal the marauding Indians a smashing blow without such sharp reminders, Mackenzie was preparing for another search, but the trip across the Staked Plains had been wearing on both horses and men, and they required time to recuperate. The horses had to be grazed, shod, and their sore backs healed, wagons and harness repaired, a court-martial for minor offenses held, and supplies accumu-

* Often referred to as "The Battle of McClellan Creek" because nearby McClellan Creek, being a short stream, more accurately pinpoints the location.

lated. On September 19 Mackenzie informed headquarters that two days later he would start for the head of the Salt and North forks of the Red River with six companies of cavalry, one company of infantry, sixteen wagons, and one month's rations. During his absence Lieutenant William Hoffman with a detachment of the 11th Infantry under the direction of Lieutenant Colonel Shafter would scout and map the region to the south of the Supply Camp.[2]

On Saturday, September 21, Mackenzie pulled out on schedule for the headwaters of the Red River with five companies of the 4th Cavalry;[3] Company I, 24th Infantry; Captain Clous, the engineer officer; and two assistant surgeons, in all, 12 officers and 272 enlisted men; the Tonkawa scouts, a Fort Richardson post guide, and prisoner Ortiz.[4] Mackenzie followed his return road from New Mexico to his August 28 camp site between Quitaque mound and the North Fork of the Pease, then turned northeast a short distance and on the 23rd camped on the north branch of the Quitaque (North Pease), where he was joined by a detachment of cavalry that he had started a day ahead of the main command. The detached unit had camped the first night out on the head of Duck Creek, circled the promontory that projects into northwestern Dickens County, and had travelled northward nearby the sites of present Dickens, Roaring Springs, and Matador. The reunited column then marched northward through the present town of Turkey, crossed the Prairie Dog or South Fork of the Red River at its junction with Mulberry Creek, and struck the Salt Fork about twenty-eight miles beyond and five miles north of the present town of Clarendon.[5]

Leaving his supplies with a detachment to guard them at a small stream just north of the Salt Fork, Mackenzie early on the morning of September 29 proceeded with 7 officers, 215 enlisted men, and 9 Tonkawa scouts under the command of Lieutenant Boehm. Twenty miles farther, in the vicinity of the present town of Alanreed, he crossed the South Fork of Mc-

Clellan Creek at a point about four miles above its confluence with the North Fork. Two miles downstream the Tonkawa scouts discovered but soon lost two fresh trails, one of two horses and the other of one mule,[6] and Mackenzie halted the column until the scouts could pick up the trails again. Captain Davis, observing along the banks of the creek vines loaded with grapes, dismounted from his horse to check for signs of Indians. From the tracks and scattered grapes he found, he concluded that the Indians had used a mule to pack grapes to their village. Led by Davis and the Tonkawa scouts, the command at a rapid gait followed the mule tracks northward for twelve miles; suddenly a large Indian village, nestled in a beautiful valley, was sighted three to five miles distant,[7] on the south side of the North Fork of Red River, about seven miles from its junction with McClellan Creek, and five or six miles east of the present town of Lefors.[8]

After halting briefly to rest, the command formed for a charge with Mackenzie at the side of Captain Beaumont of Co. A, the base troop, and Captain Davis at the head of Co. F leading, and about 4:00 p.m. galloped in columns of four toward the unsuspecting village. Upon entering a draw, the cavalrymen could see near the river hundreds of horses being driven toward the village.[9]

The village, the largest of several Kwahadi and Kotsoteka Comanche camps in the vicinity, was that of Kotsoteka Chief Mow-way, who had emphatically announced that "when Indians in here [the reservation] are treated better than we are outside, it will be time enough to come in." Nevertheless, Mow-way was anxious for peace with the whites and had gone to talk with the "peace people," leaving the village in charge of Kai-wotche, who had ridden the mule whose trail had led to the village.[10] The villagers, busy drying buffalo meat and making pemmican, had noticed clouds of dust in the distance but had assumed that some of their own men were chasing buffalo.[11]

Suddenly, the villagers heard the thunder of hooves and saw

within a half mile of them a charging wave of bluecoated "Long Knives." Some ran for their horses, others tried to hide in the brush and ravines, while still others grabbed their bows and arrows and endeavored unsuccessfully to defend their village. Sending Lee's Co. D racing after the Indian horse herd and McLaughlin's Co. I charging through a small group of lodges somewhat detached, Mackenzie with the companies of Beaumont, Davis, and Wint charged into the main village. Captain Davis' Co. F, which encountered sharp resistance throughout the fight, sustained most of the casualties.[12] As it reached the center of the village, a number of warriors hidden in the grass not more than fifteen steps away fired a volley of bullets and arrows. The four men nearest the Indians went down, killed or wounded: Private William Rankin caught a bullet that lodged near his spine; Private John Dorcas, shot through the neck, strangled on his own blood; Private John Kelley, also shot through the neck, died three days later; and the fourth man caught an arrow in his thigh.[13]

After a "brisk" fight of about half an hour the village was carried. Beaumont's Troop A, galloping in pursuit of Indians, encountered desperate resistance by seventy-five to eighty warriors sheltered under the bank of a creek where there was a waterhole eight or ten feet deep and twenty-five or thirty feet long. As the troops deployed to flank the enemy, the warriors twice charged but each time fell back with heavy losses, dumping a number of their dead in the pool, apparently to save them from the scalping knife.[14]

Meanwhile, McLaughlin, who had led his Co. I toward the head of the ravine to cut off escaping hostiles, went to Beaumont's aid, and from an advantageous position poured a withering fire in the direction of the Indians. The survivors fled, and the women began coming out of the brush with their hands in the air.[15] Mackenzie then ordered McLaughlin and Wint to pursue the fleeing Indians and Beaumont to help Lee round up their horses.[16]

The Tonkawa scouts, as soon as they thought it was safe, began appropriating trophies from the heads of their traditional enemies until Mackenzie ordered them to stop. Tonkawa Henry indignantly blurted out: "What fur you no lette me scalp heme Comanche?"[17] Although the evidence is to the contrary, Clinton Smith, the captive youth whom Tatum had hoped Mackenzie could recover, later claimed that the soldiers "tried to make a massacre of this attack, for they killed many squaws, babies, warriors, and old white headed men."[18] Mackenzie reported that the wounding of the women and children occurred accidentally, because they were mixed with the men during the battle.

Not until the companies reunited at the village about dusk was Mackenzie able to tally the results. His own losses had been relatively small: in addition to the three casualties in Co. F (Mackenzie did not regard the soldier hit in the thigh as seriously wounded), Corporal Henry A. McMasters, Co. A, was seriously wounded – a total of one dead and three wounded, one of whom would soon die. Only ten cavalry horses had been killed or wounded.

The Comanches, on the other hand, had suffered heavily. The village of 175 large and 87 small tipis and the accumulated stores of meat, equipment, and clothing, except a few choice robes, were destroyed.[19] Mackenzie reported that twenty-three dead Comanches, including Chief Kai-wotche and his wife, had been counted after the battle, that a captured warrior afterwards had died of his wounds, and that certainly a number of others had been killed.[20] An old Mexican woman taken captive stated that she saw sixty-two bodies thrown into the pool,[21] but it is difficult to believe that a woman frightened by bullets whizzing about her could count accurately. When they surrendered a few weeks later, the warriors admitted that fifty-two of their people had been killed during the battle.[22]

About 130, mostly women and children, were taken captive, some very old, and some, who had been among the men during the battle, too badly wounded to be moved. Mackenzie left the village site with 124 prisoners, of whom one man and seven women and children had died by October 12, although they had been given "the best care possible."

Evidence that the villagers had been engaged in murdering raids and costly depredations was abundant. Ortiz, the captive *Comanchero* who twice had guided Mackenzie across the Staked Plains, recognized many who had spent the previous winter at Mucha-que. José Carrión, formerly a teamster and blacksmith with the train burned at Howard's Wells during the spring of 1872 and now with Mackenzie, asserted that he recognized among the Indians' herd of livestock forty-three mules, including the saddle mule of the wagon master, that had belonged to his train. Francisco Nietto, a fourteen-year-old Mexican, said that he had been captured by these same Comanches two years before while enroute with his father's train from Fort Duncan to San Antonio; seven of the prisoners were Mexican women who had been Comanche captives so long that "practically they have become Indians." [23]

The soldiers and scouts succeeded in rounding up a great many horses and mules, the estimates ranging all the way from 800 to 3,000. Sergeant Charlton and Lieutenant Thompson both wrote later that it was 3,000, but Strong, the Richardson post guide, many years later remembered that about 1,000 had been taken, and Carter, who was not with the expedition at the time, set the number at "about 800 ponies." As usual Mackenzie's official report contained very little information. The Colonel merely noted that "We captured a very large number of horses and mules," a statement equally applicable whether the number was 800 or 3,000. [24]

Shortly after dark, the command, with the prisoners under heavy guard, moved two miles from the burned village and made a dry camp among the sandhills. Afraid to put the Indian ponies in the center of the camp lest they cause the cavalry horses to stampede, Mackenzie had them corralled, under guard of Lieutenant Boehm and his Tonkawas, about a mile from the burned village in a draw or sink in the prairie, where it appeared they could be easily held in case of attack.[25] His experience at Blanco Canyon the preceding autumn should have taught him better. The Tonkawas felt so secure that they rolled into their blankets and fell asleep. The details of what followed cannot clearly be pieced together, but unquestionably on that night and the following the Comanches successfully recovered most of their horses and in addition those of the scouts.

A Comanche participant gave his version of what happened: "One of the chiefs [who escaped from Mow-way's village] came down to the lower village and said, 'The soldiers got all our horses.' So we tied up the tails of our ponies [a custom followed by the Comanches when going into battle] and came on them at night. We got all our own horses back and some of the soldiers' too. The women and children were under close guard."[26]

The Comanches, shooting and yelling, first encircled the main camp, hoping, no doubt, to stampede the horses. Failing to achieve their objective, they soon withdrew, but about midnight they rushed the captured pony herd and succeeded in driving off the horses, including those of Lieutenant Boehm and the Tonkawa scouts. The next morning, according to Charlton, Boehm, and the Tonkawas, "looking sheepish and woefully dejected," walked into camp, leading a small burro bearing their saddles.[27] If Charlton's account is accurate, then the command must have gathered up a considerable number of the stock during the day, for while it was encamped the next night some eighteen miles to the south, on the bank of the South Fork of McClellan Creek, Comanches again succeeded in driving off a great many.[28]

On the second day after the battle Mackenzie rejoined his supply train, camping for the night on the north side of the Salt Fork of the Red River. From there, the prisoners riding bareback, he retraced his outward route, stopping for the night of October 2 on the Prairie Dog Fork of Red River, near Quitaque on the 4th, upon the Llano Estacado on the 5th, and at the mouth of the Blanco Canyon two nights later, and reached Supply Camp on the 8th, having marched 209 miles in eighteen days without any noteworthy occurrence since leaving the Salt Fork. Mackenzie, who still had fifty ponies and nine mules captured from the Indians, gave most of the ponies to the Tonkawa scouts.[29]

Well pleased with the outcome of the expedition, the Colonel was more generous than usual in citing his men for gallant conduct. Twelve officers, including Surgeon Choate and Cartographer Clous, and nine enlisted men were recommended for and received congressional medals. Even so, at least two men did not agree with the citations. Captain Davis recommended all of the non-commissioned officers of his company for Medals of Honor, but Mackenzie cut the list down to the senior sergeants and the wounded.[30] Sergeant Charlton, one of those deleted from the list and, according to his captain, "the finest soldier I ever knew during my several years of hard service," was still bitterly critical about the matter a half century later. One of the sergeants honored, he claimed, was no soldier and could neither drill his men nor hit a target; Mackenzie was a vain "autocrat" who believed that the rest of the officers and men "had no business entertaining such foolish feelings as a desire for commendation or recognition of services."[31]

Regarding his victory on the North Fork of the Red as a satisfactory conclusion to a summer of strenuous work, Mackenzie decided to finish the job the next summer if the Indians had not agreed to remain peaceably on their reservation. After allowing a week for the horses to recuperate, he broke camp and sent the men to their respective posts. Troop F reached Fort Griffin headquarters on October 18; D and I reached Concho on the 21st; and A and L reached Richardson on the 23rd.[32]

Meanwhile, the other companies of Mackenzie's cavalry per-

formed varied duties across the Texas frontier from Brownsville to the Red River. Captain Mauck's Company B, relieved
from duty with Mackenzie on September 20, after a short rest
was kept busy scouting in the vicinity of Fort Richardson.
Company E, Captain William W. Webb, and Company C,
Captain John A. Wilcox, from Richardson had been escorting
Indian prisoners to Indian Territory and cattle herds northward; Company H, Captain Sebastian Gunther, at Griffin had
engaged in a number of short scouts in the vicinity; Company
K, Captain Heyl, had spent the summer and fall guarding the
Texas and Pacific Railroad survey "near Concho;" Company
G, under the old Prussian officer, Captain Rendlebrock, had
escorted large herds of cattle from Concho to Horsehead Crossing on the Pecos River; and Captain William O'Connell with
Company M, although continuously on the move, had been
unable to check the activity of marauders who depredated the
ranches in Texas and escaped with their plunder across the Rio
Grande. The total strength of the 4th Cavalry as of August
31 was 40 officers, 882 enlisted men, and 522 serviceable horses,
but a very large number of both officers and men were absent
from various causes.[33]

Colonel Mackenzie sent the Comanche captives to Concho
because that post was better adapted for their confinement than
Griffin or Richardson. On the way one wounded Indian died,
the springless army wagon in which he was riding having jolted
the life out of him — twenty-four hours from Supply Camp
he was found stiff and immovable, sitting upright against the
side board. However, a woman who gave birth in another
jolting wagon arrived at Concho none the worse for the wear
and tear. Although the baby died, its mother uttered not one
word of complaint nor showed a sign of pain. Upon their arrival at Concho, the 115 prisoners were confined in the post
corral, where they remained throughout the winter.[34]

On October 11, while still at Camp Supply, Mackenzie received General Augur's order to report at once to San Antonio

to discuss the disposition of the Comanche prisoners and plans for further military action against their hostile kinsmen. Deciding in the conference at San Antonio to hold the captives as a trump, the two officers recommended that they not be restored to their people until all the white captives and all the public animals in the hands of the tribes south of the Arkansas River had been surrendered and the Kwahadis and other hostile Comanche bands had gone to the reservation and promised "good behavior." Sheridan endorsed the recommendation with the comment that "this chastisement will do much to stop Indian depredations" in Texas, and Sherman passed the recommendation on to the Secretary of War, commenting that "These Comanche children are as wild as coyotes, and unless taken in hand early, must grow up like their fathers, unqualified savages," and adding a recommendation that the captive children be provided for by the Indian Bureau in some place where they could be "raised with habits one degree nearer civilization than they now possess." [35] The Secretary of the Interior, upon the recommendation of the Commissioner of Indian Affairs, concurred with Sherman's proposal, but stipulated that the children must be returned to their parents as soon as the Indians had complied with Augur's demands. [36] Pending their final disposition, Augur ordered that the prisoners be well fed and kindly treated, and by December they had been provided with clothing in the amount of $250 and by army standards were "comfortably fixed." [37]

His victory on the North Fork of Red River was not only Mackenzie's greatest in a long career of Indian warfare but it also stands as one of the major Anglo-American triumphs over the Indians on the Southern Plains. Although he had failed to set the Comanches afoot, something that would have to be done before they would stay on the reservation, Mackenzie had shown them that the mounted bluecoats could find and destroy them in their remote hideouts. Within a week after the defeat, Kwahadi Chief Para-o-coom, whose camp at the time of the

battle was only a short distance from Mow-way's, brought
his band to the vicinity of Fort Sill, telling Agent Tatum that
the Comanches had had their fight with the soldiers, had been
whipped, and were now ready to remain on the reservation, to
send their children to school, and even to try a hand at farm-
ing, provided the agent would exchange the women and children taken by Mackenzie for several Mexican children held by
his people.[38]

When Agent Tatum, who knew of several Americans they
held in captivity, refused the offer and explained the terms laid
down by Mackenzie and Augur, Horseback, a Nokoni chief
who had several relatives among the captives, including his
mother-in-law and a former wife and her daughter, constituted
himself as a special agent to gain Comanche compliance with
the terms.[39] Traveling among the Comanche bands, Horseback
persuaded them to give up several captives, including Clinton
Smith. As a reward for the chief's efforts, Augur early in December released five of his relatives, one of whom died on the
way to the reservation. Delighted with Horseback's success,
other chiefs began arriving at the reservation in December with
captives and horses. By early in January they had returned
thirty-seven horses and sixteen mules, the equivalent of the
fifty-four stolen from Fort Sill by Tenawerka on the night of
June 15, 1872, and seven American and twelve Mexican captives were turned over to the agent.[40] Other Comanches during the winter straggled to the reservation to assure Agent Tatum of their willingness to change their ways — for as long,
they might have added with more honesty, as the bold and daring Mackenzie held their women and children as hostages.
Thus, all the signs indicated that at last peace had come to the
northwestern frontier of Texas.

Nevertheless, Mackenzie and Augur had not allowed wish-
ful thinking to lull them into complacency. While drawing up
the "olive branch" proposals in San Antonio in October, they
had worked out alternate plans for more effective use of the

"sword" — plans for the complete subjugation of the Comanches during the following summer. The two officers decided
that Fort Concho, which afforded advantages over Fort Richardson for campaigning, should be the headquarters and base
of operations for the 4th Cavalry during the 1873 campaign.

Mackenzie, rejoining his post on November 5, having trav-
eled via Austin and Dallas,[41] had very little time for relaxation
while he waited to move his headquarters to Concho. Small
scouting parties were kept continuously in the field, and a
number of detachments were guarding surveying parties and
escorting wagon trains. He made certain that General Augur
would find the post in satisfactory condition when he inspected
it on November 16. Ninety-two recruits, who arrived on October 25, were drilled and trained to his rigid standards, Beaumont and Thompson were dispatched to enlist more recruits,
a Horse Board was sent out to procure an additional supply
of cavalry horses, and some of the rougher element were disciplined. Mackenzie, displeased by the lack of discipline in
Company A, may deliberately have sent its officers on the en-
listment mission. While they were away some of their men were
confined to the guardhouse, court-martialed, reduced in rank,
or subjected to the usual severe punishments.[42]

In preparation for the removal, Mackenzie ordered the commanding officers at Griffin and Concho to place a supply of
forage at convenient points along the 220-mile route, including a four-day supply at Chadbourne.[43] Company L left on
December 21 for Fort Concho, and Mackenzie, traveling in an
army ambulance, followed a week later.[44]

But despite his move to a more effective post, Mackenzie's
plans to finish driving the Indians out of northwestern Texas
had to be postponed for a year. The excitement caused by
depredations along the Rio Grande frontier by Indians from
Mexico had stirred Washington to action, and soon after his
arrival at Concho Mackenzie received orders to transfer to the
Rio Grande the whole of his 4th Cavalry. His amazingly suc-

cessful campaign of 1872 had inspired his superiors to select him for what, no doubt, was to be a far more dangerous job.

FOOTNOTES — CHAPTER V

[1] Quoted in the *Dallas Herald*, August 10, 1872.

[2] Mackenzie, Camp on the Fresh Water Fork of the Brazos, to departmental headquarters, September 19, 1872, 2737 DT 1872, Army Commands, RG 98.

[3] A, Captain Beaumont; D, Captain Lee; F, Captain Davis; I, Captain McLaughlin; L, Captain Wint. For some unexplained reason, Mackenzie on the preceding day had changed his mind and sent Company B, commanded by Captain Mauck, to its Fort Richardson headquarters station, where it arrived on September 30. "Regimental Returns," September, 1872, as cited.

[4] Mackenzie, Camp on Fresh Water Fork of the Brazos, to departmental headquarters, October 12, 1872, 4546½ AGO 1872, RG 94 (hereafter cited as "Mackenzie, report, October 12, 1872"); "Regimental Returns," September, 1872, as cited; "Tabular Statement of Expeditions," September 28, 1872, as cited.

[5] Orleman, "Map of Parts of Indian Territory, Texas, and New Mexico," as cited; Gillespie, "Map of Expeditions," as cited; Lucas, "Map of Country Scouted by Mackenzie, Shafter, and Wilson," as cited.

[6] Mackenzie, report, October 12, 1872, as cited; Carter, *On the Border*, 377; Carter, *The Old Sergeant's Story*, 82.

[7] Mackenzie, report, October 12, 1872, as cited; Carter, *On the Border*, 377; Carter, *The Old Sergeant's Story*, 83; W. A. Thompson, "Scouting with Mackenzie," in *Cavalry Journal*, X (1897), 430 (hereafter cited as Thompson, "Scouting with Mackenzie"). Thompson was one of Mackenzie's lieutenants. Mackenzie reported that the village was five miles distant when sighted; Carter stated that it was three or four.

[8] Mackenzie, report, October 12, 1872, as cited; Charlton in Carter, *The Old Sergeant's Story*, 85.

[9] *Ibid.*; Carter, *On the Border*, 377–378; Thompson, "Scouting with Mackenzie," 430; Mackenzie, report, October 12, 1872, as cited.

[10] Nye, *Carbine and Lance*, 161–162.

[11] Thompson, "Scouting with Mackenzie," 430.

[12] Mackenzie, report, October 12, 1872, as cited.

[13] Thompson, "Scouting with Mackenzie," 430; Charlton in Carter, *The Old Sergeant's Story*, 85.

[14] Thompson, "Scouting with Mackenzie," 431.

[15] Mackenzie, report, October 12, 1872, as cited; Charlton in Carter, *The Old Sergeant's Story*, 83; Nye, *Carbine and Lance*, 162, quotes Cohaya and Mumsukawa, both Comanche participants in the battle.

[16] Mackenzie, report, October 12, 1872, as cited.

[17] Strong, *My Indian Fights*, 39.

[18] Clinton L. and Jeff D. Smith, *The Boy Captives* (Bandera, Texas, 1927), 128.

[19] Mackenzie, report, October 12, 1872, as cited; Carter, *The Old Sergeant's Story*, 83.

[20] Mackenzie, report, October 12, 1872, as cited.

[21] Strong, *My Indian Fights*, 38.

[22] Thompson, "Scouting with Mackenzie," 431.

[23] Mackenzie, report, October 12, 1872, as cited.

[24] Charlton in Carter, *The Old Sergeant's Story*, 86, Thompson, "Scouting with Mackenzie," 431; Strong, *My Indian Fights*, 38; Carter, *On the Border*, 378; Mackenzie, report, October 12, 1872, as cited.

[25] *Ibid.*; Charlton in Carter,*The Old Sergeant's Story*, 86; Strong, *My Indian Fights*, 39; Carter, *On the Border*, 379.

[26] Quoted in Nye, *Carbine and Lance*, 162.

[27] Charlton in Carter, *The Old Sergeant's Story*, 86; Carter, *On the Border*, 379.

[28] Mackenzie, report, October 12, 1872, as cited.

[29] *Ibid.*; "Regimental Returns," September, 1872, as cited.

[30] Mackenzie, report, October 12, 1872, as cited; Adjutant General, Washington, D.C., to Adj. Gen., Department of Texas, November 21, 1872, 2867 DT 1872, Army Commands, RG 98; Carter, *The Old Sergeant's Story*, 166–167, 188.

[31] *Ibid.*, 62, 213, 110.

[32] "Regimental Returns," October, 1872, 5228 AGO 1873, RG 94.

[33] "Regimental Returns," August, 1872, as cited; "Movement of Troops in Department of Texas during the year ending September 30, 1872," in Augur, annual report, September 28, 1872, as cited.

[34] Augur, annual report, September 30, 1873, 5228 AGO 1873, RG 94; Carter, *The Old Sergeant's Story*, 85–86; Carter, *On the Border*, 389; Joseph H. Toulouse and James R. Toulouse, *Pioneer Posts of Texas* (San Antonio, 1936), 53.

[35] *Army and Navy Journal*, X (1872), 212; Augur, annual report, September 28, 1872, as cited; Augur, Special Order No. 193, October 29, 1872, 4785 AGO 1872, RG 94; Augur to Sheridan, October 25, 1872, 4546½ AGO 1872 (filed with 4148 AGO 1872), RG 94; Sheridan, endorsement of *ibid.*, November 4, 1872; Sherman to Secretary of War, October 30, 1872 (filed with 4148 AGO 1872), RG 94.

[36] F. A. Walker, Commissioner of Indian Affairs, Washington, D.C., to Secretary of Interior, November 4, 1872, and Q. Delano, Secretary of Interior, to Secretary of War, November 23, 1872, both filed with 4148 AGO 1872, RG 94.

[37] The daily ration to each person consisted of 18 oz. of flour, 20 oz. of beef, ½ oz. of salt, approximately 1 oz. of rice, and about ⅓ oz. of soap. Augur, San Antonio, Special Field Order No. 2, November 7, 1872, 4478 AGO 1872, RG 94; Sheridan, endorsement on the War Department approval of Augur's proposal, December 7, 1872, filed with 4148 AGO 1872, RG 94.

[38] Nye, *Carbine and Lance*, 162–163.

[39] Richardson, *Comanche Barrier*, 363–364.

[40] Major G. W. Schofield, Fort Sill, to Augur, January 17, 1873, 750 AGO 1873, RG 94; Augur, annual report, September 30, 1873, as cited.

[41] "Medical History of Fort Richardson," Vol. 236, p. 289, as cited; Augur, Special Order No. 193, October 29, 1872, as cited.

[42] "Medical History of Fort Richardson," Vol. 236, pp. 289 ff., as cited; Carter, *On the Border*, 394–397.

⁴³ Mackenzie to the commanding officers at Forts Griffin and Concho, December 20, 1872, and to departmental headquarters, December 21, 1872, (index number illegible) AGO 1872, RG 94; also, in Army Commands, Fort Richardson, Letters Sent, Vol. 71, National Archives.

⁴⁴ "Movement of Troops in Department of Texas during the Year ending September 30, 1873," as cited.

CHAPTER VI

The Raid on the Mexican Kickapoos

Washington, D.C., Feb. 5, 1873.

General C. C. Augur,
Comdg. Dept. of Texas
General: —

The president wishes you to give great attention to affairs on the Rio Grande Frontier, especially to prevent the raids of Indians and Mexicans upon the people and property of Southern and Western Texas.

To this end he wishes the 4th Cavalry to be moved to that Frontier. . . . In naming the 4th for the Rio Grande the President is doubtless influenced by the fact that Col. Mackenzie is young and enterprising, and that he will impart to his Regiment his own active character.

I have the honor to be,

Your obedient servant,
W. T. Sherman,
General.

Although Sherman's order did not alter the existing Indian policy, the assignment of Mackenzie to the Rio Grande border was indicative that Washington had determined to end the deplorable situation there even at the risk of international involvement.

The principal target of the marauders was the country (generally referred to as the Upper Rio Grande Border Region) bounded on the southeast by Laredo, on the northeast by central Atascosa County, about thirty miles south of San Antonio, on the north by Bandera and Edwards counties, and on the west by Del Rio.[1] By 1870 the five counties in the region contained 4,248 residents and 90,770 head of cattle and horses,[2] too sparsely populated for defense and too well stocked for predatory Indians to ignore. Between 1865 and 1873 the rustlers swept Atascosa County clean of horses and cattle and so thoroughly terrorized the ranchers that most fled to San Antonio for safety. A Kickapoo raid on a ranch in Schleicher County during 1866 netted a thousand head of cattle.[3]

Although Mescalero and Lipan Apaches were engaged in the raiding, most of the depredations were the work of the Kickapoo Indians, who had migrated to Mexico from the United States.[4] First encountered by the French in the seventeenth century south of the Great Lakes, the Kickapoos under Anglo-American pressure moved southwest. A part of the tribe settled on the Missouri River near Fort Leavenworth, Kansas, but the majority moved into present Oklahoma and Texas. One band of eighty, which had confederated with the Cherokees in East Texas, in 1839 fled to Mexico, where they allied with the Mexicans against the incursions of Comanche and Kiowa raiders from the United States.

During the Civil War this band was joined by other groups from Kansas and Oklahoma who had become discontented with the policies of the United States. While on its way to Mexico in December, 1862, a band camped on the Little Concho, near present San Angelo, was attacked by a mounted Confederate patrol. The Kickapoos, after shooting sixteen Texans out of their saddles, hurried southward to Mexico. The Mexican government, highly pleased with the services of the first Kickapoo arrivals, gave them a grant of land in return for a pledge to defend the northern frontier against Comanches and Kiowas.[5]

Favorably impressed with the treatment accorded their kinsmen, another group of about seven hundred Kickapoos in the autumn of 1864 started for Mexico. While waiting out a snowstorm on Dove Creek, a few miles west of San Angelo, it was attacked on January 8, 1865, by about 360 Texas militia and Confederate troops. Although they soundly defeated the whites, the Kickapoos, having lost fifteen warriors, considered the attack to be a declaration of war, and once safely settled in Nacimiento Canyon at the head of the Sabinas River near Santa Rosa, Coahuila,[6] they struck back with savage fury. Soon discovering economic possibilities in their war against the Texans, they came to rely for their livelihood less on agriculture and more on Texas plunder, readily disposed of in Santa Rosa and other nearby towns, where the merchants and political officials aided them.[7] A petition from the Uvalde County jury in 1868 stated that Kickapoo depredators over a three-year period had taken the lives of at least sixty-two persons, had wounded many citizens, and had driven off thousands of dollars worth of livestock. By 1870 the raiders reportedly had wiped out the flourishing horse-raising industry of the Upper Rio Grande Border Region.[8]

Besieged by a steady stream of letters, petitions, and appeals for aid against the incursions, and fearful that unless such help was forthcoming the Texans would take matters into their own hands, the Office of Indian Affairs, the State Department, Congress, and the army in 1870 and 1871 began taking cognizance of the situation. Secretary of State Hamilton Fish, upon learning that the victimized settlers were threatening to organize retaliatory pursuits, in 1870 requested permission of the Mexican government to send troops with the owners of stolen livestock across the Rio Grande in pursuit of the marauders, but Mexican officials steadfastly refused.[9]

Since reports indicated that most depredations were being committed by the Kickapoos, the Office of Indian Affairs, operating under the Peace Policy, decided that it could solve the problem by persuading the tribe to return to the United States, but Quaker Agent John Miles, who was sent to Santa Rosa in April, 1871, found the Kickapoos not the least interested and the local Mexican officials and citizens opposed to the plan.[10] The Mexicans claimed that the Kickapoos were peaceful and aided them against the ferocious Comanches.[11] Miles' failure was assured when the Mexican officials distributed $5,000 in goods, purchased with money owed the tribe for border defense. In a meeting on June 15 in the Santa Rosa courthouse, the chiefs politely declined the invitation to return to the United States.[12]

In addition to financing the effort to return the Kickapoos, Congress authorized a commission to investigate the border situation. The findings of the commissioners, presented on June 31, 1873, alleged losses totaling more than forty-eight million dollars and reported that the Upper Rio Grande Border Region in 1872 had only one-tenth as many livestock as in 1865. Although the commissioners made no effort to compile figures on bodily injury or loss of life inflicted by the marauders, their reports contained numerous abstracts of such atrocities, and charged that the Mexican populace in the vicinity were giving aid and encouragement to the Indian marauders.[13] A similar Mexican commission, on the other hand, after months of investigation concluded that the Mexican authorities had taken every reasonable precaution to restrain the raids into Texas, and that the Mexican settlements had suffered more from depredations committed by Indians from the United States than the Texans had from Mexican Indians.[14]

Meanwhile, the raids continued and the protests of the Texans grew more and more vehement. The *Galveston Daily News* declared that there was "no shame of the times so offensive . . . as the unchecked and chronic spoliation of our population on the Mexican border." [15] These new outcries and the preliminary report of the American commission aroused the government to action. President Grant in January, 1873, announced that the military forces along the border would be redistributed and that Mexico would be held to strict account for the depredations.[16] In consequence, Mackenzie was directed to move the headquarters of the 4th Cavalry to Fort Clark. The 4th Cavalry, Sherman explained, was a more efficient scouting unit than the 9th Cavalry, the regiment then on the border.[17]

Colonel Mackenzie, who had moved his headquarters to Fort Concho on January 1, 1873, at once began preparations. On March 4 five companies (A, B, C, E, and K) of the 4th Cavalry commanded by Major Latimer pulled out of Fort Richardson for the Rio Grande. At Fort Concho Mackenzie replaced Co. K with Co. G and Major Latimer with Captain Mauck. Following the military road by way of Fort McKavett on the upper San Saba, Mauck reached Fort Clark with his column on March 31. The headquarters unit, Co. I, and a detachment of Co. K left Concho on April 17 and reached Fort Clark early in May; Co. M moved from Fort Brown to Fort Duncan, on the Rio Grande about forty miles south of Clark; Cos. D, F, H, and L left Concho on May 23 and 24 and arrived at Clark in June, too late to participate in the raid into Mexico.[18]

Mackenzie, meanwhile, had left Fort Concho for San Antonio on March 24 to confer with his superiors. Fully aware of the diplomatic danger involved, Secretary of War Belknap and General Sheridan reached San Antonio on April 7, three days after leaving St. Louis, to make an on-the-spot assessment of the situation. At Clark four days later Belknap and Sheridan expressed great pleasure with Mackenzie's command. That evening Colonel Merritt, commander of the departing 9th Regiment, honored the visiting dignitaries and the 4th Cavalry with a colorful dance.

During the next two days Belknap and Sheridan were in secret council with Mackenzie. Before leaving, according to Carter, acting regimental adjutant, Sheridan ordered Mackenzie "to control and hold down the situation, and to do it in your own way . . . When you begin, let it be a campaign of annihilation, obliteration and destruction." To Mackenzie's request for written orders, Sheridan replied with his usual impatience: "Damn the orders! Damn the authority . . . Your authority and backing shall be Gen. Grant and myself. With us behind you in whatever you do to clean up this situation, you can rest assured of the fullest support." [19]

For more than a month Mackenzie assiduously prepared for what he correctly surmised would be the most daring and arduous exploits in the annals of Indian warfare. The companies were scattered at nearby grazing camps: Beaumont's Co. A and Mauck's Co. B pitched their tents twelve miles northeast of the post on Piedras Pintos Creek; Captain Wilcox found good grass and drill grounds for Co. C on the Las Moras, twelve miles downstream from the post; Cos. E and M located their camp about twenty miles east of the post on Elm Creek.[20] The distribution of the companies served a twofold purpose: to provide more forage for the horses and to avoid arousing the suspicion of Mexican spies at Brackettville. Although the men of the 4th were tough and possibly unexcelled in discipline, Mackenzie ordered gruelling daily drills and carbine practice. While the troopers were improving their tactical skill and endurance, he devoted long hours to studying maps and information provided by his scouts and nearby ranchers.

Both officers and men went about their rigorous training entirely ignorant of Mackenzie's plans — that is, all but Adjutant Carter, in whom Mackenzie confided after exacting a pledge of secrecy. Some of the officers suspected that certain unusual preparations, such as having all the sabres in the command ground to a razor edge, portended a border crossing, but they never knew until the hour arrived.

Having gathered information from the local Mexicans and ranchers that renegade bands of Kickapoos, Lipans, and Mescaleros lived about sixty or seventy miles in the interior of Mexico, Mackenzie sent three scouts, Ike Cox, the trustworthy post guide, and Green Van and Art McLain, two half-breed ranchers who had suffered heavy losses of livestock, to locate and determine the strength of the villages and to find the best trails by which they could be reached undetected. The scouts at once made contact near Nacimiento with a community of Muscogee Seminoles, descendants of Seminoles and Negro slaves who in 1850 had migrated to Coahuila. The Muscogee Seminoles, traditionally disliked by the Kickapoos, welcomed the opportunity to inform on their arrogant neighbors. Cox, Van, and McLain scouted the country thoroughly, sketching maps of trails and gathering information about the location and strength of the three Indian villages a short distance west of Remolino, a Mexican village on the San Rodrigo River, thirty-six miles west and slightly north of Piedras Negras.[21]

At 11:00 o'clock on the night of May 16 the scouts reported to Mackenzie that the entire warrior force of the Kickapoo village had ridden off toward the west that morning, and that they were prepared to lead him to the Indian villages. Within a few minutes, Mackenzie had couriers speeding to the cavalry companies, bearing orders to report for field duty the next morning at the camp on the Las Moras. Captain Mauck, who was at Clark that evening, accompanied by Cox, rode immediately to join his command and to carry the order to Captain Beaumont. Mauck and Cox reached the camp on the Piedras Pintos sometime after 2:00 a.m., and at 3:30 the two companies marched for the designated rendezvous where they arrived about mid-morning. Shortly afterwards, Mackenzie in company with McLaughlin's Co. I, McLain and Van, and eighteen Seminoles arrived, and about the same time Lieutenant John Lapham Bullis, 24th Infantry, Civil War hero and veteran of six years' service on the Rio Grande frontier, came in from Fort Duncan with sixteen additional Seminole scouts. Co. E reached the rendezvous before noon, but Co. M did not arrive until the impatient Mackenzie was ready to start.[22]

About 1:00 o'clock the column, consisting of 360 enlisted

men, 17 officers, 24 scouts, and 14 citizens, marched.[23] The course was southwest along the Las Moras Creek toward the Rio Grande. For a spring day the heat beat down with terrific force, but Mackenzie had each man fitted out with a wet sponge in his hat. Fortunately, as yet there was no hurry, because Mackenzie did not want to reach the Rio Grande, twelve miles distant, until the fading moments of twilight. Several times he rested the command; still not a captain knew his destination. Arriving at the river crossing, eighteen miles above Fort Duncan and about midway between the mouth of the Las Moras and the town of Quemado, Mackenzie halted the column and explained to the men the objective of the expedition. It would be a physically exhausting undertaking; the risks incurred would be great. In addition to the danger of being killed or wounded, those captured faced the possibility of being hanged or riddled by bullets from a Mexican firing squad. The men were to maintain the utmost quiet.[24]

Just as darkness settled around them, the blue-coated Yankee raiders splashed their horses into the swift, belly-deep waters of the ford, scrambled up the south bank of the river onto foreign soil, and headed southwest along mule trails and cattle paths that wound through canebrakes and dense chaparral, across rocky ravines, over dusty barren stretches, and near Monclova, a village seven miles from the river. Mackenzie, his adjutant, and the three guides, Cox, Van, and McLain, were in the lead, selecting the trails and setting the pace. Close behind them rode a small escort of orderlies, followed by Lieutenant Bullis and his mixed-blood scouts with ebony faces, high cheek bones, and long black hair, unable to contain their excitement over the adventure. The cavalrymen, in columns of four when the topography would permit, came next, McLaughlin's Co. I in front.[25]

Beyond Monclova the exact route is not certain, but to reach the Indian villages without detection the column travelled sixty-three miles from the Rio Grande, twenty-three more than the airline distance. The night was warm, the moon shone only dimly through a haze, and the dust stirred up by the rapid gait of the animals made it difficult for the sergeants to keep the column closed up. Lieutenant George A. Thurston's heavily loaded pack mules refused to travel at the pace set by the nervous and irritable commander, who was aware that his best chance of success depended upon a dawn attack. Some of the captains, realizing that the lagging pack train might well endanger their safety, shortly after midnight persuaded Carter to go forward and ask Mackenzie's permission to cut the packs loose from the mules. Upon hearing about the situation, Mackenzie exploded with a burst of profanity, but, convinced that the alternative was too risky, ordered a five-minute halt during which time the men were to fill their pockets with hard bread and cut the packs loose. Although there was no further trouble, the delay prevented a dawn attack. When daybreak came, the expedition was still not in sight of the Indian villages, and the rapid pace kept by the commander for mile after mile had begun to tell on both the men and their mounts.

Upon reaching the Rio San Rodrigo (Remolino River), shortly before the sun appeared over the horizon, Mackenzie ordered a halt for the men and animals to refresh themselves in the welcome waters of the little stream and in the cool breeze floating in from the Santa Rosa Mountains to the west, and to make ready for the charge upon the village. He had the men fill their pockets with cartridges rather than carry them in their saddlebags as a safety measure in case a dismounted trooper should be cut off from his horse. (Custer failed, unfortunately, to take such a precaution later at the Little Big Horn.) At six o'clock he cautiously led his men to the top of the slope, from which point could be seen to the west, strung out along the low, south bank of the San Rodrigo, the Indian huts and wickiups of the three villages, averaging fifty to sixty lodges, the largest that of the Kickapoos about a mile away and a quarter of a mile closer than that of the Lipan. The intervening slope between the blue-coated raiders and the Kickapoo village was covered with clumps of prickly pear, Spanish bayonet, and mesquite, but not enough so to interfere with the cavalry charge. As soon as the men could move into platoon position, Mackenzie ordered the fearless McLaughlin to lead the charge upon the Kickapoo village and to follow the fleeing Indians. The remainder of the cavalry was to charge by platoons, each delivering its volley and afterwards wheeling out of the way and returning to the rear to reload and charge again when its time came.

The cavalry charge hit the Kickapoo village as swiftly and as destructively as a tornado. The surprised Indians — the warriors had left the day before — scattered panic-stricken across irrigation ditches and fields of corn and pumpkins with McLaughlin's men in close pursuit. Taking cover in the ravines and ditches, the old men and women defended themselves with whatever weapons they could lay their hands upon. When the rear companies struck the village, Mackenzie ordered them to dismount and with torches to fire the reed and grass huts. The crackling flames, the sharp crack of rifles, the thud of horses' hooves, the yells of the cheering troopers, the hysterical screams of the Indian women and children as they sought to escape all mingled to create an indescribable horror. Within a few minutes the prosperous Kickapoo village was in shambles. Meanwhile, Lieutenant Carter with a detachment of Co. A rounded up sixty-five of the Indians' horses, some marked with the brands of Texas ranchers. The captured ponies were divided among the hired guides as a reward for gathering the information Mackenzie wanted.

The destruction was complete. The lodges of all three villages were burned, at least nineteen Indians by official count were killed, and forty women and children were captured. No doubt, many others must have fallen in hiding places or, wounded, managed to escape the count. In addition, Costilietos, a principal Lipan chief, was lariated by one of the Seminole scouts, but the Lipan and Mescalero bands escaped further loss by fleeing westward to the Santa Rosa Mountains while the troops were attacking the Kickapoo village.

Mackenzie's losses were negligible. Only one trooper, a private of Co. I, was killed; another private of the same company was wounded in the arm, and a trooper of Co. E received a slight facial wound. Even the horses, which normally suffered heavy casualties in a charge upon an enemy, fared well, only two having been killed and two having died of exhaustion.[26]

By 1:00 o'clock the troops, having watered their horses, treated the wounded, including Surgeon Donald Jackson's amputating the arm of one of the privates, and placed the prisoners on their ponies, began the long march for the Texas side of the Rio Grande. From the battle ground, the raiders followed the guides eastward along the San Rodrigo River through the village of Remolino, whose inhabitants showed their displeasure at the presence of the Yankee intruders but made no effort to interfere. Beyond Remolino, the route led north-northeast, a few miles west of the Mescalero Apache village of Zaragosa and somewhat west of the incoming route, to a crossing on the Rio Grande at the mouth of Sycamore Creek and fifteen miles below Del Rio.[27] There was good reason for returning by a more western route. The area along it was sparsely settled, whereas the region around Zaragosa and just east of the entrance route was well populated; no doubt the settlers had discovered the presence of the invaders and had given the alarm, and perhaps reinforced by Mexican soldiers, were waiting in ambush at some vantage point. Mackenzie well knew that the angry Indians and Mexicans could easily make an overpowering assault on the weary cavalrymen.

The column could no longer move rapidly. Although summer was officially more than a month away, the scorching heat, untempered by any breeze, was almost too much for both men and beasts already exhausted from a seemingly superhuman feat. Night brought little relief, for only the fear of ambush and the prodding of alert, veteran officers enabled the men to endure the agony of a second night (third for some) without sleep or rest, and even then many drowsed in their saddles or fell fast asleep at every momentary halt. Late in the night when the Indian prisoners, heavily guarded in the rear, began in their sleep to fall off their horses, they were lashed to their saddles. Several times Lieutenant Bullis' hardy Seminoles, stealthily hovering on the flanks and in the rear to guard against surprise, rode in to report that groups of the enemy were nearby. "It was a long, long night" of terror, Carter recalled many years later, but as the first grey of dawn appeared on the morning of the nineteenth, the blue-coated raiders, following a narrow trail that wound through patches of mesquite, reached the Rio Grande.

Nerve-racking time was required to reach the opposite bank. The troopers had to take the narrow, elongated ford in a single file, and it was with some difficulty that the prisoners and wounded were transported across. Once on the Texas side, Mackenzie bivouacked to rest the command. Shortly, dependable Quartermaster Lawton, as previously arranged, came in with a supply wagon loaded with rations and with forage for the animals. While breakfast was being prepared, the dehydrated men bathed in the cool water of the river.

The crossing had been none too soon. During the day a crowd of Mexicans and Indians gathered on the south side of the river, apparently intent upon attacking the Americans provided a favorable opportunity occurred. Mackenzie, however, did not permit them the opportunity. He made sure this time that his horses would not be stampeded, and hid his best sharpshooters in the dense chaparral to cover the ford, which lay in full view and in range of their powerful .50 caliber Spencer rifles. The river was too deep and too wide to be crossed elsewhere nearby. After selecting a campsite that could be easily defended and throwing out picket lines, Mackenzie allowed the men to get some badly needed sleep. Early the next morning, the command leisurely took up its march for Fort Clark, where it arrived about noon on May 21.[28]

The mission was a daring display of bravery and a remarkable feat of endurance. From the rendezvous at Captain Wilcox's camp on the Las Moras to the return crossing on the Rio Grande, the command, without sleep and with only hard bread for nourishment during the last twenty-seven hours, travelled more than 140 miles in thirty-eight hours and destroyed three Indian villages. For the men of Cos. A, B, E, and M, the scouts, the guides, and Mackenzie, the raid was even a greater ordeal. The men who had been camped on the Piedras Pintos had ridden 160 miles in forty-nine hours without removing the saddles from their horses. There is no hint in the record of how long or how far the guides had ridden before the departure. In his official report Mackenzie commended all his officers and men, calling especial attention to Captain McLaughlin, who with Mackenzie had led the charge on the Kickapoo village; to Lieutenant C. L. Hudson of Co. I, who had displayed unusual bravery to the point of recklessness; to Second Lieutenant Bullis, who with his Seminoles had protected the flanks and rear of the column on the return march; to Lieutenant L. O. Parker, his adjutant; to Surgeon Jackson; and to Captain Mauck, who had left his sick bed to participate in the raid and had narrowly escaped death at the hands of a Lipan warrior.[29] The citations for "unusual bravery" may seem, however, somewhat out of order inasmuch as the only defenders were the women and a few old men.

As soon as a special courier brought word on May 20 that the expedition was back in Texas, Major J. K. Mizner, commanding at Fort Clark in Mackenzie's absence, telegraphed a brief preliminary report to departmental headquarters.[30] Two days later, General Sheridan at Chicago transmitted the information to Secretary of War Belknap with a hearty endorsement of Mackenzie's action and an anxious admonition that "it is more than probably that Mackenzie crossed into Mexico and had his fight on that side of the Rio Grande. We must back him." On May 28 Sheridan wired Belknap a confirmation that the engagement had taken place on Mexican soil, and defended Mackenzie with the argument that "there cannot be any valid boundary when we pursue Indians who murder our people and carry away our property." He also sent a strong defense of Mackenzie's action to Sherman. Although more cautious and restrained in his praise, Sherman indicated that unless the Mexicans formally complained, there was no need of further inquiry into the violation of Mexican sovereignty, and five weeks after the raid Belknap informed Mackenzie that he had been commended by the War Department for his action.[31]

When the press revealed that Mackenzie's raid had been in Mexico, most observers reacted favorably. A Washington correspondent reported that the news had created a great sensation in the city, and that Mackenzie "will be famous hereafter as a bold and fearless general, for the hearts of the people are turned towards him." [32] Most Texans were decidedly pleased. The state legislature on June 2 in a joint resolution officially extended "the grateful thanks of the people of our State . . . to General McKenzie [sic] and the officers and troops under his command, for their prompt action and gallant conduct in inflicting well merited punishment upon these scourges of our frontier." [33] Not all comments, however, were favorable. Some persons charged the national government with trying to precipitate a rupture with Mexico.[34] To the contrary, the administration had no desire for a war; nevertheless, Sheridan, convinced that the only way to stop the marauders was to destroy their villages near the border, assured Mackenzie in June that under similar circumstances he could again strike across the border.[35]

Mackenzie, without any attempt to evade full responsibility, defended his action. He assured the Mexican officials that he was friendly and wished to cooperate in every way to insure tranquility and order along the border. Peace, not war, he insisted, had been the objective of his invasion. Mackenzie also explained that there were precedents for crossing the Rio Grande: in 1869 three companies of Mexican militia, commanded by Colonel Ildofonse Fuentes and Captain Antonio Guerra, had attacked a Lipan camp in Texas near the mouth of the Pecos and carried several prisoners back to Mexico, and in 1872 Mexican troops had used Eagle Pass as a base for driving rebels from Piedras Negras. Since these violations of American territory had been settled quietly between the two governments, Mackenzie felt that his case should be granted similar treatment.[36]

The raid aroused excitement and resentment among Mexican citizens along the border. Even before Mackenzie had recrossed the Rio Grande, the inhabitants of Piedras Negras, having been summoned by drums and informed that "six hundred gringos" were south of the border, dispatched couriers to the nearby villages and to Saltillo for aid in resisting the intruders. Fortunately, United States Consul William Schuchardt at Piedras Negras persuaded the crowd to disperse by explaining that the only purpose of the United States Army on Mexican soil was to punish the Indian bands that had been depredating in Texas, and that Mexican citizens would not be harmed.[37] The large number of Mexicans and Indians who gathered near the ford shortly after Mackenzie had crossed it provoked nothing more harmful than some insulting remarks and a few ineffectual shots. For several days there were wild rumors and exaggerated reports of imminent retaliatory raids, but within a few weeks comparative calm had settled over the apprehensive Mexican communities.

The Mexican government, however, did not wish to make the affair an international issue. Ignacio Mariscal, Mexican Minister to Washington, in June expressed the belief that the incident could be settled amicably. Finally, on January 14, 1874, eight months after the raid, he sent a note to Secretary of State Fish. No similar offense against the United States by Mexican troops had been or would be authorized, the note stated, and Mexico had cooperated in efforts to solve the border problem, including the attempt to remove the Kickapoos. Although his government had postponed action on the violation of its nationality until the excitement was over, because of possible internal repercussions it could not allow American troops to trespass on its territory. The United States, however, could rely upon its support in joint measures against the offenders.[38] With this mild protest, Mexico dropped the matter.

During the interval between the raid and Mariscal's note, depredations along the border were almost nil. To the Indians, complacently accustomed to the protection of the boundary, Mackenzie's surprise attack had been a rude shock. Some of the escapees planned to commit reprisals; some, fearing another American attack, divided into small bands and scattered to the mountains in the interior of Coahuila and Chihuahua; others, mostly Potawatomies and Kickapoos, felt that they should return to the United States.

On May 18, 1873, the very day on which Mackenzie with the backing of the War Department destroyed the villages of the depredating Indians, agents of the United States Bureau of Indian Affairs were in Saltillo to seek the cooperation of Governor Victoriano Cepeda of Coahuila in settling the border problem peacefully. Henry M. Atkinson and Thomas G. Williams, who had been appointed in March to make a new effort to effect the removal of the Kickapoos, left Washington early in April and after a few days' layover in San Antonio proceeded to Monterrey, where they met Mexican Commissioner Antonio Madero. After a hospitable reception at Saltillo by Governor Cepeda, his personal deputy Alfredo Montero and the two commissioners journeyed north to begin negotiations.[39]

Upon reaching Santa Rosa, where they first learned of the raid, the American commissioners sent their congratulations to Mackenzie and expressed the belief that his success would aid them in their mission. This optimistic note inspired Mackenzie to inform General Augur that the commissioners would succeed if given adequate military support; if the Mexican officials or citizens of Santa Rosa arrested or interfered with them, he wanted permission to go to their rescue with his entire regiment and a volunteer force of Texans. Impressed with Colonel Montero's apparently earnest desire to cooperate, Mackenzie promised the commissioners that he would not hit the Indian villages again until their undertaking was completed.[40]

The Indians whose villages Mackenzie had destroyed were still in hiding, but the assurances of Montero and the free food provided by Atkinson and Williams enticed the frightened, hungry Kickapoos to meet with the commissioners. At the first session of the council on June 1 at Santa Rosa, the Kickapoos, as a prerequisite for negotiation, demanded the return of their wives and children who had been imprisoned at San Antonio. Atkinson, entirely agreeable, persuaded the Indians to send one of their chiefs with him and Montero to plead with Augur for their release.

At San Antonio, Atkinson met with a stern refusal. Mackenzie and Sheridan strenuously objected, Sheridan declaring that compliance would only lead to other demands and that "The detention of the women and children . . . would do more to bring the tribe back [to the United States] than half a dozen commissioners." [41] The War Department supported its officers. Atkinson thereupon carried his case to the Commissioner of Indian Affairs, but President Grant upheld the military.[42] A few days later, to get them removed farther from the border and to a post with better facilities, Sheridan had the prisoners (all but Costilietos, who had escaped) transferred by train to Fort Gibson, Indian Territory.[43]

Although he had failed in his efforts to get the prisoners released, Atkinson refused to abandon his mission. Remembering the concern of the tribesmen over their captive women and children, he became convinced that Mackenzie and Sheridan were right: that the detention of the prisoners would bring the tribe to terms. He decided to make it clear that the prisoners would be restored to their families, but that the reunion would not take place until after the tribe had removed to a reservation in the United States. As a further inducement, Atkinson distributed eight thousand dollars worth of goods when he reached Santa Rosa, promised more should they agree to move, and made substantial cash payments to a number of influential men in return for their support.[44]

On July 11 a group of Kickapoos and their Potawatomi confederates informed the commissioners that they were prepared to accept the offer. The first contingent of 317, about one-half of the Mexican Kickapoos and Potawatomies, escorted by Commissioners Atkinson and Williams, left Santa Rosa on August 28 for their new home in the United States. Crossing the Rio Grande west of the mouth of the Pecos River and travelling west of the settlements in Texas, they arrived safely at Fort Sill on December 20, 1873. Atkinson returned to Mexico to continue negotiations, but he was able to persuade only 115 to join their kinsmen in the United States.[45]

The continued activity of Mackenzie no doubt significantly influenced the Indians to accept the commissioners' terms. For ten days after returning from the raid, Mackenzie had three companies of troops patrolling the north bank of the Rio Grande, and in June he deployed his cavalrymen to strategic points to thwart any attempt at reprisal and to prevent further depredations. Two companies were stationed about fifty miles below Eagle Pass, two on Piedras Pintos Creek, one at San Felipe, two thirty-five miles east of Fort Duncan, and four were kept at Fort Clark. Lieutenant Bullis and his Seminole scouts remained constantly in the field, camping first at San Pedro Springs and later on Elm Creek near Fort Clark.[46]

But Mackenzie was not content with mere defensive measures. By special messenger he urged Governor Cepeda of Coahuila to cooperate in a joint military assault upon the main Kickapoo village in Nacimiento Canyon, but Sheridan disapproved of the venture, commenting that "Mackenzie has done very well," but that he should leave diplomatic maneuvering to others.[47]

Determined to put an end to the border problem with or without Mexican cooperation, Mackenzie on several occasions sent troops south of the border. A detachment of forty cavalrymen under Lieutenant Thurston on June 22 discovered a herd of stolen Texas cattle on the south bank of the Rio Grande about forty-five miles below Fort Duncan. Thurston reported that the rustlers returned the herd without his having to cross the river, but the press accounts claimed that the troops crossed the river, captured the thieves, and returned with the herd.[48] During the same month Mackenzie twice sent his scouts to search for the camps of the Lipans and Mescaleros, and advised Augur that their villages should be attacked as soon as the commissioners were out of danger. Since Mexico was inclined to overlook Mackenzie's raid and to cooperate with the commissioners, Sheridan and Sherman early in July ordered Mackenzie not to send any more spies or troops across the river.[49]

The 4th Cavalry continued to scout the Upper Border Region for nearly a year without again violating Mexican territory. Mackenzie, suffering from an attack of rheumatism, in August took an extended leave and did not return until February, 1874.[50] Five months later the impetuous commander led about one hundred troopers across the river eighty-five miles above Fort Duncan while pursuing a number of rustlers driving a herd of stolen cattle. He followed the trail to within twenty-five miles of Zaragosa, where he gave up the chase upon discovering that the thieves were Mexicans rather than Indians.[51] This was the last border scout until the resurgence of the depredators a few years later; within another month Mackenzie and the 4th Cavalry were transferred to the northwestern frontier of Texas to participate in the final settlement of the Indian problem in that area. Although he had not entirely eliminated the depredations, he had succeeded in bringing temporary peace and order, for during the next two years the reports consistently verified that "affairs were quiet" in the Upper Rio Grande Border Region.

FOOTNOTES — CHAPTER VI

[1] Report of the United States Commission to Texas, June 30, 1873, "Depredations on the Frontiers of Texas," 43 Cong., 1 Sess., *House Exec. Doc.* 257 (Washington, 1874), 13.

[2] *Ninth Annual Census of the United States* (Washington, 1872), I, 64; III, 250-262.

[3] Deposition of Joseph A. Durand, U.S. Comm., "Depredations on the Frontiers of Texas," 17, as cited; "Great Indian Raid near Fort McKavett in 1866," *Frontier Times*, IV (June, 1927), 41-43; A. M. Gibson, *The Kickapoos, Lords of the Middle Border* (Norman, 1963), 213. Gibson gives an excellent account of the Mexican Kickapoos.

[4] *Reports of the Committee of Investigation Sent in 1873 by the Mexican Government to the Frontier of Texas* (trans. from official edition; New York, 1875), 412-421 (hereafter cited as Mex. Comm., *Reports on the Frontiers of Texas*, 1873.

[5] Gibson, *The Kickapoos*, 198-201.

[6] William C. Pool, "The Battle of Dove Creek," *The Southwestern Historical Quarterly*, LIII (April, 1950), 367-385; Mex. Comm., *Reports on the Frontiers of Texas*, 1873, 412.

[7] William Schuchardt, United States Consul, Piedras Negras, to Asst. Sec. of State, July 15 and December 26, 1872, Consular Despatches, Piedras Negras, I, State Department Records, National Archives (microfilm copy in The Southwest Collection, Texas Technological College, Lubbock); for an excellent treatment of Mackenzie's 1873 raid, see Adrian N. Anderson, "Colonel Ranald S. Mackenzie on the Texas Frontier, 1873-1874" (M. A. thesis, Texas Technological College, Lubbock, 1963), 25-61 (hereafter cited as Anderson, "Mackenzie on the Texas Frontier").

[8] Gibson, *The Kickapoos*, 219; Committee on Foreign Affairs, "Report on the Relations of the United States with Mexico," April 25, 1878, 45 Cong., 2 Sess., *House Report* 701 (Washington, 1878), xiii.

[9] Hamilton Fish to Thomas M. Nelson, United States Minister to Mexico, December 12, 1870, in *House Report* 701, App. B, 198-199, as cited; Sebastián Lerdo de Tejada, Mexican Minister of Foreign Affairs, to Nelson, April 20, 1871, in *ibid.*, 200-201, 202; Fish to Nelson, June 26, 1871, in *ibid.*, 204; Ignacio Mariscal, Mexican Department of Foreign Affairs, to Nelson, April 23, 1872, in *ibid.*, 211.

[10] Charles Delano, Secretary of the Interior, to Fish, August 1, 1871, in *ibid.*, 205.

[11] Mariscal to Fish, January 14, 1874, Diplomatic Notes, Mexico City, XXIII, U.S. State Department Records, National Archives (microfilm copy in The Southwest Collection, Texas Technological College, Lubbock).

[12] Schuchardt to Asst. Sec. of State, May 6, 1871, in *House Report* 701, App. B, 205-206, as cited; John D. Miles to Enoch Hoag, Superintendent, Lawrence, Kansas, July 13, 1871, in Commissioner of Indian Affairs, annual

report, November 15, 1871, 42 Cong., 2 Sess., *House Exec. Doc.* I, pt. V (Washington, 1871), pp. 608–612.
   [13] U.S. Comm., "Depredations on the Frontiers of Texas," 3, 15–27, as cited; Gibson, *The Kickapoos*, 224.
   [14] Mex. Comm., *Reports on the Frontiers of Texas, 1873*, 379, 382–383, 414. Some of the Kickapoos were peaceful agriculturalists, but not those near Remolino and Nacimiento.
   [15] *Galveston Daily News*, December 15, 1872.
   [16] *Ibid.*, January 14 and 25, 1873.
   [17] Sherman to Augur, February 5, 1873, quoted in Carter, *On the Border*, 419; *New York Herald*, April 11, 1873, quoted in the *Galveston Daily News*, April 18, 1873.
   [18] "Post Medical Reports, Fort Concho, December 1867–June 1889," Vols. 401-3-4-7, pp. 89–97, AGO, RG 94 (hereafter cited as "Medical History of Fort Concho"); "Medical History of Fort Richardson," Vol. 238, p. 5, as cited; Carter, *On the Border*, 394–421.
   [19] *Galveston Daily News*, April 4 and 8, 1873; Carter, *On the Border*, 421–424.
   [20] *Ibid.*, 425, 428; Mackenzie to departmental headquarters, May 23, 1873, 2193 AGO 1873, RG 94. This is Mackenzie's report of his raid across the border.
   [21] Carter, *On the Border*, 424–428; Mariscal to Fish, January 14, 1874, as cited; Schuchardt to Asst. Sec. of State, March 29 and May 8, 1873, Consular Despatches, Piedras Negras, II, as cited; U.S. Comm., "Depredations on the Frontiers of Texas," 27, as cited; Gibson, *The Kickapoos*, 240; Mackenzie to departmental headquarters, May 23, 1873, as cited. The Indian Seminoles returned to the United States in the late 1850's but the Muscogees remained in Mexico. When the Kickapoos arrived in Mexico in 1865, they were allowed to settle in the Nacimiento region abandoned by the Seminoles, one village being only five miles from the Muscogees. In 1871 a group of Muscogees were prevailed upon to enlist as scouts in the United States Army and were headquartered at Fort Clark. Edward S. Wallace, "The Mackenzie Raid," *The Westerner's New York Posse Brand Book*, IV (1958), 75.
   [22] Mackenzie to departmental headquarters, May 23, 1873, as cited; "Tabular Statement of Expeditions," September 30, 1873, 5228 AGO 1873, RG 94; Carter, *On the Border*, 428–429, 465.
   [23] Apparently the eighteen Seminoles from Fort Clark, the sixteen Seminoles from Fort Duncan, Bullis, Cox, McLain, and Van comprised the twenty-four scouts and fourteen citizens.
   [24] Mackenzie to departmental headquarters, May 23, 1873, as cited; "Post Medical Reports, Fort Duncan———, 1849–October 1883," Vols. 86–87, 316, AGO, RG 94 (hereafter cited as "Medical History of Fort Duncan"); Carter, *On the Border*, 429, 432, 466.
   [25] Shafter, Fort Duncan, to Mackenzie, May 26, 1873, 2353 AGO 1873, RG 94; Mackenzie to Schuchardt, May 28, 1873, 2353 AGO 1873, RG 94; Carter, *On the Border*, 431, 437.
   [26] Mackenzie to departmental headquarters, May 23, 1873, as cited; Carter, *On the Border*, 434–447; "Tabular Statement of Expeditions," September 30, 1873, as cited; Schuchardt to Asst. Sec. of State, June 3, 1873, Consular Despatches, Piedras Negras, II as cited; Wallace, "The Mackenzie Raid," *The*

Westerners New York Posse Brand Book, 73 ff., Mex. Comm., *Reports on the Frontiers of Texas, 1873*, 425; Mariscal to Fish, January 14, 1874, as cited.

[27] Mackenzie to departmental headquarters, May 23, 1873, as cited; Carter, *On the Border*, 446-467; Carter, *The Old Sergeant's Story*, 73.

[28] Carter, *On the Border*, 455-457, 466-467, 460.

[29] *Ibid.*, 465-467; Mackenzie to departmental headquarters, May 23, 1873, as cited. Other than Mackenzie, the only officer to receive official recognition was Lieutenant Bullis, who on February 27, 1890, was brevetted captain for his bravery in the engagement. Heitman, *Historical Register*, I, 261. Lieutenant Hudson, who had distinguished himself on many occasions, was killed in an accidental shooting at Fork Clark a few months later. *Galveston Daily News*, January 4, 1874.

[30] Major J. K. Mizner to departmental headquarters, May 20, 1873, 2112 AGO 1873, RG 94.

[31] Sheridan to Belknap, May 22 and 28, 1873, 2006 AGO 1873 and 2092 AGO 1873, RG 94; endorsement of Sheridan to Sherman, June 4, 1873, on Mackenzie to departmental headquarters, May 23, 1873, as cited; endorsement on *ibid.* of Sherman to Belknap, June 13, 1873, and Belknap to Secretary of the Interior, June 24, 1873.

[32] *Galveston Daily News*, May 30, 1873.

[33] James P. Newcomb, Department of State, Austin, to Augur, June 2, 1873, 2366 AGO 1873, RG 94.

[34] *New York Times*, June 10, 1873; *Galveston Daily News*, May 23, May 30, August 6, August 30, and September 3, 1873.

[35] Fish to Nelson, January 16, 1873, *Foreign Relations of the United States, 1873*, I, pt. I (Washington, 1873), 643; Mackenzie to departmental headquarters, June 12, 1873, 2604 AGO 1873, RG 94.

[36] Mackenzie to Schuchardt, May 28, 1873, as cited; Schuchardt to Asst. Sec. of State, June 3, 1873, as cited; Augur to Sheridan, September 28, 1872, as cited; Francisco Palacio, Mexican Minister to the United States, to Fish, March 27 and April 22, 1872, Diplomatic Notes, Mexico City, XXIII.

[37] Schuchardt to Mackenzie, May 19, 1873, 2193 AGO 1873, RG 94; Schuchardt to Asst. Sec. of State, June 3, 1873, as cited.

[38] *Galveston Daily News*, June 3, 1873; *New York Times*, June 2, 1873; Mariscal to Fish, January 14, 1874, as cited.

[39] Henry M. Atkinson and Thomas G. Williams to Commissioner of Indian Affairs Edward P. Smith, October 8, 1873, in Commissioner of Indian Affairs, "Report," November 1, 1873, 43 Cong., 1 Sess., *House Exec. Doc.* I, pt. V (Washington, 1873), pp. 537-539; Mariscal to Fish, March 21 and June 12, 1873, Diplomatic Notes, Mexico City, XXIII; Gibson, *The Kickapoos*, 245; *Galveston Daily News*, May 4, 1873.

[40] Williams to Mackenzie, May 28, 1873, 2532 AGO 1873, RG 94; Mackenzie to departmental headquarters, June 6, 1873, 2332 AGO 1873, RG 94; Mackenzie to departmental headquarters, June 12, 1873, as cited.

[41] Atkinson to Commissioner of Indian Affairs, June 1, 1873. and July 9, 1874, as cited in Gibson, *The Kickapoos*, 246-247; Mackenzie to departmental headquarters, May 23, 1873, as cited; Sheridan to Sherman, June 10, 1873, 2320 AGO 1873, RG 94.

[42] Atkinson and Williams to Smith, June 14, 1873, 2473 AGO 1873, RG

94; Smith to Delano, June 16, 1873, in *ibid.*; Delano to Belknap, June 17, 1873, in *ibid.*; Belknap to Delano, June 23, 1873, in *ibid.*

[43] *Galveston Daily News*, June 29 and July 1, 1873.

[44] Atkinson to Commissioner of Indian Affairs, July 9, 1874, as cited in Gibson, *The Kickapoos*, 250.

[45] Atkinson to Augur, July 12 and 25, 1873, 2942 AGO 1873 and 3157 AGO 1873, RG 94; *Galveston Daily News*, September 5, 1873; Gibson, *The Kickapoos*, 252, 262–266.

[46] Mackenzie to departmental headquarters, June 12, 1873, as cited; "Medical History of Fort Duncan," 320–321, as cited.

[47] Mackenzie to departmental headquarters and endorsement of Sheridan to Sherman, June 6, 1873, as cited.

[48] "Tabular Statement of Expeditions," June, 1873, as cited; *San Antonio Express*, July 4, 1873; *Galveston Daily News*, July 6, 1873.

[49] Endorsements of Sheridan and Sherman on Mackenzie to departmental headquarters, June 28, 1873, 2374 AGO 1873, RG 94.

[50] Mackenzie to departmental headquarters, September 12, 1873, 3810 DT 1873 (filed with 3877 ACP 1873), AGO, RG 94; "Mackenzie's Record of Service," 1149 ACP 1884, AGO, RG 94.

[51] Schuchardt to John W. Foster, United States Minister to Mexico, August 5, 1874, Consular Despatches, Piedras Negras, II.

CHAPTER VII

The Renewal of the Comanche-Kiowa War

AFTER MACKENZIE'S VICTORY on the North Fork of the Red River the Texas border for several months enjoyed unprecedented quiet. The hostile Comanches camped during the winter of 1872–73 near the Fort Sill agency on Cache Creek, the Kwahadis south of the agency in the area of present Lawton, and the friendlier Comanches, under Chiefs Horseback, Howea, and Cheevers, north of the post near Chandler Creek. The Kiowas were divided into two groups: Kicking Bird, with about a dozen chiefs who recognized his leadership, was encamped on Two Hatchet Creek, two miles south of Fort Cobb; Lone Wolf, at the head of the hostile Kiowas, was camped north of Mount Scott.[1]

The Indians well knew that only by remaining at peace could they hope for the restoration of their people. In January, 1873, Agent Tatum wrote his superintendent that "The Indians manifest a more docile and better disposition than they have ever done before, and give strong assurance of friendship."[2] Superintendent Hoag was impressed with their attitude, and sent word in March that both the prisoners taken by Mackenzie and the two Kiowa chiefs would be released in June if the Indians remained peaceful. Realizing that his position would be untenable if Satanta and Big Tree were released, because of his request that the army punish the marauding Indians, Agent Tatum immediately submitted his resignation. His successor, J. M. Haworth, who arrived at the agency on April 1, 1873, thought the Indians so docile that he removed the military guard from about the agency buildings and replaced it with Indian police.

The Indian Bureau soon ordered the release of the prisoners and their transferal from Concho to Fort Sill. Captain Robert McClermont, commanding the escort detachment of the 11th Infantry, had a hazardous task; the Texas frontiersmen along his route had suffered a great deal at the hands of the Comanches and were anxious for revenge. Learning that angry citizens planned to take charge of the prisoners at Jacksboro, he drove into town and pretended to be waiting for the train to catch up until it had skirted the village and was safely on its way. Two squaws who escaped along the route reached the reservation a few days behind the train, not much the worse for wear despite subsisting on whatever they could find.[3] When McClermont arrived at Fort Sill on June 10 and amid great rejoicing released his charges, many of the leading braves promised henceforth to remain at peace.[4] But despite their promises, within a short time a few Comanche warriors began to make destructive raids along the Texas frontier. Agent Haworth, nevertheless, remained quite optimistic because several of the responsible chiefs worked for peace.

The renewal of Comanche raids was inspired to some extent, at least, by the Kiowas, who were becoming increasingly restless over the delay, caused by reluctant Texas officials, in releasing their chiefs Satanta and Big Tree. Lieutenant Colonel John W. Davidson, 10th Cavalry, who assumed command of Fort Sill in the spring of 1873, after a scout of the country in late August reported that "Evidence was found to spare that the Indians are constantly marauding upon the borders of Texas, that the Reservation is a 'City of Refuge' for them, that it is almost impossible for our troops to catch an enemy with the eye of a hawk and the stealth of a wolf, who knows every foot of the country, and that an effective method of stopping this state of affairs, while the government feeds and clothes the reservation Indians, is to dismount them and make them account for themselves daily." [5]

Governor Davis of Texas, pressured by public opinion for the release of the prisoners, was determined to exact a high price in return. Leaving Huntsville on August 19, 1873, in custody of Lieutenant Hoffman, the two chiefs on September 4 were lodged in the Fort Sill guardhouse. On October 6 Governor Davis, Commissioner of Indian Affairs Edward P. Smith, and Superintendent Hoag met at Fort Sill to decide their fate. Davis at first proposed that "all of the horse [mounted] Indians bordering on Texas be gathered into reservations, their arms and horses taken from them, and supplies be issued to them for not longer than one day at a time," but finally demanded that the Kiowas return Satanta and Big Tree, or chiefs of equal rank, whenever it should appear that their people had been raiding in Texas; and that the agent would make roll calls at such short intervals that it would be impossible for the warriors to go as far away as Texas without detection. Davis also demanded that the Comanches, who had permitted some of their young men to raid in Texas after their kinsmen had been restored to them, surrender five of the guilty leaders as a guarantee against further hostilities. These and several other proposals being mutually acceptable to the Indian Bureau officials and the Indians present, Davis on October 8 paroled the Kiowa chiefs and Smith ordered the Comanches to deliver within one month the five guilty war leaders.

A troop of cavalry was detailed to assist the Comanches in finding the culprits, but after scouring a wide sector of the wild Comanche country the troopers returned to Fort Sill. Washington thereupon instructed Agent Haworth to withhold not only the annuity goods but, at the end of ten days, the daily rations also unless five warriors had been given up, and to turn the tribe over to the military if it did not comply. This order placed the friendly Indians in a precarious predicament, as Comanche Chief Cheevers said: "I have tried very hard to do right, have done everything I can to get my people to do as Washington asked us to, and only a few have done wrong and they are now far out on the plains; we can't catch them, let us try as hard as we may, if the soldiers should kill them, we would not cry or care, but Washington must be crazy to want to kill all the Comanches because a few have done wrong." [6]

The frightened Comanches, with the exception of a few like Horseback, who told Haworth he was too old and sick to run or fight, promptly moved a safe distance away from the reservation. When the Quakers intervened, the Federal government revoked the order on condition that the Comanches would bring in the stolen stock. This retreat from a firm position, construed as a sign of fear or weakness, encouraged the Comanches again to take the warpath, and soon several raiding parties defiantly set out to plunder the frontier settlements of Texas and northern Mexico.

One party of twenty-one Comanches and nine Kiowas included Tau-ankia and Guitan, Lone Wolf's favorite son and his nephew. Leaving their spare animals at Kickapoo Springs on the West Fork of the Nueces, the raiders crossed the Rio Grande, killing, capturing prisoners, and taking horses. As they retreated northward on December 6, they killed two Americans, but two Mexican prisoners escaped and alerted Lieutenant Charles L. Hudson, who was scouting in the vicinity with forty-one men of the 4th Cavalry. The next day Hudson found the Indian ponies near Kickapoo Springs. Taking them in charge, he planned to wait in ambush but, learning of the raiders' movements, surprised them with 150 captured horses and mules. After about ten minutes' hot fire the Indians broke and ran, leaving nine of their comrades dead on the field and losing eighty-one of their animals. Hudson had one trooper slightly wounded. [7] On the way to the agency, the

Indians suffered another loss of eleven warriors and sixty-five horses at the hands of Lieutenant Colonel George P. Buell near Double Mountain.[8]

When on January 13, 1874, news of the disaster reached the Kiowa camps, the whole tribe wailed dolefully. Among the Indians killed by Hudson's troops were Lone Wolf's son and his nephew. Lone Wolf cut off his hair, killed his horses, burned his wagon, lodges, and buffalo robes, and vowed to get revenge.[9] Although he did not know it for some time, the slayer of his son, Lieutenant Hudson, was also dead, accidentally shot in his quarters at Fort Clark by his roommate, who had just finished cleaning a gun.[10]

In addition to the desire for revenge, several other reasons led the Indians to go to war again in the spring of 1874. Social prestige among the Plains Indians rested on individual exploits in warfare, and a number of the younger warriors, now convinced that the United States did not intend to fight them, were anxious to attain recognition. On January 28 a small detachment of troops were fired upon near the agency, presumably by Comanches, and on March 27 Indians fired into a company of soldiers near Fort Sill. A majority of the Indians resented being confined to a reservation, and the slaughter of the buffalo, which was just getting underway on the Southern Plains, they could not tolerate. Indian trails were seen near the settlements, and the Texans began losing stock.

When on March 28 it was learned that Lone Wolf was organizing a party to recover the bodies of his son and nephew, cavalry detachments were sent out to intercept him. Captain Beaumont with seventy men of his Co. A went south and west from Fort McKavett; a detachment of the 4th Cavalry from Fort Clark went to the burial site, but arrived too late, for the bodies had already been removed. Upon discovering that they were about to be overtaken by the troopers, the Indians left the two bodies buried on a mountainside. The cavalrymen followed Lone Wolf's trail for 240 miles, finding water only twice, to

Johnston's Station, twenty-eight miles above Fort Concho, where the fleeing party of Indians had killed a trooper and captured twenty-two horses. The commanding officer, fully aware that he could not overtake the Indians who had fresh mounts, gave up the chase.[11]

The situation at the agency in the spring of 1874 was unusually bad. Heavy rains interfered with freight service, and at a critical time the agent was forced to issue half rations. As a result, the Indians had to kill their horses and mules for food, and some resorted to killing beeves belonging to whites. Furthermore, the Cheyennes, who were committing depredations in Kansas, endeavored to incite the Comanches.[12] The Indians suddenly became aware that their old way of life was slipping away from them; they were ripe for a movement of nativistic revivalism.

As so often happens in the history of oppressed peoples, a messiah came forth. A young and as yet untried Kwahadi warrior-medicine man, Ishatai (Coyote Droppings), who had been brooding over the future, told his people that the tribes who had adopted the white man's road were rapidly going down hill, and asserted that the Comanches could remain strong only if they killed all the whites. He had received the power to lead them to victory, he claimed; he was immune from bullets, and had brought back the dead from the After World. But real prestige came with his accurate prediction that a comet attracting much attention early in 1873 would disappear in five days and be followed by a summer-long drought. In their despair the Comanches were willing to turn to him for the kind of leadership their established chiefs could not give. When he belched forth a "wagonload" of cartridges and swallowed them again in the presence of several Comanches, it was soon common talk that Ishatai had such powers as no other Comanche had ever possessed.[13]

Ishatai, having stirred up the Comanches with his inflammatory talk, called for a sun dance to make strong medicine. Every band was represented when in May the ceremony began on the North Fork of the Red River not far from the reservation. Although a few of the Comanches refused to accept the Prophet and left the dance before it was over, large numbers of Kiowas, Arapahoes, and Cheyennes were won over.

In planning their all-out war, some of the warriors wanted first to annihilate the Tonkawas, but that proposal was rejected for fear of encountering troops in Texas. Young Quanah Parker then suggested that they first clean out a party of white buffalo hunters encamped at Adobe Walls on the Canadian River in the Texas Panhandle. The suggestion met with enthusiasm, and as Para-o-coom, the principal Kwahadi war chief, lay dying at the time, Quanah and Ishatai took command of the war party.

The warriors, 200 to 250 Comanches and Cheyennes, set out on the second day following the close of the sun dance for Adobe Walls. At daybreak on the morning of June 27, "the noise of the horses' hoofs was like thunder" as the Indians attacked. Fortunately, some of the men (twenty-eight men and one woman were at the post) were up and dressed at the time, and the hunters were armed with new large-bore, long-range buffalo rifles. When the battle ceased that afternoon, the raiders had killed only three whites, but in turn had nine dead, whom the whites could count, possibly more, and a number wounded — a crushing spiritual defeat for the Comanches, whose hopes had been so falsely raised by Ishatai.[14] The warriors lingered around the post for several days, but did not dare attack it again, and in time Lieutenant Frank D. Baldwin came south from Kansas with a detachment of troops and rescued the buffalo hunters. But the fighting on the Southern Plains was far from over. Adobe Walls was the opening of the Great Red River War of 1874–1875.

Although their initial attack on the whites had failed, the Comanches, Kiowas, and Cheyennes were not dismayed; they plundered and killed over a wide area from Texas to Colorado.

A party of Cheyennes and Comanches burned a wagon train loaded with supplies and killed the four teamsters about fifty miles north of the Cheyenne agency at Darlington, and then raided through the ranch country of southern Colorado, killing an estimated thirty to sixty persons.[15] The frontier settlers in Kansas, after suffering a number of deaths, resorted to "forting up" for safety, and Cheyenne agent John D. Miles in alarm sent for troops.

The Texas frontier did not escape the wrath of the hostile Indians. When the Kiowas had finished their sun dance on July 7, Kicking Bird with about three-fourths of the tribe left immediately for Fort Sill to stay clear of the coming war. Lone Wolf, still anxious to revenge the death of his son, was finally able to get Mamanti to lead a war party into Texas. In high spirits the party started on the night of July 10. Crossing the Red River near the present town of Quanah, it passed near present Seymour and proceeded to Cox Mountain, on the wagon road between Jacksboro and Griffin, the place where the teamsters had been massacred in 1871. Here, the Kiowas, while chasing four cowboys who escaped in Lost Valley, discovered that they were being trailed by another party of white men. The latter were Texas Rangers led by Major John B. Jones, commander of the Texas Frontier Battalion, who was looking for a Comanche raiding party. Jones had picked up the trail of the Kiowas on Salt Creek. Mamanti, realizing that the Rangers had not seen him, quickly prepared an ambush, killed two of the Rangers, and, having fulfilled the obligations of a revenge war party, made good his escape to the reservation.[16]

After the Lost Valley raid, Lone Wolf, afraid of being punished, camped several miles east of Fort Sill. The reservation Indians now became increasingly hostile. On July 13 Indians attacked J. S. Evans' wood camp, eleven miles from the post, and one of the cattle herders near the agency was scalped and filled with arrows.[17] The situation became so serious that the military called for an end to the Quaker Peace Policy. Sherman

on July 15 asked Sheridan, "Don't you think it would be well
. . . to converge on Fort Sill and settle this matter at once." [18]
Sheridan was ready. On the next day, Sherman asked the sec-
retaries of War and Interior for permission for troops to follow the raiding parties onto the reservations.[19] Four days later,
he advised Sheridan that Secretary of War Belknap had ordered the punishment of guilty Indians "wherever found . . .
the Reservation lines should be no barrier." Immediately,
Sheridan directed General John Pope, commander of the Department of the Missouri, to have the 6th Cavalry operate
southward from Kansas into Indian Territory and Texas and
requested General Augur to have Mackenzie move with his
4th Cavalry from Fort Clark into northwestern Texas.[20] With
this command, the Quaker Peace Policy, which for more than
five years had protected the guilty as well as the innocent, was
dead.

To assure the protection of those Indians who were peaceful, Colonel Davidson, acting on instructions from the Commissioner of Indian Affairs, on July 26 directed all friendly
Indians to enroll at their agencies by August 3 and thereafter
to answer daily roll call. The Indians, traditionally opposed to
being enrolled, were hesitant to comply. On July 30 Davidson
with a detachment of cavalry enrolled at their camps without
difficulty the Comanche bands of Horseback, Cheevers, and
Quirts-Quip. On August 3 some Kiowas came in, but were in
an ugly mood. Although the registration period was extended
until August 8, only 173 Kiowas, 108 Apaches, and 83 Comanches had been enrolled by that date. All the enrolled Kiowas, except Kicking Bird's band, after committing some murders went north to the Wichita agency at the site of Anadarko.

On August 21 Davidson received an urgent message from
the Wichita agency that a band of sixty lodges of Nocona
Comanches, in addition to the Kiowas, were camped there and
that trouble was expected. The next day Davidson arrived
with a detachment of his cavalry and ordered the Comanches

and Kiowas to surrender. A resulting skirmish brought a clear line between hostiles and friendly Indians; the hostiles now fled into the wild unknown country to the west and southwest, while the friendly bands completed their enrollment. Before the end of September some 479 Comanches, exclusive of the friendly Penatekas, 585 Kiowas, and 306 Kiowa-Apaches were at Fort Sill. More than half the population had fled to their favorite haunts along the headwaters of the Red and Brazos rivers in western Oklahoma and along the eastern edge of the Llano Estacado of Texas.[21] By this time, however, the military in five columns was converging from as many directions upon the Indian hideout. Commanding three of these columns, and personally leading one, was Colonel Mackenzie, who had been ordered up from Fort Clark to complete the job he had planned to finish in 1873.

In fact, General Sheridan and General Augur organized the campaign, which called for the cooperation of General Pope, very closely in accordance with the plan which Mackenzie had worked out in the autumn of 1872.[22] Pope ordered Colonel Nelson A. Miles to move southward from Fort Dodge, Kansas, with eight companies of cavalry and four of infantry to the headwaters of Red River, and Major William R. Price to move east from Fort Union, New Mexico, along the Canadian River with four companies of cavalry, scouting the country between the Canadian and Red rivers and joining Miles on the Texas-Indian Territory border.[23]

Augur sent toward the area three columns under the command of Colonel Mackenzie. Lieutenant Colonel Davidson was directed to operate westward from Fort Sill with six companies of cavalry and three of infantry between the main forks of Red River and the Canadian as far as the Llano Estacado. Lieutenant Colonel Buell, 11th Infantry, was to move six companies of cavalry and two of infantry from Fort Griffin and to establish a camp near the junction of Wanderer's Creek and the Red River, and from there to scout the area south of Miles and between Davidson and Mackenzie. Mackenzie with eight companies of cavalry and five of infantry was to reestablish his base on the Freshwater Fork of the Brazos and search out his old familiar haunts along the eastern edge of the Llano Estacado, overlapping Miles in the Red River country.[24] Altogether forty-six companies, about three thousand troops, were sent into the field against the hostile Indians.

On July 23 Mackenzie received the order from Augur to start his cavalry northward.[25] While Mackenzie met with Augur in San Antonio during the next few days for further planning, preparations for moving went forward, and on August 6 and 9 six companies of the 4th Cavalry (D, F, G, I, K, and L) left Clark and Duncan for Fort Concho, by way of McKavett, where Companies A and H were stationed.[26] On August 15 Augur and Mackenzie met the column at McKavett.[27] Leaving two days later, the column, joined by Co. C from Kerrville and Cos. A and H and two infantry companies from McKavett, proceeded toward Fort Concho.[28] The command reached Concho on August 21 and went into camp near the post.[29] The next day, while Davidson battled the defiant Comanches and Kiowas at the Wichita Agency, Mackenzie organized his expedition, which he thereafter designated as the "Southern Column." It consisted of Troops A, D, E, F, H, I, K, and L of the 4th Cavalry; and A, C, I, and K of the 10th Infantry and H of the 11th Infantry, under the command of Major Thomas M. Anderson, 10th Infantry.[30] Mackenzie fortunately had hired an additional scout, a half-breed Lipan and Mexican ex-*Comanchero* named Johnson, who had intimate knowledge of the country where the Southern Column was headed. The scouts, commanded by Lieutenant Thompson, in addition to Johnson, consisted of Sergeant Charlton, Strong, the Fort Richardson post guide, three other white men, thirteen Seminole Negroes who had given valuable assistance in the raid on the Mexican Kickapoos in May, 1873, twelve Tonkawas, and a few Lipans.[31]

The Southern Column, except Captain Boehm's Co. E which

was on a scout and did not join the column until September 17, took the field on the morning of August 23. About a mile out, it paused for inspection by Augur and Mackenzie, and then breaking into columns of four with the scouts in the lead, it headed northward for the Freshwater Fork of the Brazos, following the wagon road whose ruts in places had been cut deep by Lawton's supply trains during the campaigns of 1871 and 1872.[32] No other military expedition of equal experience, toughness, and preparation had ever gone forth to battle the Southern Plains Indians; when it returned from the field four months later, the Comanche-Kiowa supremacy over the Southern Plains had been completely destroyed.

FOOTNOTES — CHAPTER VII

[1] Nye, *Carbine and Lance*, 164.

[2] Tatum to Enoch Hoag, Superintendent of Indian Affairs, Central Superintendency, January 11, 1873, Indian Territory, Miscellaneous, Kiowa and Comanche Papers, 1869–1874, Office of Indian Affairs, National Archives.

[3] Carter, *On the Border*, 389–390.

[4] Thomas C. Battey, *The Life and Adventures of a Quaker among the Indians* (Boston, 1875), 164; Nye *Carbine and Lance*, 166.

[5] Davidson to Asst. Adj. Gen., Department of Texas, September 16, 1873, as quoted in Nye, *Carbine and Lance*, 168.

[6] Haworth to Cyrus Beede, December 8, 1873, as quoted in Richardson, *Comanche Barrier*, 369–370.

[7] Hatch to departmental headquarters, December 15, 1873, 5184 AGO 1873, RG 94; Sheridan to Sherman, December 16, 1873, 4997 AGO 1873, RG 94.

[8] P. H. Sheridan, *Record of Engagements with Hostile Indians within the Division of the Missouri from 1868 to 1882* (Washington, 1882), 39.

[9] Nye, *Carbine and Lance*, 183.

[10] *Galveston Daily News*, January 4, 1874.

[11] Nye, *Carbine and Lance*, 189–190.

[12] Richardson, *Comanche Barrier*, 371–372.

[13] Wallace and Hoebel, *The Comanches*, 318–319.

[14] *Ibid.*, 325–326.

[15] Richardson, *Comanche Barrier*, 382; Report of F. W. Smith and J. W. Smith to the Commissioner of Indian Affairs, September 26, 1874, Central Superintendency, S 1328, National Archives.

[16] Nye, *Carbine and Lance*, 192–200.

[17] *Ibid.*, 201.

[18] Sherman to Sheridan, July 15, 1874, in Joe F. Taylor (ed.), *The Indian Campaign on the Staked Plains, 1874–1875* (compilation of military records

contained in 2815 AGO 1874, RG 94; Canyon, Texas, 1962), 10 (hereafter cited as Taylor, *Indian Campaign*).

[19] Endorsement of the Secretary of War, July 16, 1874, on Sheridan to Sherman, July 16, 1874, in *ibid.*, 11.

[20] Sherman to Sheridan, July 20, 1874, in *ibid.*, 11–12; Sheridan to Sherman, July 21, 1874, in *ibid.*, 12–15; Augur, Special Orders No. 113, July 23, 1874, 2854 AGO 1874 (filed with 2815 AGO 1874), RG 94.

[21] Augur, annual report, September 28, 1874, 5604 AGO 1874, RG 94; Nye, *Carbine and Lance*, 206–211.

[22] "Extract of a Memo Prepared in Nov., 1872," in Mackenzie to departmental headquarters, August 4, 1874, (index number illegible) DT, Army Commands, RG 98.

[23] General John Pope, annual report, September 7, 1874, in Secretary of War, "Report," 1874, 43 Cong., 2 Sess., *House Exec. Doc.* I, pt. 2, p. 30; Special Order, 114, Department of the Missouri, July 27, 1874, in Taylor, *Indian Campaign*, 14–16.

[24] Augur, annual report, September 28, 1874, as cited.

[25] Special Order 113, July 23, 1874, in Taylor, *Indian Campaign*, 13–14.

[26] "Regimental Returns," August, 1874, 5604 AGO 1874, RG 94; "Movement of Troops in the Department of Texas from August 31, 1874, to August 31, 1875, 5689 AGO 1875, RG 94. Companies B (Captain Mauck) and G (Captain Rendlebrock) were left at Clark. Co. D went directly to Concho, where it arrived on August 19.

[27] Carter, *On the Border*, 474; "Scouting on the 'Staked Plains' (Llano Estacado) with Mackenzie in 1874," *United Service*, XIII (1885), 400 (hereafter cited as "Scouting with Mackenzie in 1874").

[28] "Post Medical Reports, Fort McKavett,——1852 to June, 1883, "Vols. 192–4–5, 181 (hereafter cited as "Medical History of Fort McKavett").

[29] Carter, *On the Border*, 474.

[30] "Movement of Troops in the Department of Texas," August 31, 1874, to August 31, 1875, as cited; Carter, *On the Border*, 474. Co. C, 4th Cavalry, was left at Concho.

[31] Carter, *On the Border*, 475; Strong, *My Indian Fights*, 50; Charles A. P. Hatfield, "The Comanche, Kiowa and Cheyenne Campaign in Northwest Texas and Mackenzie's Fight in Palo Duro Canyon, September 26 [sic], 1874," in West Texas Historical Association *Year Book*, V (1929), 118 (hereafter cited as Hatfield, "Mackenzie's Fight in Palo Duro Canyon"). Hatfield was a second lieutenant in Co. E, 4th Cavalry, at the time.

[32] Carter, *On the Border*, 474.

CHAPTER VIII

The Battle of Palo Duro Canyon

TRAVELLING WITHOUT its commanding officer, who accompanied General Augur to Fort Griffin, the Southern Column moved up the North Concho about sixteen miles to the "Stone Ranch" before camping for the first night. Continuing very leisurely up the North Concho beyond present Sterling City, it turned northward and camped for the night of August 26, 1874, in southern Mitchell County at Rendlebrock Springs, named for the Prussian-born captain of Co. G. The command remained in camp the next day to rest the men and horses. It was a hot, dry summer, the water was bad where the soil was loose, and the command was enveloped in a fog of dust. A high wind that night ignited from a campfire the sun-parched grass, which for a few minutes threatened to destroy the camp. The men, armed with wet blankets and sacks, succeeded in putting out the fire, but not before it had destroyed the tent of Captain Wint.

Starting at 5:30 the next morning, the cavalry went into camp before noon about five miles from the Colorado River to wait for the infantry and the heavily loaded wagons to catch up. Early the next morning the command forded the sandy Colorado near present Colorado City, getting the wagons across with some difficulty, continued northward through the heavy sand, and camped two nights later, "glad enough to get anything to drink," at a brackish waterhole on Hemphill's Creek, named for Lieutenant Hemphill of Co. G, opposite Kelly's Creek. Travelling up the valley of a ravine north of present Snyder and east of the Caprock, the column skirted the west base of Mt. McKenzie, about twenty miles north of Snyder, and camped on August 31 on the Double Mountain Fork of the Brazos, southwest of present Aspermont. After twelve hours in the saddle the next day, the cavalry reached its Freshwater Fork of the Brazos destination, a day ahead of the wagon train and infantry, having travelled during the last two days through immense herds of buffalo which furnished plenty of meat for the entire command.[1]

As soon as he had unloaded on September 2, Quartermaster Lawton pulled out with his six-mule wagons for more provisions from Fort Griffin via the Mackenzie Trail. While Lawton headed for Griffin, the command busied itself with establishing a camp. Two days later, the cavalry, having made camp on a plateau about a mile above the infantry, had a long drill, after which it attended the funeral of Private William Max, Co. K, 4th Cavalry, who was buried about a mile upstream from camp and not far from the grave of Private Gregg, killed in the battle with the Comanches three years before.[2]

While the troops on the Freshwater Fork were drilling, establishing their camp, overhauling their equipment, and scouting the vicinity for signs of Indians, Mackenzie and Augur at Fort Griffin completed their plans for the expedition. Augur instructed Mackenzie to "pay no regard to Department or Reservation lines. You are at liberty to follow the Indians wherever they go, even to the Agencies." If the Indians returned to the agency at Sill, Mackenzie was "to assume command of all troops there, and take such measures as necessary to control them."

Because of Mackenzie's familiarity with Indian warfare and, to some extent, with the country in which he was to operate,

Augur gave him considerable freedom to carry out the campaign as he saw fit. Consequently, the Colonel prepared for the information of the departmental commander a "Memorandum" in which he sketched some details of his plan. From the Freshwater Fork of the Brazos, he would operate with five companies of infantry, keeping one or two with the wagon train, and eight companies of the 4th Cavalry. He would move north with the first column along the eastern edge of the Staked Plains by Quitaque, across the Main Fork of the Red River, to the Salt Fork of the latter stream, and perhaps to Supply Camp, Indian Territory, on the Canadian near the Texas line. Buell was to cross the Pease River and march up the Main Red approximately to the High Plains. Both columns were to move out on September 18. Before leaving Concho, Mackenzie had directed Captain Boehm to send some of his Seminoles to scout the head of the Double Mountain Fork of the Brazos; should they find any Indians camped there, the column at the Freshwater Fork might be a few days later in starting than anticipated.[3]

Mackenzie, who had gone to Griffin also to arrange for adequate supplies, was delayed there because he had difficulty in finding forage to load his wagon train. On September 17 Augur from Fort Sill wrote Sheridan of Mackenzie's difficulty and requested that four thousand more bushels of corn be sent by way of Denison or Dallas to Griffin.[4] On the same day that Augur wrote for corn, three wagonloads, the first the horses had had in several days, arrived at the Freshwater Fork Supply Camp. Boehm with Co. E reached the Supply Camp that same afternoon, and on the 19th Mackenzie, Major Hatch, and Major Anderson arrived at camp with two companies of infantry.

Mackenzie immediately organized the Southern Column for the campaign. The cavalry was divided into two columns: the first, composed of companies D, F, I, and K, was placed under the command of Captain McLaughlin; the second, composed of companies A, E, H, and L, was placed under the command

of Captain Beaumont.[5] Both officers had distinguished records
of service and had been tested under fire. McLaughlin had been
a brigadier general of volunteers during the Civil War, and had
been the hero in the attack on the Kickapoo Indian village at
Remolino, Mexico, in 1873; Beaumont, a graduate of West
Point in 1861 and a veteran of the Battle of Gettysburg and of
Sherman's campaign through Georgia,[6] had with Mackenzie
led the charge on the Comanche village on the North Fork of
Red River in 1872. Major Anderson, who afterwards became
a major general, was placed in command of Supply Camp in
Mackenzie's absence.[7] His foot soldiers would escort wagon
trains to and from the field. The expedition now numbered 47
officers, 560 enlisted men, 3 acting assistant surgeons, and 32
scouts.[8]

On the same day that Mackenzie arrived at Supply Camp,
the Seminole Negro scouts, who had been ranging to the north,
reported that they had discovered three Indian trails in the vicinity of the head of the Pease River. Although the trails were
small, Mackenzie, hoping that they might lead to a village, decided to start the expedition at once in that direction.[9] Not
these, but other trails did lead him to a village in the Palo Duro
Canyon.

In fact the country along the eastern edge of the Staked
Plains from the Pease River northward to the Washita was
swarming with hostile Indians pushed southwestward into
these badlands by Miles, Price, and Davidson, who already had
their columns in the field. Leaving Fort Dodge on August 14
with 750 men, Colonel Miles on August 27 discovered at Sweetwater Creek near present Wheeler, Texas, a large, fresh Indian
trail that led to the southwest. Three days later in a five-hour,
twelve-mile fight along Battle Creek, opposite the junction of
the Tule and Palo Duro canyons, he defeated four to six hundred mounted warriors, killing seventeen and destroying a large
amount of the Indians' badly needed provisions. Miles followed
the fleeing Indians to the head of Tule Canyon, but realizing

that he could not overtake them, he turned back, leaving them to Mackenzie.[10]

Two weeks later Captain Wyllys Lyman and about sixty men — a detachment escorting Miles' wagon train — fought off an attack of three to four hundred Comanches and Kiowas for three days in present Hemphill County near the Washita River.[11] After giving up the siege, the Indians headed for the Palo Duro Canyon. While Lyman was "corralled" at the Washita, Major Price engaged another large body of Indians between Sweetwater Creek and the Dry Fork of the Washita River on September 12, killing two warriors, wounding six, and capturing twenty horses.[12]

On the same day that Price had his engagement with the Indians, Colonel Davidson with 610 men left Fort Sill, and moved along the divide between the Washita and the North Fork of the Red River to the Texas line and then turned southwest and scouted the North Fork, McClellan Creek, and Mulberry Creek to the base of the Staked Plains.[13] Thus, Mackenzie could hardly miss finding the hostiles.

Leaving Major Anderson with three infantry companies to guard Supply Camp, Mackenzie's entire command, consisting of 450 enlisted men, 21 commissioned officers, the three surgeons, a detachment of scouts, and the wagon train, escorted by two companies of infantry and commanded by Lieutenant Lawton, crossed to the east side of the Freshwater where final preparations were completed.

At 6:00 a.m. the next morning, Sunday, September 20, the cavalry column, with its Colonel in the lead, climbed the Caprock and headed northward along its old familiar road. About noon, after having marched fifteen miles, it caught up with the wagon train, which had started earlier, at a waterhole near present McAdoo, and halted for lunch.[14]

As the troops were preparing to resume the march about 2:30 p.m., four scouts who had been operating ahead of the column rode into camp and reported that they had been attacked by a party of twenty to twenty-five Comanches, one of their number having barely escaped when his horse was shot. Mackenzie ordered Lieutenant George Albee, 24th Infantry, a New Hampshire veteran of the Civil War, to take some Seminoles and track the hostiles. While Albee followed their trail, the cavalry set out at a trot, and at 5:00 p.m., having descended the Caprock and failed to sight any Indians, it bivouacked for the night near present Roaring Springs on the South Pease, still erroneously designated as the Big Wichita, thirty miles from where it had started that morning. Late in the evening Albee rejoined the command after having followed the trail for several miles without sighting any Indians.[15]

After waiting in camp the next morning until the arrival of the wagon train and then allowing the horses time to consume two quarts of corn each, Mackenzie sent the First Battalion under Captain McLaughlin in pursuit of the Comanches whose trail Albee had quit, while the remainder of the expedition continued northward along the Quitaque road to the Middle Pease, near present Matador, where it halted for two hours while Captain Boehm investigated another fresh trail that led to the west. When Boehm returned with a report that the trail had been made by a hunting party from the north, Mackenzie, leaving Lawton's supply train trailing far behind, resumed the march and late that evening, having travelled about twenty miles that day, made camp on the good, clear, running water of the Quitaque.

That night there was a thunderstorm with "sheets of flame" that illuminated the entire camp and torrents of rain that swelled the streams and turned the hard ground into soft, sticky mud. Mackenzie remained in camp the next day to wait out the storm, and to allow the supply train to catch up and the First Battalion to rejoin him. Lawton reached camp with one wagon loaded with beef, but the others were mired in mud eight miles in the rear, and there was no news of McLaughlin.

After Lawton had pulled the remainder of his wagons into

camp on the following morning, September 23, Mackenzie, impatient at the delay, broke camp and moved seven miles to the base of the Caprock on the Santa Fe Trail near the present town of Quitaque. There the troops were forced to seek whatever shelter they could find against another "tremendous" rainstorm and the accompanying cold wind.[16] In five hours Lawton managed to get his supply wagons through seven miles of mud, and just before sundown the First Battalion rejoined the command. McLaughlin reported that he had followed the Comanches for thirty-five miles, forcing them to abandon several horses and considerable equipment, but that they had escaped under cover of darkness.[17]

The rains which persisted throughout the night continued to hamper the movement of the column, which delayed starting until 1:00 p.m. Staking out their mounts to graze, the cavalrymen by means of ropes helped the "doubled up" teams pull the wagons up the slippery Caprock, and late in the afternoon made their ascent, halting for the night only three miles from the last camp.

At sunrise on the next morning, September 25, Mackenzie, leaving his wagons mired in the mud, led his cavalrymen, who walked part of the distance to preserve their mounts, northwest about twenty miles to Tule Canyon. About sundown, while Mackenzie was selecting a campsite, Strong, the Fort Richardson post guide, galloped in to report that Indians were east of the Tule with a herd of 150 horses and that Lieutenant Thompson with most of his scouts was checking on them. About dark Thompson reported to Mackenzie that during his sixty-mile scout that day he had found many trails of Indians leading in all directions, the largest made by an estimated 1,500 horses headed east.[18]

Leaving the First Battalion camped in Tule Canyon, Mackenzie ordered Captain Beaumont's weary Second Battalion to climb back into their saddles and follow the big trail. The long, dark column, moving under a full autumn moon over the thick buffalo grass that muffled the sound of the horses' hooves, expected at any moment to encounter the enemy. After following the trail five miles without discovering any Indians, Mackenzie gave up the search and, picketing their horses under a strong guard and spreading their blankets in a series of ravines designated in the records as "Boehm Canyon," the men with their boots on and their weapons in reach slept without disturbance through the rest of the night.

With his quarry hovering all about him but as difficult to pin down as phantom ghosts, Mackenzie remained in camp the next day. While the Colonel waited for Lawton to bring the wagon train through the mud, the horses refreshed themselves on the nutritious prairie grass and the scouts searched the area for Indian signs. About 5:00 p.m. the Second Battalion moved a few miles south of Boehm's Canyon and camped at a depression or lake full of good rainwater, where it was joined before night by McLaughlin's First Battalion, which had exchanged shots with seven Indians while on its way from the Tule Canyon. About night Johnson, the half-breed Mexican scout, reported that he had seen buffalo running west of the Tule as though they were being chased, and other scouts reported that Indians were beginning to gather around the command and during the night probably would attack. Mackenzie possibly recalled his unfortunate nights in Blanco Canyon and on the North Fork of the Red, for on this evening he ordered measures to prevent a recurring stampede. Each horse was tied with a one-inch rope to an iron stake, hobbled, and cross side-lined, and pickets at five-yard intervals ringed the bivouac. In addition, "sleeping parties" of from twelve to twenty men each were posted around the horseherd to rush the enemy in case of attack and to serve as skirmishers until the command could come to their support.[19]

At ten o'clock an estimated 250 Indian warriors, firing and yelling, charged the camp in an attempt to stampede the horses, but Captain Beaumont's Co. A checked the main assault. Faced with withering rapid fire from every direction, the attackers resorted to circling tactics, still hoping to stampede the horses. They wounded three cavalry horses, but what injury the troopers did to the screeching, circling redmen in the dim moonlight could not be determined. After about half an hour, the attackers withdrew a short distance, but sporadically broke the calm of the prairie night with a volley of gunfire.

About midnight a most enigmatical incident occurred. The rattling of wagons, the cracking of whips, and the cursing of teamsters, who were completely unaware of the battle, announced the approach of the wagon train sharply and clearly, perhaps due to atmospheric conditions, as the wagon wheels cut through the rain-soaked mesquite sod. Unmolested by the Indians for some inexplicable reason, wagonmaster James O'Neal brought in his ten wagons as if it were a routine affair.[20]

Between one and two o'clock the Indians ceased firing and withdrew to the ravines north of the cavalry encampment, allowing the troopers time to roll themselves into their blankets and snatch a bit of badly needed sleep. At daylight, however, an estimated three hundred hostiles reappeared on the surrounding ridge and began sniping ineffectually at the command. When the tempo increased, Mackenzie ordered the troopers to saddle up and counter-attack. Captain Boehm with his Co. E and Lieutenant Thompson at the head of his scouts led the charge. When the Indians saw the troops coming toward them, they lost their heart for battle, ran for their ponies, and after retreating some distance to the level prairie, formed a battle line about a mile long.[21]

At this moment a bit of humor was injected into the realism of the skirmish. Tonkawa scout Henry with a well-placed bullet knocked to the ground a horse mounted by an elaborately-feathered Comanche warrior who had been cut off from his comrades. Henry, carelessly failing to reload his rifle, approached the prostrate Comanche, who suddenly sprang to his feet, dragged Henry from his mount, and began flailing him with his bow while the troopers paused to look on in amusement. With every blow, Henry yelled at his nearby friends: "Why you no shoot? Why you no shoot?" A sympathetic cavalryman finally dispatched the Comanche.

While Henry salved his embarrassment with a scalping knife to make sure he would not meet his antagonist under less fortunate circumstances in the Happy Hunting Ground, Mackenzie at the head of other troops rode out to join in the battle. He was too late, however, for the Indians had scattered and disappeared as completely as if the ground had swallowed them in the vast expanse of the prairie. Realizing that pursuit was impossible, he led his men back to camp to breakfast and to wait for further information from his scouts. The first battle of Mackenzie's 1874 campaign was over. The Indians had suffered one dead for certain, one horse captured, and several horses wounded; Mackenzie had had three horses wounded.[22]

However, the cavalry did not unsaddle; Mackenzie intended to take the offensive. With his order to prepare for an extended campaign, horse equipage was checked, every man drew his quota of ammunition, and in addition to the regular supplies carried by each cavalryman on a scout, the company pack mules were loaded with twelve days' rations. Leaving one cavalry company with the infantry and wagon train, Mackenzie at 3:00 p.m. on Sunday, September 27, ordered the other seven cavalry companies to mount up. From the campsite he led his troopers slowly southwest up the Tule Canyon, the pack animals trailing closely behind. No doubt the Indians, whose camps were mostly in the opposite direction, were deceived into a feeling of false security by the movement. Mackenzie, however, was in reality merely taking the most practical route around the head of the Tule Canyon to his destination – the upper Palo Duro Canyon. At dusk, when the Indians could no longer easily observe his movements, he abruptly turned northward, crossed Tule Canyon at its head in his 1872 tracks, and

headed slightly west of north across the muddy plains toward
Palo Duro Canyon.

Mackenzie's strategy, which was almost identical with that
used in the raid on the Mexican Kickapoo Indians in 1873, indicates that the scouts had discovered the location of the Indian
village in the Palo Duro before the command left the Tule, but
the inadequate records make it impossible to determine when
Mackenzie first learned its location.[23] When at 2:00 a.m., September 28, after having marched twenty-five miles in eleven
hours, the scouts lost a "very large" Indian trail they had been
following for two hours, Mackenzie halted the column for the
men and horses to get some needed rest while the untiring
scouts hunted for the elusive trail. The troopers unsaddled and
staked out their horses at a spot where there was no grass, unpacked the mules, and then rolled into their blankets on the wet
ground.

They got very little sleep, for it was not long before Charlton and two of the Tonkawas reported that they had relocated
the trail, which had led them to a large concentration of Indians in Palo Duro Canyon, four miles to the north-northwest.
As the first faint streaks of day appeared in the east, the command came to the precipice of Palo Duro Canyon just below
its junction with Blanca Cita (Cita) Canyon,[24] about five miles
below the present limits of the state park.

Peering over the rim of the chasm, which had a vertical drop
of seven hundred to nine hundred feet, Mackenzie and his men
were overawed by what they beheld. Ninety million years of
erosion had created in the depths below an ideal haven for the
Indians.[25] Palo Duro (hard wood) Canyon, at this point approximately six miles from rim to rim, and Blanca Cita, more
than a half mile in width, had a good supply of cottonwood,
cedar, wild cherry, mesquite, and hackberry trees from which
the Indians could obtain firewood, lodge poles, and arrows. At
the bottom of the gorge meandered a stream of good water, fed
by springs along the canyon walls. Extending for two or three

miles along the banks of the stream stood an estimated two hundred tipis, roughly grouped into five villages, and hundreds of horses grazed nearby.[26] Deceived by the distance, one of the Seminoles exclaimed: "Lor' men, look at de sheep and de goats down dar."[27]

The encampment on the floor of the canyon consisted of a Kiowa band led by Mamanti, a large band of Comanches under O-ha-ma-tai, and a small band of Cheyennes led by Iron Shirt. After the Anadarko fight on August 22, a majority of the Kiowas and Comanches had fled westward by way of the head of Elk Creek, wandered aimlessly between the Canadian and Washita for several days, and then headed southwest toward Palo Duro Canyon, where Mow-way, Tabananica, and others were known to be, camping on the night of September 7 fifteen miles from and within sight of the Llano Estacado and intending to reach the breaks on the following day. After a delay of a day spent in search of one of the party who had been captured by Lieutenant Baldwin, 5th Infantry, serving under Colonel Miles, the Indians on September 9 near the crossing on the Washita River attacked Miles' wagon train, escorted by Captain Lyman's infantry company. On the third day of the siege Botalye, a young Kiowa, dashed his pony through the troopers' trenches four times and returned safely. When on September 12 the Indians gave up the siege, some of the band, including Woman's Heart and the parolees Satanta and Big Tree, left the group and headed east to surrender. Managing to miss the soldiers, they led their bands to the Cheyenne agency at Darlington and on October 24 surrendered.

While the medicine men and leaders debated policy, the remainder of the rain-drenched, exhausted people lay down in mud and water at the head of Elk Creek to get some sleep. The next morning in clear weather they proceeded to Palo Duro Canyon, entering the gorge by a trail from the north rim. O-ha-ma-tai's band of Comanches, numbering about forty lodges, camped at the mouth of the Blanca Cita; next came the Kiowas, and then the Cheyennes under Iron Shirt. The Comanche bands of Mow-way, Tabananica, and Wild Horse were farther south engaging Mackenzie on the Tule.[28]

Mamanti, the Kiowa medicine man, was in general charge. After "making medicine," he assured the people that no blue-coated soldiers would ever disturb them in the canyon. Thus assured, the women erected their tipis, began preparing new lodge poles from the cedars in the canyon and getting ready for winter, and at daylight on the morning of September 28 the unsuspecting villagers slept without fear while from the rim of the canyon high above them the tenacious and daring Mackenzie, bent upon their complete destruction, decided to take the most daring risk he had yet encountered and lead his hardened cavalrymen into what one of them later called the "jaws of death." [29] A mistake in strategem could turn the canyon into literal "jaws of death;" perhaps the Indians, reputedly well-armed, were prepared to man advantageous barricades and pick off each intruder as he scrambled almost helplessly down the narrow trail!

The command had to march along the canyon rim about a mile before finding a trail, directly above the Comanche tipis, leading down the canyon wall. Meanwhile, the chance of an early dawn attack had gone. The sun had changed the eastern sky from rose to ochre, and finally rose above the opposite rim of the canyon as the men moved down the tortuous trail. When he found the narrow, zig-zag path, Mackenzie quietly turned to Lieutenant Thompson, in command of the scouts, and said: "Mr. Thompson, take your men down and open the fight." "Very well, sir," came the quick and confident reply. Captain McLaughlin with his First Battalion was instructed to stand guard at the head of the trail, and Captain Beaumont and Mackenzie at the head of the Second Battalion followed closely on the heels of the indomitable Thompson and the thirty-two scouts.

The descent, which required nearly an hour, was an unforgettable nightmare. Stumbling and sliding, leading their horses, the troops single-filed slowly down the narrow zig-zag path. About two-thirds of the way down, a startled Indian look-out on a bluff in the canyon wall sprang from behind a rock, "war-whooped," and waved a red blanket in an effort to warn the village below of the approaching danger. His "war-whoop" and the quick shot that ended his life shattered the stillness of the early morning and abruptly aroused the sleeping villagers.[30]

When K'ya-been (Older Man), headman of the family group at the bottom of the trail, saw the troopers scrambling down, he fired his gun twice and then rushed into his tipi to don war paint—no proud warrior could engage in battle without war paint and the proper ceremonies. The Kiowas farther down the valley paid no heed to the shots, thinking they were fired by some early-rising deer hunter. A few moments later four more shots startled the villagers,[31] who became panic-stricken upon seeing the blue-coated troopers at the foot of the trail mounting their horses and forming into battle formation.

Thompson's scouts, Beaumont's Co. A, and Boehm's Co. E were the first to get formed. Companies H and L, led by Mackenzie, were close behind. A scene of utter chaos greeted the troopers as they charged through the village, already totally abandoned, and up the floor of the canyon. Many warriors had grabbed their weapons and scattered for safety among the cedars and boulders that lined the canyon walls, while others fled on their ponies or were attempting to drive their horseherd away. The women and children had leaped on their ponies and fled up the valley, or attempted to find safety by scaling or hiding in the northwest canyon wall. Everywhere the ground was strewn with blankets, clothing, cooking utensils, buffalo robes, shields, weapons, ammunition, and other articles dropped or discarded by the frightened

Indians in their desperate flight. Pack animals whose hastily
tied burdens had slipped below their bellies ran wildly through
the brush, while those securely tied to trees lunged desper-
ately at their ropes.[32]

After a running four-mile skirmish, during which Thompson's scouts killed three warriors, the only bodies found on
the field, the Indians finally abandoned the horseherd and
dashed for the pass at the western end of the canyon.[33] An-
zai-te ducked behind a tree and shot the horse of one of the
officers at the head of the troops, and as the men opened fire
on the fleeing Indians, Poor Buffalo hid behind a pile of rocks
and, although a Kiowa, sang the Blackfoot Society death
song. His comrades found him there a few moments later,
dead from a bullet hole through his head, a finger on which
he had worn a ring cut off but not scalped, and took him up
the trail to the top of the hill where the people danced to
honor his bravery.[34]

At this point Captain Beaumont ordered the men to round
up the Indians' horses and drive the herd back down the valley toward the camps. The frightened animals ran wildly in
every direction and could not be bunched until after the leaders had been shot and the others surrounded by the cavalrymen. Two miles down the canyon, the returning troopers
met Colonel Mackenzie at the head of Cos. H and L coming
up the valley at a gallop.

As the troops reunited and Mackenzie paused to survey the
situation, a few Indians, from the vantage of the higher eleva-
tion in the canyon walls, opened a galling fire on the cavalrymen, forcing the two companies with Mackenzie to withdraw
to a safe distance. As they wheeled to the left by fours,
Trumpeter Henry E. Hard, Co. L, caught a bullet in his
bowels, but thanks to the skill of Surgeon Choate he lived to
sound his bugle calls for many more years. Companies H and
L fell back about two hundred yards to the bed of a dry
arroyo, but again the hostiles found the range and made their

position untenable. Dismounting and throwing their reins to horse-holders, the troopers formed a skirmish line across the stream bed. Although not a man was wounded, six or eight horses were hit in as many minutes, Concluding that there was no other way ever to get out alive, German-born Captain Sebastian Gunther ordered a detachment of his dismounted Co. H to clear the hostiles from the bluffs, but seeing them start, Mackenzie ordered them back with the explanation that "Not one of them would live to reach the top." One frightened trooper, realizing that the command might well be annihilated before it could get out of the canyon, expressed aloud his despair: "How will we ever get out of here?" Overhearing the remark, Mackenzie snapped out a confident reassurance: "I brought you in, I will take you out." When the firing finally diminished, the troops moved toward the camps with Cos. H and L deployed to protect the flanks.[35]

By noon Mackenzie was ready to destroy the lodges and supplies and leave the canyon. Anticipating that the Indians would attempt to block their exit, he sent Beaumont and Boehm with Cos. A and E to the bottom of the trail and Captain Gunther with his Co. H to the top to prevent any such possibility. When the troops reached the foot of the "Jacob's Ladder" pathway out of the canyon, Co. H dismounted and began its perilous ascent. Between a half and three-quarters of an hour later it reached the plains. Not an Indian was in sight.[36]

Meanwhile, a part of McLaughlin's First Battalion, Cos. D, I, and K, descending too late to get into the first phase of the fight, was ordered to dismount and deploy as skirmishers against a party of Indians who had been working their way down the canyon wall to a position nearer the troops, behind a pile of huge boulders. As the skirmishers kept up a desultory fire that gradually drove the Indians from their position, another detachment was ordered to pull down the lodges and to destroy all of the equipment and supplies and still another to guard the horseherd. This time Mackenzie allowed his men to move against the warriors. As the blue line of skirmishers advanced, the Indian warriors retired, finally giving up the duel and fleeing up Blanca Cita Canyon, the escape route used by many earlier in the day.

The troopers who had the less dangerous job of destroying the villages found that the Indians had stocked their larder well for the winter. In the lodges they found bows and arrows, all sorts of robes, new reservation-issue blankets, stone china, kettles, tools and implements, including even a pair of tinner's snips, modern breech-loading rifles with ammunition, bales of calico, sacks of flour, and several other kinds of groceries. Huge bonfires roared as the soldiers heaped vast quanities of dried buffalo meat and Indian Department flour and sugar on the flames. Some of the items were appropriated by the women of the Tonkawa scouts, who had accompanied the expedition in violation of Mackenzie's order.

When the destruction of the village had been completed, the command began the climb up the narrow trail, taking the horseherd with them. About four o'clock all the troops were again on the Staked Plains. Half an hour later, the column, forming itself into a living square corral around the captive horseherd, started for the wagon train, which was supposed to be at the head of Tule Canyon. One company moved in front of the herd; two rode on each side in columns of two; and another rode in line in the rear. In this manner, the weary troopers rode slowly across the more than twenty miles of prairie to the head of Tule Canyon, rejoining the wagon train and guard about 12:30 on the morning of September 29. Turning the herd over to the infantrymen, who placed them in a corral formed by the wagons, the exhausted troopers, having spent thirty-one of the preceding thirty-three hours in the saddle or in battle and without food, unsaddled, picketed and fed their mounts, gulped down some scalding black coffee, and rolled into their blankets for a well-earned rest, some of the men having slept very little since the night of the 25th. A late breakfast that morning was the first meal for the men in over forty-eight hours.[37]

After breakfast the troopers had a most unusual experience. Mackenzie had no desire for a repetition of his experiences in Blanco Canyon in 1871 and on the North Fork the next year when the Indians recovered their herds, but to keep the ponies securely guarded would hinder his campaigning. He decided, therefore, that all of the 1,424 captured animals, 1,274 horses and 150 mules, except 376 of the finest, must be destroyed. He had promised the scouts a share of the spoils for their hazardous work, and because he had located the Indian village in Palo Duro Canyon, Johnson, the ex-*Comanchero*, was allowed the first choice. Johnson selected his allotted forty, then immediately sold them to some of the officers. The other scouts and guides then selected five animals each. Ironically, through carelessness they later lost a majority of these animals while on their way to Fort Griffin. Of the mules turned over to Lawton, ten six-mule teams were formed, some were given to the cavalry for pack mules, some were used to replace broken-down animals in the wagon train, and about forty of the poorest were sent to Fort Griffin. Some of the horses were used to replace jaded cavalry mounts, and the remainder were eventually sold and the proceeds apportioned among the several companies for extra spending money. Actually, very few of the animals were of excellent quality.[38]

The gory job of killing the remaining 1,048 head was assigned to Lieutenant Lawton. Firing squads shot the animals as fast as a troop of infantry could rope and get them to the designated spot. As the guns boomed and the herd grew proportionately smaller, the crazed animals became increasingly difficult to handle, but by 3:00 p.m. the slaughter was over.[39] The bone-pile marking the site of the horse slaughter near the head of Tule Canyon remained for many years a gruesome landmark signifying the end of Indian dominance over northwestern Texas. It has also brought forth an eerie but fascinating legend of a phantom herd of riderless steeds that on moonlight nights can sometimes be seen galloping along the rim of the canyon with uncanny speed, their heads high and their manes flying in the wind.[40]

With the slaughter of the horses, the first phase of Mackenzie's 1874 campaign had been completed. At daring risk the commander had lost not one man and had only one wounded; the hostiles had succeeded in killing three and wounding ten of his horses. Although only four Indians whose bodies "fell into our hands" had been killed, the finding and destroying of the village in Palo Duro Canyon, seemingly a secure hideout, was a devastating blow. Instead of spending the winter amidst the comfortable surroundings of the canyon, this group was cast adrift to cope with the harsh winter blizzards of the plains without lodges, provisions, robes, or horses. They could no longer find safety east of the Llano Estacado, for other columns of blue-coated troopers led by Miles, Davidson, and Buell were scouring every valley and hideout untouched by Mackenzie, and without horses the hostiles could neither reprovision themselves nor outrun the dogged cavalrymen. Faced with such alternatives, most of the Indians straggled back to the reservation and surrendered, but others thought they could find safety at the widely scattered waterholes on the inhospitable and treacherous Plains. Their strategy, however, did not take into account the indomitable Mackenzie.

FOOTNOTES — CHAPTER VIII

[1] "Medical History of Fort Concho," 154, as cited; Carter, *On the Border*, 478-479; "Scouting with Mackenzie in 1874," 401-402; Gillespie, "Map of Expeditions," as cited; Lucas, "Map of Country Scouted by Mackenzie, Shafter, and Wilson," as cited.

[2] "Scouting with Mackenzie in 1874," 403-404; Jerry Hall in the *Lubbock Avalanche-Journal*, July 7, 1960. The original inscribed sandstone grave marker has been moved recently to Crosby County Museum.

[3] Augur, Fort Griffin, to Mackenzie, August 28, 1874, quoted in Carter, *On the Border*, 475-476; Augur, annual report, September 28, 1874, as cited;

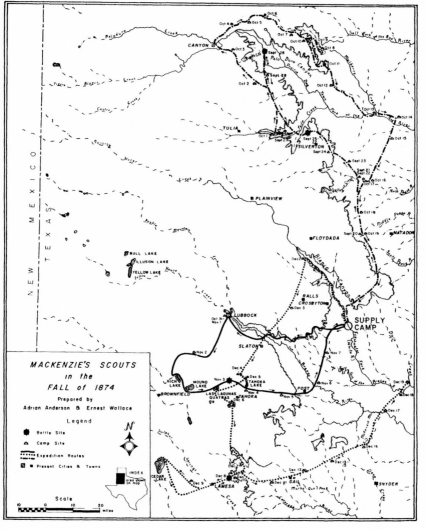

Map of 1874 Scouts and Battles

Mackenzie, "Memorandum for the information of the Departmental Commander, Department of Texas," n.d., quoted in Carter, *On the Border*, 476–477; Sheridan to Sherman, September 5, 1874, 3625 AGO 1874 (filed with 2815 AGO 1874), RG 94.

⁴ Augur to Sheridan, September 17, 1874, quoted in Carter, *On the Border*, 480–481.

⁵ "Scouting with Mackenzie in 1874," 404.

⁶ *Times-Leader* (Wilkes-Barre, Pennsylvania), August 17, 1926, quoted in Carter, *On the Border*, 24–27.

⁷ Although Mackenzie always designated his base on the Freshwater Fork of the Brazos as "Supply Camp," it became known also as "Anderson's Fort," because, according to Carter, of "the many boxes, barrels, bales and filled bags piled up for defense." Carter, *On the Border*, 474, 481; "Scouting with Mackenzie in 1874," 404.

⁸ "Tabular Statement of Expeditions . . . during the Year ending August 31, 1875," September 10, 1875, 5689 AGO 1875, RG 94.

⁹ Mackenzie to departmental headquarters, September 19, 1874, 3926 DT 1874, Army Commands, RG 98.

¹⁰ Miles to departmental headquarters, September 1, 5, and 11, 1874, in Taylor, *Indian Campaign*, 21–24, 26–28.

¹¹ Wyllys Lyman to Commanding Officer, Camp Supply, September 10, 1874, and Miles to departmental headquarters, September 17, 1874, both in *ibid.*, 31–32, 34–35.

¹² Price to departmental headquarters, September 23, 1874, in *ibid.*, 46–55.

¹³ Davidson to departmental headquarters, October 10, 1874, 4622 AGO 1874 (filed with 2815 AGO 1874), RG 94.

¹⁴ Mackenzie, "Memorandum of March of the Column from Camp on Freshwater Fork of the Brazos," September 20–29, 1874, September 29, 1874, 4050 DT 1874, Army Commands, RG 98 (microfilm copy, courtesy of Lessing H. Nohl, Jr., Albuquerque, New Mexico; hereafter cited as Mackenzie, "Memorandum," September 20–29, 1874); "Scouting with Mackenzie in 1874," 404–405.

¹⁵ *Ibid.*, 405; Gillespie, "Map of Expeditions," as cited; Mackenzie, "Memorandum," September 20–29, 1874, as cited; *Galveston Daily News*, October 22, 1874, gives an account of Mackenzie's movements from September 20 to September 29, 1874, originally printed in the *New York Herald*, October 16, 1874. Although the source of the information is not known for certain, Lieutenant George Albee has been given the credit. Marvin J. Hunter, "The Battle of Palo Duro Canyon," in *Frontier Times*, XXI (January, 1944), 177.

¹⁶ "Scouting with Mackenzie in 1874," 405–406; Mackenzie, "Memorandum," September 20–29, 1874, as cited; Gillespie, "Map of Expeditions," as cited; Carter, *On the Border*, 483. Mackenzie stated in his journal that he camped on the Pease River, but since he was only slightly more than seven miles from the base of the Caprock where he ascended onto the High Plains, the site necessarily would have been the Quitaque, a headstream of the North Pease.

¹⁷ *Galveston Daily News*, October 22, 1874; Carter, *On the Border*, 483; "Scouting with Mackenzie in 1874," 406.

¹⁸ *Ibid.*, 407; Mackenzie, "Memorandum," September 20–29, 1874, as cited;

Carter, *On the Border*, 484; Hatfield, "Mackenzie's Fight in Palo Duro Canyon," 119.

[19] Gillespie, "Map of Expeditions," as cited; Mackenzie "Memorandum," September 20-29, 1874, as cited; "Scouting with Mackenzie in 1874," 408; *Galveston Daily News*, October 22, 1874; Carter, *On the Border*, 484-486.

[20] Mackenzie, "Memorandum," September 20-29, 1874, as cited; Strong, *My Indian Fights*, 56, 58; "Scouting with Mackenzie in 1874," 408-409; Charlton in Carter, *The Old Sergeant's Story*, 105; Hatfield, "Mackenzie's Fight in Palo Duro Canyon," 119-120; Carter, *On the Border*, 486.

[21] Mackenzie, "Memorandum," September 20-29, 1874, as cited; Carter, *The Old Sergeant's Story*, 105; Hatfield, "Mackenzie's Fight in Palo Duro Canyon," 120; "Scouting with Mackenzie in 1874," 409; Mackenzie to departmental headquarters, October 1, 1874, 3973 DT 1874, Army Commands, RG 98; Anderson, "Mackenzie on the Texas Frontier," 62-113, is a scholarly account of Mackenzie's 1874 campaign.

[22] Charlton in Carter, *The Old Sergeant's Story*, 105-106; Hatfield, "Mackenzie's Fight in Palo Duro Canyon," 120-121; "Scouting with Mackenzie in 1874," 409; Mackenzie, "Memorandum," September 20-29, 1874, as cited; Carter, *On the Border*, 487.

[23] *Galveston Daily News*, October 22, 1874; Hatfield, "Mackenzie's Fight in Palo Duro Canyon," 129-131; "Scouting with Mackenzie in 1874," 409-410. Sergeant Charlton, one of the scouts, claimed that he and two Tonkawas, Johnson and Job, had discovered the village and had brought the information to Mackenzie before he left camp. (Carter, *The Old Sergeant's Story*, 106.) Hatfield claimed that Johnson, the Mexican half-breed, had reported the location of the village about thirty minutes before the Comanches attacked Mackenzie near the Tule on the preceding night. This appears to be a likely story, for as previously noted Johnson did rejoin the command at 9:30 that evening, and Mackenzie, after chasing the Indian warriors away from camp, the next morning began packing for the march without allowing the horses to be unsaddled. Haley, in *Fort Concho*, 220, states that the scouts were directed to the Indian camp by José Piedad Tafoya, a *Comanchero*, who disclosed the location after being hanged three times on a propped-up wagon tongue. Mackenzie credited Johnson with the discovery.

[24] Mackenzie, "Memorandum," September 20-29, 1874, as cited; Hatfield, "Mackenzie's Fight in Palo Duro Canyon," 121; "Scouting with Mackenzie in 1874," 410; Carter, *On the Border*, 488.

[25] Estimate made by Archaeologist Jack T. Hughes (Canyon, Texas) to Charles Townsend, May 7, 1962.

[26] Mackenzie to departmental headquarters, October 1, 1874, as cited; "Scouting with Mackenzie in 1874," 410; Nye, *Carbine and Lance*, 284.

[27] Strong, *My Indian Fights*, 59.

[28] Nye, *Carbine and Lance*, 213-221.

[29] Charlton in Carter, *The Old Sergeant's Story*, 64.

[30] Mackenzie, "Memorandum," September 20-29, 1874, as cited; Hatfield, "Mackenzie's Fight in Palo Duro Canyon," 121-122; "Scouting with Mackenzie in 1874," 410; Charlton in Carter, *The Old Sergeant's Story*, 107; Strong, *My Indian Fights*, 60; Nye, *Carbine and Lance*, 222; Carter, *On the Border*, 488-489.

[31] Comanche Mumsukawa's account in Nye, *Carbine and Lance*, 22.

³² Mackenzie, "Memorandum," September 20-29, 1874, as cited; "Scouting with Mackenzie in 1874," 410-411; Hatfield, "Mackenzie's Fight in Palo Duro Canyon," 122; Mackenzie to departmental headquarters, October 1, 1874, as cited; Nye, *Carbine and Lance*, 22.

³³ Mackenzie, "Memorandum," September 20-29, 1874, as cited; Thompson, "Scouting with Mackenzie," in *Cavalry Journal*, X, 431; Charlton in Carter, *The Old Sergeant's Story*, 108.

³⁴ Comanche Mumsukawa's account in Nye, *Carbine and Lance*, 223-224.

³⁵ Charlton in Carter, *The Old Sergeant's Story*, 108; "Scouting with Mackenzie in 1874," 411; Carter, *On the Border*, 489-491; Mackenzie, "Memorandum," September 20-29, 1874, as cited. In 1924 forty Indians who visited the Palo Duro identified the location of the battlefield and the trail used by Mackenzie. Bruce Gerdes to Frank Collinson, May 24, 1935, Panhandle-Plains Historical Museum, Canyon, Texas.

³⁶ Carter, *On the Border*, 492.

³⁷ "Scouting with Mackenzie in 1874," 412, 532; *Galveston Daily News*, October 22, 1874; Mackenzie, "Memorandum," September 20-29, 1874, as cited; Hatfield, "Mackenzie's Fight in Palo Duro Canyon," 122; Charlton in Carter, *The Old Sergeant's Story*, 110; Carter, *On the Border*, 494.

³⁸ Mackenzie, "Continuation [of Memorandum] Itinerary of the march of the 1st Southern Column," September 29-November 8, 1874, 4262 DT 1874, Army Commands, RG 98 (microfilm copy, courtesy of Nohl; hereafter cited as Mackenzie, "Itinerary," September 29-November 8, 1874); Mackenzie to departmental headquarters, October 26 and November 16, 1874, 4310 DT 1874, and 4956 DT 1874, Army Commands, RG 98; Hatfield, "Mackenzie's Fight in Palo Duro Canyon," 122; Mackenzie to departmental headquarters, October 1, 1874, as cited; "Scouting with Mackenzie in 1874," 532; Anderson, Commanding Supply Camp on the Freshwater Fork of the Brazos, to departmental headquarters, October 24, 1874, (Box 16) DT 1874, RG 98.

³⁹ Mackenzie, "Itinerary," September 29-November 8, 1874, as cited; Mackenzie to departmental headquarters, October 26, 1874, as cited; Strong, *My Indian Fights*, 62; Carter, *On the Border*, 494-495; "Scouting with Mackenzie in 1874," 532; "Tabular Statement of Expeditions and Scouts . . . during the Year ending August 31, 1875," as cited.

⁴⁰ *Texas Writers' Project* (New York: Hastings House, 1940), 521.

CHAPTER IX

Searching the South Plains for Indians: The End of the Red River War

WHEN THE SLAUGHTER of the horses had been completed at midafternoon on September 29, to get away from the stench Mackenzie moved his camp up Tule Creek six miles, where he remained two days before moving another three miles. Observing Indians near the bivouac about sundown that evening and fearing another night attack, the Colonel closed up the command, penned the animals in a corral improvised by ropes attached to the wagons, and surrounded the camp with "sleeping parties" and skirmishers.[1]

There was no attack, however, and concluding that men and horses were sufficiently recuperated, Mackenzie at noon on October 2 launched a series of phenomenal but exhausting marches that brought to a successful end the great Red River War. Leading his command slightly west of north seventeen miles, he bivouacked for the night at a waterhole on the Quitaque-New Mexico road, seven miles from the head of Blanca Cita Canyon, where Lieutenant Thompson and his scouts, after picking up ten stray horses, pushed on ahead to trail the escaping Indians. When the column reached the Blanca Cita crossing the next day, Thompson was waiting with word that no sign of the Indians or their route of flight had been discovered. After halting that evening at a waterhole ten miles northwest of Blanca Cita, the command marched the next morning at daylight, crossed the Palo Duro at the present city of Canyon, where the men had a late Sunday breakfast and the horses grazed on the luxuriant grass, then travelled northeasterly, following a cart trail along the rim of the canyon for six miles before stopping for the night as ominous clouds appeared above the horizon. After a deluge that drenched some of the troopers, the next morning the command, while moving along the 1872 trail of Colonel J. J. Gregg, encountered a few Indians driving a small herd of horses. The Indians escaped into the canyon, but seventeen horses were taken, two bearing a government brand. Leaving the cumbersome supply wagons bogged in mud, Mackenzie then veered away from the canyon, and for two days trudged slowly toward the northeast across prairies soaked by forty-eight hours of heavy rains.

On the morning of October 7, the cavalrymen, about half of whom were leading their tired horses through the sticky mud, encountered fifteen Mexicans driving six ox-carts loaded with dried meat and provisions. Three of the Mexicans, who claimed that they were not part of the train, joined the column as guides; the others, who convincingly insisted that they were buffalo hunters, were released. After leaving the Mexican outfit, the command struck an Indian trail leading in a southeasterly direction. While still following this trail the next morning, the troopers reached at the edge of the High Plains a small headstream of Mulberry Creek, thought to be the North Fork of the Red, where they encountered five Mexicans with an empty ox-wagon, eight oxen, and a burro. Obtaining a confession that they had been hauling supplies to the hostiles, Mackenzie placed the men under arrest, had the wagon broken up for fuel, and turned the oxen over to the troops for beef. A burly trooper appropriated the burro for his mount, but although they laughed at the amusing spectacle, other cavalrymen, their horses exhausted by the mud, were walking much of the time.

Short of supplies, his horses exhausted, and without any favorable report from his scouts, Mackenzie on October 9 turned back, soon meeting three of his wagons loaded with corn; when on the next day he joined the remainder of the train near the Caprock, he learned that his Mexican prisoners had met an estimated one hundred Indians with three times as many horses. Turning fifty-five exhausted horses and the disabled men over to Lawton and drawing rations for twelve days, Mackenzie on October 11 led his troops south-southeast along the Indian trail parallel to and midway between Palo Duro Canyon and Mulberry Creek. The command stopped the first night at a waterhole on a promontory of the Llano Estacado, and the next in very rough gypsum country a few miles below the Caprock, near the present community of Paloduro, where the quarry had camped not more than three days before. From here, Mackenzie sent the wagon train with an infantry escort and the disabled men and horses to his supply camp, instructing Lawton to hurry back with badly needed supplies.[2]

The signs indicated that at this campsite either Miles, Davidson, or Buell had quit an Indian trail. Had Mackenzie not been forced to turn back to meet his wagon train, it is quite likely that he would have encountered Colonel Buell's column somewhere in the breaks east of the Caprock. Buell at the head of the Fort Griffin column, consisting of 15 officers, 211 enlisted men, and 27 scouts, had established his supply camp near the junction of the Red River and its Salt Fork, northwest of present Vernon, and from there had marched up the Salt Fork. On October 9 he struck a small camp of Indians, killing one and destroying fifteen lodges. Pursuing the Indians up the Salt Fork to the foot of the Caprock and then northward across McClellan Creek and the North Fork

of the Red, Buell during the next few days fought them twice
more, destroying 82 lodges in the first and about 400 in the
second encounter.[3]

From the site of the Indian camp, Mackenzie on October
13 followed Byrnes Creek twelve miles to the Prairie Dog
Fork of the Red River, seeing along the way several worn-
out ponies abandoned by the Indians, doubled across the river,
and camped for the night near the mouth of Mulberry Creek,
where there was no grass for the tired animals. During the
next day the command encountered a small party of hostiles,
capturing three of their broken-down ponies, and followed
them eastward to the vicinity of present Memphis. Here Mackenzie, because he had crossed into the area where Miles,
Davidson, and Buell were campaigning, his horses were jaded,
and his supplies almost exhausted, abandoned what appeared
to be a futile chase and turned his troops southward to meet
Lawton and the wagon train.

On the night of October 16 he camped on the North Pease,
where he grazed the horses until the 18th and then moved to
the Middle Pease near present Matador, where the next day
a wagon arrived with rations, a little forage, and the mail. Although the supplies were meager, the mail, the first in several
weeks, revived the spirits of the weary men. In the afternoon
the column moved a few miles to a tributary of the South
Pease, probably Dutchman's Creek in the vicinity of present
Roaring Springs. On the 20th Lawton brought in fifteen days'
rations but only enough corn for three to five days.[4] The wagon train mules also were weak, requiring eight to the wagon,
and many wagons were teamless.[5] After allowing his horses
to recuperate on corn and good grass for three more days,
Mackenzie broke camp early on October 23 and at 11:00 p.m.
that night reached the site on the east side of the Freshwater
Fork from which he had started more than a month before.[6]

The first scout of the campaign was over. In thirty-four
days Mackenzie had led his troopers nearly 450 miles in the

very heart of the Indian country. Nevertheless, a large band of hostiles was still at large, possibly on the Double Mountain Fork of the Brazos in the vicinity of present Lubbock,[7] and it must be found and chastised as soon as Lawton brought in enough supplies and the men and horses had recuperated.

To graze the animals better, the Colonel scattered the companies for some distance along the valley of the Freshwater Fork, and for a week kept the men busy overhauling their equipment, shoeing horses, and performing other routine duties. On October 26 he sent his "spies a long distance away with the promise of a large reward of horses in case of success" for such dangerous work.[8]

Because of the lack of transportation for hauling adequate forage from Griffin, Mackenzie concluded that he could not maintain the eight companies of cavalry in the field, and on October 29 informed Augur that, subject to his approval, he had ordered Cos. E, F, and K of the 4th Cavalry to Richardson and Concho for recuperation, and requested Co. M at McKavett and Co. C at Concho to report to him at Supply Camp. He would start on another scout with the five remaining companies at the Freshwater camp soon after the forage arrived, and scout until December, by which time many of the horses would be dead or thoroughly broken down unless he had replacements.

Before he had finished his letter, the scouts returned with the information that the Indians were encamped to his west, possibly on the Double Mountain Fork of the Brazos. He decided, therefore, to send Co. E to Concho, keeping the other two for a while longer, and to start immediately without waiting for the train. No time was lost. That same afternoon, the serviceable cavalrymen in the seven companies, a little over half the total, were concentrated at the Supply Camp, where each was given twelve days' rations and the company mules were packed,[9] and just after sundown Mackenzie led his troopers southwesterly toward where the Double Mountain

Fork of the Brazos cuts a saw-tooth channel in the eastern edge of the Llano Estacado near present Slaton. In the darkness just before midnight, thirteen miles from Supply Camp, the column struggled up the Caprock, then skirted it for seventeen miles before camping at its base in a well-sheltered arroyo, where the grass and water were good, approximately on State Highway 122. At sundown the command climbed back up the Caprock, but soon descended it again and struck the canyon of the Double Mountain Fork about eight miles east of Slaton, emerged on the west side of the canyon north of Slaton at midnight, and then after riding on the level plains west of but generally parallel to the river for eighteen miles camped on October 31 at the head of the canyon, at present Lubbock, where there was no firewood to ease the suffering from an "indescribable norther" but plenty of good water and grass.[10]

Allowing his horses a day to recuperate, Mackenzie at mid-morning on November 2 headed southwest. Sighting a few Indians off to the right, the command gave chase, but soon resumed its course, and at sunrise, having ridden forty-five miles since leaving the Double Mountain Fork, arrived at Laguna Rica (Rich Lake), seven miles northeast of present Brownfield, where it halted for breakfast. From Rich Lake Mackenzie turned eastward, travelling by Mound Lake and through sand and shin oak, to Lagunas Quatras, four small lakes about ten miles west of present Tahoka.

As Mackenzie prepared to bivouac at the first "sufficient" water since leaving the Double Mountain Fork, the scouts discovered a herd of horses that led the command to eight Indian lodges four miles to the northeast. Charging the surprised Indians, the troopers killed 2 braves, captured 19 women and children, and rounded up 144 horses. Among the captives were some whom Mackenzie had taken on the North Fork of Red River two years earlier.[11] The command camped at the site of the "village," where there was good grass and water, until the next afternoon, and then moved eastward ten miles to Tahoka Lake, five miles northeast of the present city of Tahoka. On the following day, November 5, Lieutenant Thompson with nine scouts surprised a small camp, killing two Indians and capturing twenty-six horses and mules.[12]

When the women prisoners informed Mackenzie that most of the Comanches were on their way to the reservation and that the two small bands still on the Staked Plains intended to avoid the soldiers and go there in a few days,[13] Mackenzie, hampered by the captives and the inadequate corn for his weary mounts, decided to return to his supply camp. Leaving Tahoka Lake at noon on November 5, he stopped for the night sixteen miles to the southeast, descended the Caprock on the next day at present Post, and turning northeastward arrived late on November 8 at his Freshwater Fork base.[14]

With the arrival of several detachments on the next day, the second scout of Mackenzie's 1874 campaign had been completed. In ten days the troops had travelled more than 225 miles, had killed 4 Indians, and had captured 19 women and children and 170 horses. Although they had failed to find a large band of hostiles, their rapid movement had not allowed the frightened Indians any opportunity to prepare for the coming winter. Mackenzie reported that the captured horses had been given to the scouts, principally to two Mexicans who had been induced to join the expedition for a share of the plunder and to Tonkawa Johnson and three Lipans; some had been given to the other Tonkawas and the Seminole Negroes, and some had been assigned to the companies.

His own horses, having gone the entire ten days with less than one day's forage, were very weak, but as soon as he could feed them corn for a few days he would make one more scout between the heads of the Brazos and Red Rivers.[15] He was highly irritated at not having ample corn. The campaign had already cost him forty-four animals, and he was in need of two hundred good replacements, unnecessary had forage been supplied to Fort Griffin in accordance with his instructions. An adequate supply of corn, he wrote, should be kept on hand at Griffin and at least two thousand bushels should be kept in reserve at Concho and McKavett. "Some one must be much to blame that this has not been done;" the Colonel wanted a departmental investigation.[16]

The forage problem on the western frontier was not unique with Mackenzie, however. Adequately supplying rapidly moving cavalry for hundreds or perhaps thousands of miles in an unknown Indian country was next to impossible, particularly during the wet and cold autumn when the wagon trains had difficulty getting through the sticky prairie mud. The use of big, grain-fed horses made the cavalry dependent upon the wagon train, especially when grass was scarce. Consequently, Mackenzie had to remain in camp until his jaded mounts had revived on grain.

The men were not allowed to remain idle. Horses were shod, equipment repaired, and for two days the men were drilled on foot. On the 11th Lawton left for Griffin with one wagon train; another was already en route from Griffin. With the prospect for supplies looking good, Mackenzie prepared to leave on November 16 for a thirty-day scout.

A series of northers, however, made it "worse than useless" to attempt to travel over the boggy ground. One of the worst storms some of the men had seen struck on November 12, making it necessary to keep both men and animals sheltered as much as possible, and then another moved in on the 16th before the troops could start. Confined to his tent most of the day by the inclement weather, Mackenzie took time to inform General Augur, in a letter longer than usual, of his situation and plans. One of his trains had reached Supply Camp on the previous day with plenty of corn for a new start, and he hoped to get off on the morrow. Although his horses were "much worn," he was still able to mount 262 men on horses able to last under ordinary circumstances, and that

morning he had started forward the wagon train escorted by
thirty-seven infantrymen. He intended to scout the head of
the Double Mountain Fork of the Brazos and the lakes toward Fort Sumner and then swing back by way of the Palo
Duro, but the trails might lead elsewhere; one of his Mexican
guides believed that the hostiles were in Palo Duro Canyon
while another thought that they were at waterholes south and
west of Mucha-que. If he did not find any Indians on his
northern swing, he would then search the country toward
Fort Concho. There had not been enough hostiles yet killed,
in his opinion, to cause them to return to the reservation in
good faith; to bring the Indian problem to a final and satisfactory conclusion would likely require most of the winter.
In anticipation of permission to buy two hundred fresh horses
and of the long campaign ahead, he had decided not to send
any more companies to their posts.[17]

But Mackenzie did not start on the morrow nor even the
next because the storm did not let up for several days. The
morning of the 19th dawned clear, but the Freshwater Fork
country had the appearance of an arctic region. The tents
were enwrapped in a solid sheet of ice, and the horses, although each was covered with a blanket, "were nearly froz-
en." [18] In the Red River country not far to the north, Colonel
Davidson had twenty-seven mounts frozen on the picket
line.[19] By the next day the storm had passed, and Mackenzie
was fairly confident that he could start on the following
day.[20]

On the 22nd, Mackenzie had his cavalrymen draw one
hundred rounds of ammunition each, the infantrymen two
hundred rounds each, packed another ten thousand cartridges on the mules and in the wagons, and headed into an
icy gale, with 13 officers and 265 enlisted men of the 4th Cavalry, 38 infantrymen, including 2 officers, and 14 guides and
scouts. The route was up the valley of Blanco Canyon, thirteen miles the first day, to its head near present Floydada, about

thirty miles by the winding trail, where he remained a week because he could not get his wagons through the sticky mud.[21]

While waiting for another piercing-cold norther accompanied by heavy snow to pass and the mud to dry, Mackenzie on the 25th sent out three parties of spies. Two Mexicans and three Seminole Negroes were sent westward along the Double Mountain Fork of the Brazos to Salado Lake, just west of the Texas-New Mexico line; a Lipan and four Tonkawas were sent to scout the Palo Duro between the Tule and Blanca Cita Canyon; and Strong, Charlton, and three enlisted men were sent to the Quitaque region. If the scouts succeeded in finding an Indian camp, he intended to attack it at once. His cavalry horses had recuperated, thanks to the arrival of adequate forage, and the men were in fine spirits.

At the head of Blanco Canyon Mackenzie learned from Augur that Sheridan was thinking of having him move his Supply Camp to McClellan Creek and take over full responsibility for the remainder of the Red River War and for the military government of the Comanches and Kiowas. Augur, rather vaguely, asked for Mackenzie's opinion. The Colonel liked the idea of moving his Supply Camp to McClellan Creek, but he was anxious to finish the scout he was on; the fatigued men should then be sent to their stations to recuperate and be replaced with another column composed of the two companies of his cavalry at Clark and the three at Concho and McKavett. With the Indians on the run, the military should keep up the chase, even in the midst of winter, as long as any were off the reservation. "It is very important," he wrote, "that this business be got through with satisfactorily before we let go of it." [22]

Augur was not in complete accord with Sheridan's suggestion, particularly relative to supplying Mackenzie from Fort Dodge, Kansas. At least, he had written his superior, he wanted to ascertain Mackenzie's recommendation first, and Mackenzie was a long way from either train or telegraph sta-

tions. Sheridan shot back a reminder that the route from
Dodge to McClellan Creek would be closer and better than
any other, but he would leave the decision to Augur and Mackenzie. He was of the opinion that eight to twelve companies
would be adequate for McClellan Creek, and wanted a decision so that he could dispatch the necessary supplies.[23]

While Augur hedged, Sheridan began shipping supplies
for Mackenzie by way of Caddo to Fort Sill, and demanded
"If it cannot be done, *let me* hear, but whatever I hear must
be without conditions — I mean positive." Apparently not realizing the inconvenience of contacting Mackenzie during bad
weather on the Plains, by December 1 he had decided to go
ahead with the plan. Fearing the supplies passing through
Fort Sill would not be adequate, he directed that 120,000 rations and 800,000 pounds of grain be sent to Camp Supply
in Indian Territory, and sent fifty six-mule teams from the
Dakotas to haul the supplies to McClellan Creek. With these
steps taken, the impetuous Sheridan demanded of Augur an
immediate decision.[24]

Learning of Sheridan's desire for a "radical change" on
December 1 when several letters and copies of his superiors'
telegrams caught up with him, Mackenzie at once informed
Augur of his plans and wishes. Since his Supply Camp should
not be moved until the Indians in the Mucha-que country had
been "disturbed," he was altering his plans and would start on
the morrow on a scout of that area for ten to fifteen days.
Unless the matter of moving was urgent, he desired to establish the new camp on McClellan Creek with the five fresh
companies then at Clark, McKavett, and Concho. They could
be started for Fort Griffin at once, by slow marches to save
their horses. In consequence of the change of plans he was
reorganizing five companies from the seven, relieving those
left in Cos. F and K of further field duty and starting them at
once for Fort Richardson. Although the remaining men and
horses would be badly worn by the time he reached his Fresh-

water Supply Camp, he would entrain at once for McClellan Creek if it was thought best, but would need more forage than he currently had on hand.[25]

Later in the day Mackenzie again wrote Augur, emphasizing the need for a fresh command, including infantry, and for strong horses. He wanted Major Anderson, who had gone to Concho in October, sent back to replace one of the infantry captains who "is a good man but has no head." He would bring the troops in the field with him to Griffin as soon as he could complete the scout to the southwest, and he then wanted personally to discuss the plans with the General. Mackenzie also advised Augur to send a good command to the lower Pecos and the Guadalupe Mountains because some of the Kwahadi Comanches would join the Mescaleros at one of those places as a result of his next scout.[26] Upon receipt of this information, Sheridan, who had high regard for Mackenzie's judgment and military ability, wired Augur that Mackenzie and the other columns could go to their posts and that Colonel Miles would keep a small camp on Sweetwater Creek in the eastern Texas Panhandle during the winter.[27]

Meanwhile, the scouts, who had been far to the northeast, north, and west, returned without having found any sign of Indians except where a party on their way south several weeks before had camped between Salado Lake and Muchaque.[28] Thus, on the morning of December 3 Mackenzie had the supplies on the wagon train transferred to two hundred cavalrymen and the pack mules, started Cos. F and K, the empty wagons, and the infantry on the back trail, and headed southwest, straight for Tahoka Lake and Las Lagunas Quatras. After spending the first night at a small pond of good water fifteen miles from the starting point, just west of present Ralls, the command broke camp early the next morning and marched another fourteen and a half miles before halting for "breakfast" at mid-day in the Rescate Canyon of the

Double Mountain Fork of the Brazos where it had been on October 31.

Despite a heavy rain and sleet storm that afternoon, Mackenzie moved rapidly for Lake Tahoka, but darkness and the storm compelled him to bivouac before he found it without wood, water, or grass. Here, where some of the horses froze to death, the men spent one of the most miserable nights they ever experienced in the Southwest. When at daylight the scouts reported that some Indians were camped at Lake Tahoka, only three miles away, Mackenzie set out at once to charge the camp. Not an Indian was there, but something more welcome was found — a ravine on the west edge of the lake that provided some shelter against the sleet, snow, and cold wind. Although there was no wood to warm the numbed men nor grass to fill the hungry horses, Mackenzie decided to take advantage of the windbreak and wait out the storm.[29]

The weather having cleared by the next morning, Mackenzie followed a fresh trail thirteen miles southwest to Las Lagunas Quatras where, again finding no Indians, he turned sharply to the southeast and camped on December 6 a short distance south of present Tahoka. While descending the arroyo toward Mucha-que the next day, one of the scouts surprised and killed an Indian.[30] After camping that night on a "large arroyo" at the edge of the Caprock, about midway between Gail and Lamesa, the command on the 8th moved five miles southwest to the Colorado River, about twelve miles northwest of present Lamesa. Learning from a scout that five Comanche braves were lurking about three miles from the camp, Mackenzie ordered Lieutenant Lewis Warrington, Co. I, who had been with the regiment since 1867, to take ten men and attack the Indians. The hostiles fled upon seeing the detachment, but after about two miles one of the braves, his horse having become exhausted, covered another mile on foot before being overtaken and captured by Warrington.[31] Turning the prisoner over to one of his men whose horse had failed,

Warrington and two of his men in a six-mile chase managed to wound one Indian while he was changing to a fresh horse, and to overtake and kill two who had abandoned their exhausted mounts. After shooting one of them through the lungs, Warrington dismounted to reload his carbine. While he fumbled frantically for his cartridges, which had slipped into the lining of his coat, the fallen brave jumped to his feet and charged his assailant with an arrow. When the Lieutenant beat him off with his rifle, the Indian attempted to escape on the cavalryman's horse, but a well-placed shot by another trooper foiled the attempt. Meanwhile, the other two had disappeared, and the troopers, whose horses were jaded, made no further effort to follow them. Mackenzie thought that Warrington's "excellent conduct" deserved some recognition.[32]

This encounter and other Indians seen in the distance by Warrington led to the conclusion that a large band of hostiles might be camped at one of the lakes to the west. Hoping to surprise them, Mackenzie made an all-night march, arriving before noon at Lagunas Sabinas (Cedar Lake), a favorite campsite about eighteen miles northwest of present Lamesa, where he found a supply of dried buffalo meat but no Indians. Since the Mucha-que valley was his main target, the disappointed commander turned back on his trail and on the 10th camped on the Colorado where Warrington had had his encounter with the Comanches.

Continuing down the valley of the Colorado until he was about fourteen miles west of present Gail, Mackenzie on the morning of the 12th turned to the northeast and headed for the mouth of Duck Creek, where he expected to rejoin the Freshwater camp contingent of his column, and in accordance with the approval given by Sheridan on December 8, send his men to the posts for a rest. Moving leisurely to watch for signs of Indians, he stopped for the night on an arroyo just north of Mucha-que Peak, and after eighteen miles the

next day halted his weary column near present Fluvanna
where there was water and good grass. Here he spent three
days to wait out a severe rain and snow storm and to await
the arrival of the wagon train. Lack of corn, long marches,
and the blizzard made it impossible for the horses to continue,
and the men, now subsisting largely on buffalo meat and con-
tinually hungry and almost barefooted, were in no condition
to travel in the blizzard. Several worn-out horses had to be
shot during the storm. Fortunately, the overdue wagon train
rumbled into camp on the night of the 14th in time to save
most of the horses and the cold and hungry troopers a great
deal of misery.

The storm having let up on the morning of the 16th and
his men and horses having been well fed for a day, Mackenzie
resumed the march, but after nine miles through snow and
sticky mud stopped for the night on the Fort Concho road at
McKenzie Mountain, about twenty miles north of present
Snyder, then circled to the east side of the mountain, forded
the Double Mountain Fork of the Brazos on the 17th after
breaking ice one and a half inches deep, halted for the night
on the north bank of the river, trudged eleven more miles
through mud and snow on the next day to the Salt (Main)
Fork of the Brazos, where the command was blanketed with
a "heavy fall" of snow during the night, and on the morning
of the 19th crossed the Brazos and three or four miles beyond
joined the wagon train near the mouth of Duck Creek.[33] The
third and final scout of the 1874 campaign had been completed. For seventeen days Mackenzie and his blue-coated
cavalrymen had searched the southern part of the eastern
Llano Estacado from present Floydada on the north almost
to Snyder on the south, travelling more than 225 miles, killing
three and capturing one hostile.

Having received orders to be in San Antonio with his maps
and reports by Christmas day, Mackenzie paused at Duck
Creek only a few hours and then left by way of Fort Griffin

to keep his appointment with Augur. On the following morning, December 20, the Southern Column broke camp and
headed for a well-deserved rest at its posts, the infantry for
Concho and McKavett, the 4th Cavalry eastward on the Mackenzie Trail. The cavalry arrived at Griffin on December 28,
where Lee's Co. D went into quarters. Wint's Co. L continued its march and reached Fort Richardson on January 6,
1875, but Gunther's Co. H. and McLaughlin's Co. I laid over
at Griffin until January 7 before proceeding to Richardson,
where they arrived on January 12, encountering on the way
another snowstorm that dropped the thermometer to ten below zero. Two days later the weary troopers moved into
crude but to them comfortable quarters.³⁴

Except for some minor activity in the eastern portion of
the Texas Panhandle and western Indian Territory by Colonel Miles' troopers, the Red River War was at a successful end,
and to Mackenzie belonged the major credit. In four months
of hard campaigning the Colonel and most of his 4th Cavalry
had marched well over 900 miles, had fought one battle and
four skirmishes, had killed 11 and captured 22 Indians, and
had taken over 1,600 horses and mules, despite a short supply
of forage and the worst weather conditions imaginable. The
number of casualties inflicted in the four months of serious
campaigning is amazingly, almost unbelievably, small. The
psychological and economic results on the Indians, however,
rather than casualties were the factors that undermined Comanche and Kiowa resistance. Unable without their many
horses to obtain either food, clothing, or lodging during a
severe winter, or even to find a place on the unexplored Llano
Estacado where they could stop unmolested for more than a
few nights, they lost their desire for war honors and gradually drifted to the reservation. There was no need to establish a supply camp at McClellan Creek; Mackenzie instead
could assume military command at Fort Sill of the Kiowas
and Comanches. General Sheridan, who seldom lavished un-

due praise on his subordinates, was elated with the results of Mackenzie, Miles, Davidson, and Buell, and in his report for 1875 stated that "This campaign was not only comprehensive, but was the most successful of any Indian campaign in this country since its settlement by the whites; and much credit is due the officers and men engaged in it." Less than two years later Charles Goodnight attested to the accuracy of Sheridan's evaluation by establishing his ranch in the heart of the former dominion of the wild Kwahadis.

FOOTNOTES — CHAPTER IX

[1] Mackenzie, "Itinerary," September 29-November 8, 1874, as cited; "Scouting with Mackenzie in 1874," 532–533.

[2] Mackenzie, "Itinerary," September 29-November 8, 1874, as cited; "Scouting with Mackenzie in 1874," 533–539. The account of this phase of the campaign in the article "Scouting with Mackenzie in 1874" is almost identical with Carter, On the Border, and both amazingly are very closely in agreement with Mackenzie's "Itinerary," except that they include considerably more information. However, neither Carter nor the Adjutant General's Office of the National Archives at the time that Carter wrote the book were able to locate Mackenzie's report. Thus, the author of the article must have kept an excellent daily journal of the campaign; if not written by him, Carter obviously drew heavily from the article.

[3] "Tabular Statement of Expeditions . . . during the Year Ending August 31, 1875," as cited; Sheridan to Army Headquarters, October 19, 1874, in Taylor, Indian Campaign, 80; Lt. A. Raphall, "Map of Second Column, Indian Territory Expedition, 1874, commanded by Lt. Col. Buell" (photocopy in The Southwest Collection, Texas Technological College, Lubbock).

[4] Mackenzie, "Itinerary," September 29-November 8, 1874, as cited; "Scouting with Mackenzie in 1874," 536–539.

[5] Anderson to departmental headquarters, October 19, 1874, quoted in Carter, On the Border, 504.

[6] "Scouting with Mackenzie in 1874," 539; Carter, On the Border, 503.

[7] Anderson to departmental headquarters, October 19, 1874, as cited; "Scouting with Mackenzie in 1874," 540; Carter, On the Border, 505.

[8] Mackenzie to departmental headquarters, October 26, 1874, as cited.

[9] Mackenzie to departmental headquarters, October 29, 1874, 4437 DT 1874, Army Commands, RG 98; "Scouting with Mackenzie in 1874," 540. Both Carter and the author of "Scouting with Mackenzie in 1874" erroneously give the date as October 31.

[10] Mackenzie, "Itinerary," September 29-November 8, 1874, as cited.

[11] Ibid.; Augur to division headquarters, November 17, 1874, 2815 AGO 1874, RG 94; Mackenzie to departmental headquarters, November 9, 1874, 4530 DT 1874, Army Commands, RG 98.

[12] Ibid.; Sheridan to Col. W. D. Whipple, November 17, 1874, relaying

Mackenzie's telegram to Augur, November 8, 1874, 4883 (filed with 2815 AGO 1874), RG 94. In his report on November 9, Mackenzie erroneously stated that Thompson's skirmish with the Indians was on November 4.

[13] Mackenzie to departmental headquarters, November 9, 1874, as cited; Sheridan to Whipple, November 17, 1874, as cited.

[14] Mackenzie, "Itinerary," September 29-November 8, 1874, as cited; Gillespie, "Map of Expeditions," as cited.

[15] Mackenzie to departmental headquarters, November 9, 1874, as cited; Sheridan to Whipple, November 17, 1874, as cited.

[16] Mackenzie to departmental headquarters, November 9, 1874, as cited.

[17] "Scouting with Mackenzie in 1874," 540-541; Mackenzie to Augur, November 16, 1874, 4956 DT 1874, Army Commands, RG 98.

[18] "Scouting with Mackenzie in 1874," 541.

[19] Sheridan to Augur, December 1, 1874, 4676 DT 1874, Army Commands, RG 98.

[20] Mackenzie to Augur, November 21, 1874, postscript to the letter of November 16, as cited; Mackenzie to departmental headquarters, November 21, 1874, 4652 DT 1874, Army Commands, RG 98.

[21] "Scouting with Mackenzie in 1874," 541; "Regimental Returns," November, 1874, 5689 AGO 1875, RG 94; Mackenzie, Head of Fresh Fork Canyon, to Augur, November 27, 1874, filed with 2815 AGO 1874, RG 94; Carter, On the Border, 508; Mackenzie, "Itinerary of March of the First Column," December 3-19, 1874, to departmental headquarters, January 7, 1875, 252 AGO 1875, RG 94 (hereafter cited as Mackenzie, "Itinerary," December 3-19, 1874).

[22] Mackenzie to Augur, November 27, 1874, as cited.

[23] Sheridan to Augur, November 10, 12, 15, 18, and 21, 1874, 4394 DT 1874, 4415 DT 1874, 4452 DT 1874, 4468 DT 1874, and 4557 DT 1874, Army Commands, RG 98.

[24] Sheridan to Augur, November 28, December 1, and December 2, 1874, 4672 DT 1874, 4676 DT 1874, and 4726 DT 1874, Army Commands, RG 98.

[25] Mackenzie, Camp in Blanco Canyon, to Augur, December 2, 1874, printed copy filed with 2815 AGO 1874, RG 94.

[26] Mackenzie, Camp in Blanco Canyon, to Augur, December 2, 1874 (2d letter), printed copy filed with 2815 AGO 1874, RG 94.

[27] Sheridan to Augur, December 8, 1874, 4790 DT 1874, Army Commands, RG 98.

[28] Mackenzie to Augur, December 2, 1874 (2d letter), as cited.

[29] Gillespie, "Map of Expeditions," as cited; Mackenzie, "Itinerary," December 3-19, 1874, as cited; Carter, On the Border, 514-515. Again, Carter either had access to Mackenzie's journal (which he later disclaims) or he kept a very accurate journal of his own, because the daily journal reproduced in his book is in very close agreement with Mackenzie's.

[30] Mackenzie credited the deed to Strong, but Carter claimed that Strong appropriated the victim's scalp and claimed credit after one of the Lipans had killed him.

[31] The captive, a fifteen-year-old boy named Vidot, was later returned to his people at Fort Sill.

[32] Lewis Warrington to departmental headquarters, December 19, 1874,

submitted with Mackenzie, "Itinerary," December 3–19, 1874, as cited; Mackenzie to departmental headquarters, January 7, 1875, as cited.

[33] Mackenzie, "Itinerary," December 3–19, 1874, as cited; Carter, *On the Border*, 518–519; Gillespie, "Map of Expeditions," as cited.

[34] "Medical History of Fort Richardson," Vol. 238, p. 116, as cited; "Regimental Returns," December, 1874, as cited; "Scouting with Mackenzie in 1874," 542; Carter, *On the Border*, 519–523.

CHAPTER X

Trouble again on the Rio Grande

AFTER CONFERRING with General Augur relative to the Comanche-Kiowa war and his transfer to Indian Territory, Mackenzie on January 15, 1875, boarded a train for a well-earned vacation in Washington. In his absence, his cavalry, scattered from Clark to Richardson, were engaged in minor scouts, in securing and training recruits, in obtaining additional horses and supplies, and in transferring to Fort Sill. Captain Mauck with ninety-seven men from Fort Clark made a 450-mile scout of the lower Pecos River from December 28, 1874, to January 23, 1875, without seeing any Indians.[1] At Richardson, Lieutenant J. H. Dorst was helping the sheriff capture horse thieves, and Captain Heyl spent most of the time purchasing horses in the eastern part of the state.[2]

The transfer to Fort Sill took place slowly. The headquarters of the 4th Cavalry with the regimental band left Fort Clark on January 30, followed three weeks later by companies B and G. On March 14 three other companies started from Fort Richardson, and by May 6 all twelve companies had departed.[3]

Mackenzie assumed command at Fort Sill on March 16,[4] at a time when the impoverished and defeated Indians were still straggling in. Lone Wolf and his Kiowas had arrived in Feb-

ruary, and in April, 170 Kwahadi Comanches surrendered
themselves and over 700 horses.[5] Mackenzie sent word to the
holdouts camped at present Quitaque that if they would come
in, there would be no punishment, but if they did not, he
would exterminate them. Mow-way's band went to the post
at once, and on June 2 Quanah Parker reached Fort Sill with
407 of his people and 1,500 horses. Quanah's surrender marked
the end of Comanche resistance; there were only about fifty
holdouts remaining.[6] This time there was no peace council, no
parleying. In accordance with Sheridan's order, Mackenzie
on April 28 sent seventy-four warriors in charge of Lieutenant R. H. Pratt and two companies of cavalry to prison at San
Augustine, Florida.[7]

In the autumn of 1875 Mackenzie suffered an accident
from which he may never have fully recovered. When a
horse started suddenly, he toppled from a wagon, landing on
his head, and remained in a stupor for two or three days. It
was rumored that thereafter he became increasingly sensitive
and irritable. Certainly he reacted violently in 1876 when
anonymous critics associated him with the war department
frauds that led to the resignation of Secretary of War Belknap. The Colonel demanded an investigation, but Sherman,
knowing his innocence and not wanting him to become involved, cautioned him to keep quiet.[8]

Mackenzie ruled with an iron hand, but sympathetically
and justly; the Indians understood and respected him because
he was a successful warrior and because he worked for their
welfare. In December, 1876, while the Colonel was absent
from Fort Sill, a small band of Comanches left the reservation
and spent the rest of the winter in Thompson (Yellowhouse)
Canyon. Learning the next summer that the band had sneaked
back to the reservation, Mackenzie ordered the chiefs to arrest the leading offenders. Instead they came to parley. After
quietly listening for half an hour, the Colonel secretly had his
cavalry prepare for battle. As soon as the troops were ready,

he arose from his desk, picked up his hat, and calmly announced that "If you do not bring the renegades in in twenty minutes, I will go out to their camps and kill them all." Then he left the room. The Indians hastily complied.

On the other hand, Mackenzie worked zealously to help the Indians along the White Man's Road. Hoping to transform the nomads into herdsmen and to promote a weaving industry, he sold at public auction the Indian horses that had not been shot or kept by the military and scouts for about $23,000, and with the proceeds purchased 3,500 New Mexico sheep. Apparently, he never considered that the Indians detested mutton stew and that not one knew how to weave a rug or cared to learn. Many of the sheep died for lack of care, boys shot some for sport, and dogs and coyotes got the rest. He also issued the Indians 800 head of cattle, which they appreciated.[9]

Mackenzie was highly displeased with the criminally insufficient quantity and poor quality of the annuities issued the Indians. For example, cattle for beef, issued on foot, were so emaciated that there was little meat. Determined to have fair treatment, he complained to authorities, warning that "The pressing emergency would eventually goad the Kiowas and Comanches into a stampede from the agency." To alleviate as much misery as possible, he issued to the prisoners of war full rations, knowing that they would share with others, and sent detachments of troops with the Indians to hunt buffalo.[10]

By the time Mackenzie had the Indians within his jurisdiction quietly accepting the White Man's Road, he was sent north to help subdue the defiant Sioux and Northern Cheyennes, who were dissatisfied with their annuities, with the advance of the railroad, and with trespassing goldseekers in the Black Hills. After negotiations broke down, the United States opened some of the lands to miners and ordered the Indians, regardless of treaty guarantees, to return to their reserve by February 1, 1876. When Sitting Bull and Crazy Horse ignored the order, Sheridan sent three converging columns of troops under General Alfred H. Terry toward the Big Horn country where the two hostile Sioux chiefs were reported to be. Discovering signs in mid-June that Sitting Bull was encamped on the Little Big Horn, Terry sent Colonel George C. Custer with 265 men to block his escape into the Big Horn Mountains while he moved directly against the village. Custer, violating orders and not waiting for Terry, attacked the village on June 25, 1876, but Sitting Bull with his 2,500 warriors annihilated the entire command and then escaped. His success encouraged other Indians to leave the reservation or to show increasing defiance.

In July the Department of the Interior, aware of the growing hostility, turned over to the military the jurisdiction of the Red Cloud Sioux and Northern Cheyenne Agency. Sheridan immediately ordered Mackenzie to take six companies of his 4th Cavalry and assume command both of the District of the Black Hills and of Camp Robinson, Nebraska, the post that stood guard over the Red Cloud Agency. Reaching Camp Robinson on August 17, Mackenzie at once took a census of the agency and discovered that less than half as many Indians were on the reservation as the agent had reported in July. One large group of escapees, encamped about twenty-three miles from the agency, scoffed at Mackenzie's orders to return — but not for long. During the late summer and autumn Mackenzie built up his force to eighteen companies and "whipped" it into shape.[11] The defiant band, awakening on October 23 to find their village completely surrounded by Mackenzie's blue-coated soldiers, surrendered without a fight. Two hundred thirty-nine men, exclusive of women and children, were taken to the agency and 722 horses confiscated. The Indians at the Red Cloud Agency had been humbled in one stroke.

With the reservation quiet, General George Crook, commanding the Department of the Platte, placed Mackenzie in command of a winter campaign, known as the Powder River Expedition, against a large band of Northern Cheyennes under Chief Dull Knife, who had fled the Red Cloud Agency in time to participate in the slaughter of Custer's troops. In a blinding snowstorm on November 14, Mackenzie with 1,552 men, 6 surgeons, almost 400 Indian scouts, and 168 supply wagons rode out of Fort Fetterman on the upper North Platte for the Powder River, one hundred miles to the north. Eight days later scouts located Dull Knife's camp on the Red Fork of Powder River.[12] Packing rations for ten days and taking 363 Indian scouts and 818 troops, including his tough and reliable 4th Cavalry, Mackenzie in subzero temperature marched for the village. When he attacked soon after daylight on the 25th, the surprised warriors rushed to a sheltered spot surrounded by an open stretch of level prairie. After Dull Knife refused to surrender, Mackenzie ordered his men to burn the village, with its 173 lodges, huge quantities of hides and robes, and "tons" of buffalo meat, and then with Cheyenne bullets flying all around him led the dangerous assault against the Indian stronghold. One officer, at least, concluded that Mackenzie deserved the star of a brigadier general for the courage and skill he demonstrated on that day. The band escaped, but in the fight it lost twenty-five known dead and about five hundred ponies, while Mackenzie in turn lost one officer and five enlisted men killed, twenty-six men wounded, and fifteen cavalry horses killed. General Crook reported that he could not commend too highly Mackenzie's "brilliant achievements;" his victory would be a terrible blow to the hostiles.[13]

Through a new eight-inch snow on the next morning Mackenzie led his troopers back to the wagon train, where the dead were buried, and for the next few days searched the Powder River valley for the hostiles. On the 12th the temperature climbed to 8 degrees below zero — during the "warm spell" he shed his overcoat and overshoes. Further campaigning, however, was impossible, because neither the Union Pacific trains nor the wagons could deliver through the heavy snows the 30,000 pounds of forage needed each day. Thus Mackenzie turned back, spending Christmas Day, with the temperature as low as 42 degrees below zero, in the saddle.

Upon reaching Fort Laramie, Mackenzie found orders from Secretary of War J. D. Cameron to proceed to Washington where President Grant wanted him to command the troops in the event a national emergency resulted from the disputed presidential election between Rutherford B. Hayes and Samuel J. Tilden. When the crisis passed on February 23, Mackenzie was ordered to return to the field, and resumed command of Camp Robinson and the District of the Black Hills on March 13.[14] When he learned that Mackenzie had returned, Dull Knife, stripped of food, shelter, and clothing, led his people to Camp Robinson on April 21 and surrendered. During the surrender parley, he reportedly said to Mackenzie: "You are the one I was afraid of when you came here last summer." [15] Two weeks later Crazy Horse surrendered 889 of his people and 2,000 ponies to Mackenzie at the Red Cloud Agency. The Sioux and Northern Cheyenne war was over — less than nine months after Mackenzie had assumed command at Camp Robinson. On May 26 Mackenzie with his 4th Cavalry headed again for Fort Sill, and a few weeks later he handed over to the agent at Fort Reno, Indian Territory, 937 destitute Northern Cheyenne with the admonition that they be well fed and well treated.

Mackenzie was not long allowed to remain quietly at Fort Sill. After he left Texas, depredations along the Rio Grande border had been renewed with increasing intensity, and the Texans were anxious to have him returned to that troublesome area. In May, 1876, William Steele, Adjutant General of Texas, and Governor Richard Coke requested Sherman to send Mackenzie and the 4th Cavalry to the Rio Grande. Steele reported that Mackenzie's action in crossing the Rio Grande "after robbers has made him more popular in Texas than any other officer in the U. S. Army," and Coke stated that his presence "would give a feeling of security," on the Rio Grande border. Sherman, still dubious about the intentions of the Kiowas and Comanches, replied that Mackenzie "is protecting the frontier of Texas better where he is than he could by serving in that Department." [16]

The situation by the autumn of 1877 had grown sufficiently serious to claim the attention of the Congress. General Ord had been given authority on June 1 to send troops across the river when in hot pursuit of bandits, but thus far the attempts had been ineffectual. [17] During a hearing of the House Committee on Military Affairs, General Sherman stated that Mackenzie and the 4th Cavalry should be sent to replace one of the cavalry regiments then stationed along the Rio Grande, because "it would give us a commanding officer there who would secure peace by his very presence; . . . General Mackenzie is a man of untiring energy, and the Texas people want him there." [18] When he obtained the authority needed for aggressive action, Sherman immediately called Mackenzie to Washington and ordered him to move his headquarters and six companies (A, D, E. K, L, and M) of the 4th Cavalry to Fort Clark at once, [19] to assume command of the District of the Nueces, and to put an end to the intolerable situation along the border.

As soon as he returned from Washington, Mackenzie started from Fort Sill in a pouring rainstorm on December 17, 1877, with his cavalry and a wagon train; the command was thirteen days reaching Red River and three crossing it, but the Colonel, furious over the delay, would not wait for fair weather. At Henrietta the grateful citizens insisted on honoring Mackenzie and his officers with a banquet and a ball. While the officers dined and danced, many of the troops to Mackenzie's disgust and irritation became "dead" drunk on cheap bootleg whiskey. From Henrietta, the command proceeded through Jacksboro and Fort Griffin, and then southward along the old military road through Fort Mason. At Fredericksburg, Mackenzie sent the command directly to Fort Clark, while he went to San Antonio for a conference with General Ord.[20]

Upon his arrival at Fort Clark, Mackenzie at once began preparing to carry out his assignment. He directed his trustworthy subordinate at Fort Duncan, Lieutenant Colonel Shafter, to accept any Lipan Indian prisoners offered him by Mexican officials and to "use every exertion to capture" any marauders.[21] As a further defensive measure, he established at strategic sites eight subposts, manned by alert detachments of cavalry.[22] Always anxious to negotiate with Mexican officials, Mackenzie in March asked Brigadier General A. R. Falcon of the Mexican Army, whom he regarded as an honest officer, to cooperate in an effort to destroy the marauders.[23] Falcon, however, as Mackenzie expected, replied that he lacked authority and could do no more than forward the request to his superiors.[24] His effort to secure Falcon's cooperation having failed and the raids by the Lipans having continued despite the energetic defensive efforts of his troops, Mackenzie by May was convinced that he could secure peace only by destroying the Lipan village near Santa Rosa.[25] Early in May, he sent a "reliable" *Comanchero* who had been a valuable scout on the Plains to Santa Rosa as a spy.[26] Although he planned to attack the village as soon as he had gathered the necessary information, he requested Ord's "explicit approval" for the "moral support" it would give him.[27] Ord assured Mackenzie of his full support, and advised him that if he crossed the river in pursuit of raiders, to take advantage of the opportunity and attack the Lipan village.[28]

Thus assured, Mackenzie organized into two columns a formidable force, just in case he should encounter Mexican opposition. The larger column, consisting of three battalions of infantry, three batteries of artillery, two companies of cavalry, and forty wagons filled with thirty days' rations under the command of Shafter, was to move 150 miles to Santa Rosa and there establish a supply base.[29] The scouting column, consisting of four companies of the 8th Cavalry, two of the 4th, and a group of Seminole Negro scouts, led by Mackenzie and Captain Samuel Young, 8th Cavalry, was to search the region between the Rio Grande and the *Serranias del Burro* before joining Shafter.[30]

The scouting column on June 11 moved from its rendezvous camp to Winker's Crossing on the Rio Grande, fifteen miles above the mouth of Devils River. Delayed twenty-four hours by high water, it forded without incident the next evening and pushed ten miles onto foreign soil before making a dry camp.[31] Marching at six o'clock the next morning, it found excellent water seven miles to the south-southwest in Sora Cañon, and from there rode west for twenty-four miles before making another dry camp.[32]

Here the surgeon announced that the guide was too ill to travel during the heat of the day. Thus Mackenzie broke camp at 2:00 a.m. on the 14th and marched nine miles to Burro Mountain where the guide expected to find an abundant supply of water, but there was only enough for coffee and for the pack mules. The horses went thirsty. Assured that water could be found about thirty-five miles distant, Mackenzie set out for the spot but after following the incompetent guide for twelve miles across the desert he was only four miles from Burro Mountain.[33] Fearing that his animals would perish, Mackenzie headed for the Rio Grande and sent a courier off to Shafter with an order to return to the American side.

Not long thereafter, however, he struck good water, and finding his horses in better condition than expected, he decided to search the region between the San Diego and San Rodrigo rivers, headquarters for a large group of cattle thieves. Upon receiving word that Mackenzie had again changed plans, Shafter led his force across the Rio Grande on June 15 and proceeded slowly up the San Diego until he met Mackenzie two days later.[34]

Heavy rains on the 18th limited the march to six miles, but after starting at 1:00 A.M. the next morning in hope of making a surprise attack, Mackenzie reached Remolino, near the location of his 1873 raid, to find himself confronted with a small force of Mexican troops commanded by Colonel Pedro Valdez ("Colonel Winker") rather than a body of surprised and frightened Indians.[35] He sent to Valdez, whom he regarded as a gallant but corrupt soldier, a message asking his cooperation against the cattle thieves. Valdez courteously replied that although he opposed cattle stealing, he was under orders to repel the American invaders. Seeing that Valdez was too weak to attack him, Mackenzie shot back word that he intended to rest his men and horses and for him to stay on the opposite side of the village.

Soon after lunch, Mackenzie sent word to Valdez that he intended to set out at 3:00 p.m. and that the Mexican troops were directly in his line of march. Colonel Jésus Nuncio, who with additional troops had joined Valdez, replied that he would not allow him to pass without his "word of honor in public" to "give satisfaction" to Nuncio's superiors and to the Mexican people; when this was done, he would escort Mackenzie's troops to the Rio Grande.[36] Mackenzie, as might be expected, unhesitatingly rejected the Mexican officer's proposal.[37] At three o'clock Mackenzie moved forward, Shafter's column along the right bank of the San Rodrigo and Captain Young's cavalry column along the left bank. Upon seeing their approach Nuncio, whose force was no match for the blue-coated raiders, withdrew and was nowhere in sight when Mackenzie encamped for the night nine miles down the river. The next day at noon, as the column was continuing down the Rio Rodrigo, the Mexican cavalry was seen in the rear, but it never approached nearer than five or six miles.

On the next morning, the 21st, having come within a mile and a half of Monclova Viejo, about seven miles from the Rio Grande, Mackenzie sent one of his lieutenants to assure the villagers that he intended no harm. The emissary soon returned with a report that Nuncio had stationed his troops on a hill

RANALD SLIDELL MACKENZIE, 1876
(*U.S. Signal Corps photo, National Archives*)

overlooking the American line of march, and a few minutes later Valdez came to the camp with a new demand from Nuncio for a public apology and reparations for the violation of Mexican territory. Mackenzie curtly informed him that any apology or reparations would have to be made by higher officials. Valdez thereupon warned Mackenzie to be ready to guard himself against attack and terminated the interview. Undisturbed by the implied threat, Mackenzie ordered Captain Young to advance on the Mexican position with a part of his 8th Cavalry and the Seminole scouts while Colonel Shafter moved to flank it. When Nuncio saw the Americans advancing, he hastily retreated without firing a shot. Mackenzie had planned for Shafter to recross the border at Piedras Negras, but to avoid the possibility of a clash and the further humiliation of Colonel Nuncio, he crossed the entire command near Monclova Viejo without further incident.[38]

The expedition, largely due to the incompetence and illness of the guide, failed to accomplish any tangible results; in 1873 Mackenzie had taken every possible precaution to avoid an encounter with Mexican troops: this time he not only made no effort to avoid them but even dared them to attack.[39] Indirectly the reappearance below the border of Mackenzie, Sherman and Sheridan's favorite warrior, influenced the Mexican government to take steps to break up the cattle stealing. President Porfiro Diaz, largely as a gesture for home consumption, denounced the invasion as an "unwarrantable outrage," and announced that he had ordered the army to repel any invaders. Diaz, however, was determined to establish law and order in his country, and to encourage foreign investments that would bring industrial development and economic prosperity, and he expected most of the capital to come from the United States. The achievement of his goal, therefore, was dependent upon amicable relations with his northern neighbor. Thus, it was no surprise that he let the matter drop with only a note from the Secretary of Foreign Affairs to John W. Foster, the United

States minister to Mexico, mildly complaining that Mackenzie at Remolino had taken sixty head of cattle, burned some fences, and destroyed sixty *fanegas* of cultivated land.[40]

After Mackenzie returned to Fort Clark, General Ord cast aside his caution and recommended that not only should the depredators be punished but also those who abetted them. Sheridan, even more drastic, thought that Congress should authorize the military occupation of the country between the Rio Grande and the Sierra Madre Mountains, but Sherman disagreed.[41] While his superiors were discussing alternatives, Mackenzie decided to make another effort to catch the depredators. Although the river was so high that he lost several of his pack mules, he began fording it on July 4. Before all his command was across, however, a courier arrived from Fort Clark with orders from the War Department to halt the movement,[42] pending what steps President Diaz might take to settle the border problem.

The American government was willing for its troops to cross the border only if in hot pursuit of marauders and if they avoided conflict with Mexican troops. With these restrictions, troops under Mackenzie on several occasions did enter Mexico. Captain J. M. Kelley, 10th Cavalry, with fifty-two men on July 25 crossed the Rio Grande near the mouth of the San Felipe River, and succeeded in recovering seventeen horses.[43] Confident that the Mexicans would not fire upon a strong force, Mackenzie, upon learning on August 15 that the bandit Areola had driven another herd of Texas cattle across the river to sell to Nuncio for feeding his troops, sent Lieutenant Thompson and Captain Young with six companies of cavalry in pursuit. On the next morning the Americans seized Newtown, a small village near the mouth of the San Diego River, but failed to catch Areola, who reportedly clad only in his hat, had made his exit on seeing the approaching blue-coated cavalry.[44] But again Mackenzie recalled his troops to the American side of the river—this time because of a combination of factors:

the inability to track the stolen cattle beyond Newtown, high water in the Rio Grande that interfered with the transportation of supplies, Lieutenant Thompson's incapacitation due to a sunstroke, and Colonel Nuncio's assurance that he would do all within his power to punish the thieves.[45] In reporting this incident, Mackenzie revealed his exasperation with the entire situation. Under his existing orders, he complained, he could do nothing to prevent Mexican troops from eating American beef. The best way to end the depredations would be to seize the territory as far south as Saltillo,[46] but he was not fully aware of Diaz's desire to establish peaceful relations with the United States.

Within another month tension along the border had relaxed. The Mexican press began blaming the laxity of its own officials for the trouble and calling for the extermination of the marauders, and Mexican officials established a number of posts and sent word to Mackenzie that they were anxious to cooperate in putting an end to the lawless situation. In response to the request for a conference, Captain Young, Mackenzie's emissary, met with Colonel Felipe Vega, one of the Mexican commanders in the area, and worked out procedures for cooperative action.[47]

Depredations had continuously diminished from the time Mackenzie had arrived at Fort Clark, and with Mexican cooperation they almost ceased. In October General Ord reported that thirty-four fewer Americans had been killed by the raiders than during the preceding year, and that most of the murders had occurred before Mackenzie had taken to the field; a few days later General Sherman reported a "most satisfactory condition of affairs . . . along the Rio Grande frontier." [48]

For another year there was little for Mackenzie to do except maintain vigilance and carry out the routine affairs of a commander of a military district, but Sherman and Sheridan kept him at Fort Clark to assure the continuation of peace. The knowledge that he would cross the border whenever conditions were not satisfactory spurred the Diaz government and local Mexican authorities to make serious efforts to prevent any further depredations in Texas.

FOOTNOTES — CHAPTER X

[1] "Mackenzie's Record of Service," as cited; Mackenzie to Adj. Gen., February 5, 1875, 545 ACP 1875 (filed with 3877 ACP 1873), AGO, RG 94; Brig. Gen. E. O. C. Ord, commanding the Department of Texas, annual report, September 10, 1875, 5689 AGO 1875, RG 94.

[2] "Medical History of Fort Richardson," Vol. 238, pp. 125, 116, as cited.

[3] "Movement of Troops in the Department of Texas from August 31, 1874, to August 31, 1875," 5689 AGO 1875, RG 94. Fort Sill was transferred on March 11 to the Department of the Missouri, commanded by General Pope.

[4] "Mackenzie's Record of Service," as cited; Nye, *Carbine and Lance*, 231, gives the date as March 22.

[5] Mackenzie to Pope, April 21, 1875, 2162 AGO 1875, RG 94.

[6] Agent J. M. Haworth, annual report, September 20, 1873, in 44 Cong., 1 Sess., *House Exec. Doc.* I, pt. V, Vol. I, pp. 773-777; Richardson, *Comanche Barrier*, 394; Carter, *On the Border*, 526; Carter, *The Old Sergeant's Story*, 113-114.

[7] Nye, *Carbine and Lance*, 231.

[8] Dorst, *20th Reunion*, App., 18; Mackenzie to Adj. Gen., May 11, 1876, and Sherman's reply, Mackenzie's ACP file, as cited.

[9] Parker, *The Old Army*, 48-49; Nye *Carbine and Lance*, 250; Ernest Wallace, "The Comanches on the White Man's Road," in West Texas Historical Association *Year Book*, XXIX (1953), 14 ff.

[10] Report of John P. Hatch, printed in the *New York Times*, May 4, 1875; Mackenzie to Sherman, August 31, 1875, (index number missing) AGO 1875, RG 94.

[11] Mackenzie to General George Crook, August 18, 1876, Army Commands, RG 98; Mackenzie to Crook, September 30, 1876, 6003 AGO 1876 (filed with 4163 AGO 1876), RG 94; Secretary of War, "Report," November 10, 1876, 44 Cong., 2 Sess., *House Exec. Doc.* I, pt. 2 (Washington, 1876), p. 48. For an excellent account of Mackenzie's service on the Northern Plains, see Lessing H. Nohl, Jr., "Bad Hand, The Military Career of Ranald Slidell Mackenzie, 1871-1889" (Ph.D. dissertation, University of New Mexico, Albuquerque, 1962).

[12] Crook to Adj. Gen. Townsend, November 28, 1876, filed with 4163 AGO 1876, RG 94.

[13] Mackenzie to Crook, November 26, 1876, and Crook to Townsend, November 28 and December 1, 1876, 6866 AGO 1876 and 7182 AGO 1876 (filed with 4163 AGO 1876), RG 94; Dorst, *20th Reunion*, App., 12; Crook, annual report, August 1, 1877, in Secretary of War, "Report," 1877, 45 Cong., 2 Sess. (Washington, 1877), pp. 84-86.

[14] Dorst, *20th Reunion*, App., 18; "Mackenzie's Record of Service," as cited; Sherman to Mackenzie, January 23, 1877, and Sheridan to Sherman, February 23, 1877, both filed with 3877 ACP 1873, AGO, RG 94.

[15] *New York Tribune*, April 23, 1877.

[16] William Steele, Adj Gen. of Texas, to Army Headquarters, May 30, 1876,

endorsement of Richard Coke, Governor of Texas, and Sherman's reply, June 9, 1876, 3228 AGO 1876, RG 94.

[17] Secretary of War, "Report," 45 Cong., 2 Sess., *House Exec. Doc.* I, pt. 2 (Washington, 1877), p. xiii.

[18] Testimony by Sherman, November 23, 1877, Committee on Military Affairs, "The Texas Border Troubles," June 6, 1878, in 45 Cong., 2 Sess., *House Misc. Doc.* 64 (Washington, 1878), 47-48.

[19] Sheridan, Chicago, General Order No. 10, December 3, 1877, filed with 1653 AGO 1875, RG 94.

[20] Parker, *The Old Army*, 86-98.

[21] Mackenzie to Shafter, February 25 and 26, 1878, 2431 AGO 1878 and 1926 AGO 1878 (both filed with 1653 AGO 1875), RG 94. The Records of the War Department cited hereafter in this chapter are microfilm copies in possession of Ernest Wallace. Unless indicated, the index and record group numbers are either missing or not legible.

[22] Ord, annual report, October 2, 1878, in Secretary of War, "Report," November 19, 1878, 45 Cong., 3 Sess., *House Exec. Doc. I*, pt. 2 (Washington, 1878), pp. 81 ff.

[23] Mackenzie to A. R. Falcon, March 10, 1878, 2431 AGO 1878 (filed with 1653 AGO 1875), RG 94; Mackenzie to departmental headquarters, March 19, 1878, 2431 AGO 1878 (filed with 1653 AGO 1875), RG 94.

[24] Falcon to Mackenzie, March 13, 1878, 2431 AGO 1878 (filed with 1653 AGO 1875), RG 94.

[25] Mackenzie to departmental headquarters, May 18 and 28, 1878, 3848 AGO 1878 and 3953 AGO 1878 (both filed with 1653 AGO 1875), RG 94.

[26] Mackenzie to departmental headquarters, May 9, 1878, DT, Army Commands, RG 98.

[27] Mackenzie to departmental headquarters, May 28, 1878, as cited.

[28] Ord to Mackenzie, May 30, 1878, 3953 AGO 1878 (filed with 1653 AGO 1875), RG 94.

[29] Parker, *The Old Army*, 104.

[30] Mackenzie to departmental headquarters, June 23, 1878, 4712 AGO 1878 (filed with 1653 AGO 1875), RG 94. In this letter, hereafter cited as "Mackenzie, report," Mackenzie gives, for him, a rather detailed account of the expedition.

[31] *Ibid.; Galveston Daily News*, June 27, 1878.

[32] Mackenzie, report, June 23, 1878, as cited.

[33] *Ibid.*

[34] *Galveston Daily News*, June 27, 1878; Mackenzie, report, June 23, 1878, as cited.

[35] Mackenzie, report, June 23, 1878, as cited.

[36] Jésus Nuncio to Mackenzie, June 19, 1878, enclosure with Mackenzie, report, June 23, 1878, as cited.

[37] Mackenzie, report, June 23, 1878, as cited.

[38] *Ibid.*

[39] *Galveston Daily News*, June 25 and 27, 1878; Sheridan to Sherman, June 24, 1878, 4505 AGO 1878 (filed with 1653 AGO 1875), RG 94.

[40] *Galveston Daily News*, August 22, 1878; J. W. Mata, Secretary of Foreign Affairs, Mexico, to John W. Foster, United States Minister to Mexico,

July 12, 1878, in "Foreign Relations of the United States," in 45 Cong., 3 Sess., *House Exec. Doc.* I, pt. 1, pp. 555–557.

⁴¹ Ord to Sherman, July 1, 1878, 4772 AGO 1878, Sheridan to Sherman, July 2, 1878, 4772 AGO 1878, and Sherman to George W. McCrary, Secretary of War, July 6, 1878, 4772 AGO 1878 (all filed with 1653 AGO 1875), RG 94.

⁴² Parker, *The Old Army*, 109.

⁴³ J. M. Kelley to Headquarters, District of the Nueces, July 26, 1878, 5585 AGO 1878 (filed with 1653 AGO 1875), RG 94.

⁴⁴ *Galveston Daily News*, August 20, 1843; Thompson to Mackenzie, August 16, 1878, 6392 AGO 1878 (filed with 1653 AGO 1875), RG 94; Deposition of Bonifacio Galan, August 7, 1878, enclosure with Mackenzie to departmental headquarters, 6392 AGO 1878 (filed with 1653 AGO 1875), RG 94.

⁴⁵ Ord to Sheridan, August 17, 1878, 5851 AGO 1878 (filed with 1653 AGO 1875), RG 94; *Galveston Daily News*, August 20, 1878; Thompson to Mackenzie, August 16, 1878, as cited.

⁴⁶ Mackenzie to departmental headquarters, August 19, 1878, as cited; endorsement of Ord to Sheridan, August 22, 1878, on same; endorsement of Ord to Sheridan, August 27, 1878, on Mackenzie to departmental headquarters, August 22, 1878, 6276 AGO 1878 (filed with 1653 AGO 1875), RG 94; Sherman to Sheridan, August 9, 1878, 5465 AGO 1878 (filed with 1653 AGO 1875), RG 94; McCrary to Sherman, August 19, 1878, 5465 AGO 1878 (filed with 1653 AGO 1875), RG 94.

⁴⁷ Colonel Felipe Vega to Mackenzie, September 7, 1878, enclosure with Mackenzie to departmental headquarters, September 9, 1878, 6867 AGO 1878 (filed with 1653 AGO 1875), RG 94; Mackenzie to departmental headquarters, September 9, 1878, as cited.

⁴⁸ R. B. Myers to Mackenzie, October 19, 1878, 7706 AGO 1878, RG 94; Ord to division headquarters, December 27, 1878, 8859 AGO 1878 (filed with 1653 AGO 1875), RG 94; Ord, annual report, October 1, 1879, and Sherman, annual report, November 1, 1879, both in Secretary of War, "Report," 46 Cong., 2 Sess., *House Exec. Doc.* I, pt. 2 (Washington, 1879), pp. 90, 6.

CHAPTER XI

An Epilogue

THE RESTORATION of peace on the Rio Grande border marked the end of Mackenzie's career on the Texas frontier, for Sherman and Sheridan sent their favorite Indian fighter elsewhere to settle crises. Three years later, after having removed the Utes from much of western Colorado and quieted the Apache and Navajo disturbances in Arizona and New Mexico without a single battle, Mackenzie returned to San Antonio to command the Department of Texas, but less than two months later he was on his way to an asylum, his plans and dreams for the future abruptly destroyed by tragic illness.

On October 2, 1879, Mackenzie was ordered to move six companies of his cavalry to Colorado. The Utes at the White River Agency in northwestern Colorado three days before had killed Agent N. C. Meeker and nine of his employees, captured several women and children, and then had ambushed a relief column of troops, killing eleven and wounding thirty-three others. With the permission of the Interior Department, General Sherman ordered Sheridan to send Colonel Merritt, 9th Cavalry, with a strong force to the White River Agency, and another "preferably under Mackenzie," to Fort Garland in southern Colorado to prevent an outbreak among Los Pinos Agency Utes who lived along the Uncompahgre River between the present cities of Montrose and Ouray. Starting from Fort Clark on October 6, the 4th Cavalry travelled by train to Fort Garland where Mackenzie joined his command on October 27.[1]

Sherman instructed Mackenzie to allow the Indian Bureau time to negotiate a removal treaty, but to be prepared at any moment to move to the Los Pinos Agency. While negotiations dragged, Mackenzie accumulated supplies and built up a force of fifteen hundred well-drilled men, and then in May, 1880, led his troops across the Cochetopa Pass to the Agency, where he passed a quiet and uneventful summer writing letters in which he contemptuously denounced both the Indian commissioners and the government for their mild policy toward renegade Indians. The awe he generated, however, by his frequent scouts and by the way he drilled and handled his men seemingly inspired the Indians in August to agree to move to Utah.

The Indians having agreed to move, Mackenzie in September left Colorado to serve as a witness before a court of inquiry and to visit with his family in New York City, and the 4th Cavalry went to winter quarters in Kansas. While Mackenzie was in the East, a strong movement developed to get him appointed to a vacancy in the brigadier general rank. The Colonel greatly coveted the promotion, not only because he felt that it was well deserved but also because his old wounds might cause him less suffering if he had a less strenuous life. However, a young officer's attempt at wit upon seeing his commander gazing at the stars — "I'm afraid, General, there's Miles between you and that star"— proved prophetic. Nelson A. Miles got the appointment.

As a result of these developments, no doubt, Mackenzie, after a prolonged conference with Sheridan, on January 15, 1881, assumed command of the Department of Arkansas, apparently created for his benefit. In May the department was abolished and Mackenzie was ordered to resume his old command and to return to the Los Pinos Agency where the Utes were showing indications that they did not intend to move. Mackenzie reached the Agency on June 6 to find the Utes "hostile, well-armed, and dangerous."

When on August 22 the agent informed them that they must start for their new reservation in Utah within three days, the Utes began preparing for war. Mackenzie, having anticipated resistance, fortunately had made it possible to communicate with Washington by completing eighty miles of telegraph line on the day the crisis arose. When the tribal headsmen appeared at the agency post on August 25 to learn if they had been granted permission to remain in their ancestral homeland, they were told that the Secretary of Interior had turned them over to the War Department and that they would have to see Mackenzie.

A few minutes later Mackenzie, backed by only a few of his unarmed officers, coolly informed the delegation that he expected the tribe to draw rations and start their trek two days later. The armed and defiant chiefs proposed compromise and delay. After listening a few minutes, the Colonel interrupted:

I have been ordered by the Army to see that you move to the new reservation. . . . It is not necessary for me to stay here any longer. You can settle this matter by discussion among yourselves. All I want to know is whether you will go or not. If you will not go of your own accord, I will make you go. When you . . . have arrived at a conclusion, send for me.

With that Mackenzie strode away. The dumbfounded chiefs, unaccustomed to such summary treatment, quickly decided to move. Two days later 1,458 Utes left their beloved homeland. Even before they reached their new reservation hundreds of whites had swarmed over the beautiful valley they left behind. By his firmness and coolness Mackenzie had possibly averted an Indian war. The settlement of the Ute problem without bloodshed Mackenzie afterwards regarded as the greatest deed of his life.

There were, however, other Indians still unsubdued and Sherman and Sheridan were still at the head of the army. On

September 2, as the Utes approached their new reservation, a courier galloped into Mackenzie's camp. The Apaches in Arizona were on the warpath and General O. B. Willcox, commanding the Department of Arizona, was not able to handle the situation. The Colonel with his 4th Cavalry was to proceed at once to Arizona.

Starting with six companies of the 4th Cavalry on September 5, Mackenzie travelled by train to Fort Wyngate with instructions to keep the road open to Fort Apache and to prevent the Navajoes from joining the Apaches. By the time he reached Wyngate, however, General Sherman, disgusted with Willcox's confusion and determined to crush the disturbances if it took the whole army, ordered Mackenzie to take command of all troops in the field in Arizona, despite the fact that the Department of Arizona was within the Division of the Pacific. Highly indignant over Sherman's action in placing Mackenzie in command of the field forces, Willcox and General Irvin McDowell, commanding the Division of the Pacific, protested to Secretary of War Robert T. Lincoln, who hesitantly accepted Sherman's argument that the arrangement must be kept until "the moral effect intended by sending Mackenzie there has been fully accomplished." Mackenzie likewise was not happy with the arrangement, but was not ordered to withdraw until he reported in October that, inasmuch as the White Mountain Apaches had surrendered and the Chiricahuas had gone to Mexico, additional troops were no longer needed in Arizona. Although the Arizona campaign added little glory to Mackenzie's reputation, it is significant that Sherman thought enough of his ability to place him in command of all field forces even at the cost of friction among his officers, and that within one month peace had been restored.

On October 30 Mackenzie assumed command of the District of New Mexico, a position that made him an administrative officer rather than a field commander. The Indian problem in New Mexico was peculiarly difficult. Not only was there a

large number of Indians (26,000 to 28,000), many of whom
were hostile, but the Apaches, both in and out of the Territory,
ignored military departmental and international lines, making
pursuit extremely difficult. Determined to keep peace, Mackenzie kept spies in contact with the hostiles, and sent Lieutenant Colonel George A. Forsyth with the 4th Cavalry into Mexico in 1882 in an "indefatigable pursuit" of Apaches from Arizona who had been raiding in New Mexico, an action that
General Sheridan applauded.

During this uprising, Sherman suggested the possibility of
adding New Mexico to the Department of Arizona and making Mackenzie, "who would make quick work of the Apache
matter," brigadier general in command, but Secretary of War
Lincoln did not think it advisable, possibly because of arousing
anew the friction among the officers concerned. At any rate,
the uprising was crushed, and some runaway Jicarillas, Navajoes, and Mescaleros were forced to return to their reservations.
In his report that autumn, General Pope attributed the relatively peaceful situation in New Mexico to Mackenzie's judicious management.

The grateful citizens of the Territory wanted Mackenzie
promoted for his services. At their convention in September,
1882, the Republicans incorporated into their platform an endorsement of the "judicious administration" of military affairs
in New Mexico by the "faithful and efficient" Mackenzie, and
a few days later Governor L. A. Shelton wrote Lincoln that
Mackenzie

is vigilant, able, and just as an officer, and possesses perfect integrity
and high character as a man. He has in a superior degree all the ele-
ments in a military and administrative officer. During his brief period he has been in command he has won the confidence and gratitude of the people of New Mexico. This promotion would . . .
greatly tend to the promotion of efficiency in the Army.[2]

Major General Thomas W. Hyde, under whom Mackenzie
had served for a time during the Civil War, wrote the President

that Mackenzie was the "best man in service after Sheridan for a large command in case of trouble," and that the Texas delegation in Congress was united in wanting him promoted.[3] On October 26 Mackenzie was informed of his promotion. The recommendations, no doubt, helped, but Mackenzie obtained the promotion, according to Dorst, through the influence of U. S. Grant, who told President Chester A. Arthur that the reward was a matter of simple justice and that he wanted it as a personal favor.

By the time he received the news, which carried with it no specific assignment, Mackenzie was in sad condition, both physically and mentally. Immediately, the local citizens began a movement to have him retained in New Mexico, but the General wanted duty on a court or a retiring board in Washington or New York, because he had suffered "much harder in the last two years than anyone has any idea of." He also needed to know his assignment in time to make arrangements for his mother and sister who were with him at Santa Fe and to "transfer" his property.[4]

Since affairs in New Mexico were quiet, Mackenzie was granted a leave on November 17. The records do not reveal his activities during the next three months, but presumably most of the time was spent at the home of his brother Morris in New York City. He returned to his post in February, 1883, but nothing of military significance in the District occurred before he was reassigned on October 27 to command the Department of Texas.

Mackenzie reached San Antonio on October 30 and two days later took command. Since there was no longer any Indian problem in Texas, his first concern was to bring to a satisfactory conclusion the sporadic raiding along the Rio Grande border. Toward this end, he at once conferred with Colonel Valdez of the Mexican Army,[5] but whatever plans that were made, if any, were never known, for it was the General's only military act of any significance in his new command.

In fact, shortly after his arrival at San Antonio, the General's behavior became a strange contrast to that of the Fighting Colonel whom the Texans had known a few years before. His efficiency and devotion to his job was noticeably less; instead of total abstinence, his drinking became "worthy of the name of dipsomania;" his "eccentricity" was notably pronounced; and for the first time in his career he was spending much time in the company of a lady. Surgeon Passmore Middleton, recognizing his unusual behavior, at times irrational, began treating the General on December 9; on the next day the Chief Quartermaster at the post also became convinced of his insanity.

The General's lady friend was the young widow of Dr. Redford Sharpe, the former Florida Tunstall, whom he first met in 1868 while boarding in her parents' home in San Antonio. Later she married Dr. Sharpe, an army surgeon who was stationed at Fort McKavett while Mackenzie was in command of that post. By December 18, it was common knowledge that the forty-three-year-old bachelor general, who had never had time for social affairs, was to be married to the thirty-four-year-old Mrs. Sharpe.[6] Apparently with the intention of retiring in Texas, the General had bought a ranch north of San Antonio near Boerne.

The marriage, however, was never consummated; the excitement was too much for the deteriorating mind of the overworked and physically debilitated General. On December 18, Mackenzie indicated to Adjutant Thomas M. Vincent that he was not in his usual mental condition, although Dr. Middleton thought he seemed much better. That evening while visiting in San Antonio Mackenzie "escaped" the two officers with whom he had gone. Soon after midnight he became involved in an altercation with two owners of an establishment who, thinking the violent stranger was drunk, with the aid of some passing Mexicans beat him into submission and then tied him to a cart where he remained unidentified until the police arrived at daylight and returned the General to his post.[7]

Later that morning Medical Director James R. Smith found that Mackenzie tended in his discourse to be "entirely personal and braggadocio." He diagnosed the trouble as a continuation of the cerebral attack that the General had suffered while in New Mexico, and concluded that he was no longer mentally capable of continuing in command. Adjutant Vincent immediately reported the Medical Director's findings to his superiors with his own endorsement. By the 22nd Vincent decided that it might be necessary to send him to an asylum, and two days later, after three physicians concluded that there was no hope for a speedy recovery, Harriet Mackenzie, who was in San Antonio, asked Sheridan, who had succeeded Sherman as General of the Army, to send her brother to the asylum in Washington.

Mackenzie was tricked into going quietly. During some of his delusions he raved that the army needed reorganization, a job that only he and Sheridan could do. Vincent asked Sheridan to order Mackenzie to come to Washington for such a conference. On Christmas Day the Secretary of War, "in the best interest of the service," directed Mackenzie to come to Washington.

Early the next morning Mackenzie, his sister Harriet, two aides, two orderlies, and Dr. Middleton boarded a special pullman car on the Missouri Pacific. At Sedalia, Missouri, Dr. Middleton was handed a telegram directing him to take his patient to Bloomingdale Asylum in New York City. The change was ordered by the Secretary of War upon the recommendation of Admiral C. P. Rodgers and other "friends" of the family after they had conferred with Sheridan, Adjutant General R. C. Drumm, and army physicians. Miss Mackenzie, who had not been consulted in the matter, protested to Sheridan and Secretary of War Lincoln, but in vain.

At St. Louis the Mackenzie party changed to the Pennsylvania's "St. Louis Express." When the eastbound train rolled into Pennsylvania's Jersey City station on Saturday evening, December 29, it was met by a physician, an attendant, and

Morris Duer, a relative of Mackenzie. The party at midnight reached Bloomingdale Asylum at Boulevard and 11th Street, New York City, where Dr. Charles A. Nichols, Medical Superintendent of the institution, took charge.

Mackenzie failed to respond to treatment. On February 22, 1884, Nichols informed the anxious Sheridan that in his opinion it was unlikely that the General would ever recover sufficiently to "reliably discharge any of the duties of his office." On the basis of this and other reports and a number of private letters, Sheridan asked the Secretary of War to have a retiring board consider Mackenzie's case.

The retiring board, headed by Major General Winfield S. Hancock and including two army surgeons, convened at Bloomingdale Asylum on March 5. Early in the hearing, Mackenzie, upon being asked if he had anything to say, replied:

I think that I am not insane. I think that I have served faithfully as any body in the Army. I would rather die than go on the retired list. The Army is all I have got to care for, — I don't wish to stay here.

The Board, however, agreed with Dr. Nichols, who had been associated with institutions for the insane for thirty-seven years, that the General was suffering from general paresis, or "general paralysis of the insane," incurred from "wounds received and exposure in the line of duty as an officer of the Army." [8] When the Board informed him of its decision, Mackenzie pleadingly protested, but to no avail:

You all know me, and have known me a great many years, and I think it very harsh if I am left out of the Army where my services have always been gallant and honest and faithful, and for a few months sickness.

In accordance with the Board's recommendation, Mackenzie was retired from the army on March 24. In acknowledging the order, Mackenzie complained that he had been treated in a "most unprecedented way," and expressed the hope that he would be restored to active service as soon as he recovered.

While hopefully waiting for the impossible, he remained quite comfortable at Bloomingdale, receiving friends and attending places of amusement, until June 14, when he went to live at his boyhood home at Morristown, New Jersey. In September he informed army headquarters that he had spent a quiet and pleasant summer at Morristown, where he would remain until the next April when he would probably go to San Antonio to look after "my interests." He never made the trip to San Antonio.

In 1886 Mackenzie was moved to the home of Morris Duer at New Brighton, Staten Island, where, attended by his sister Harriet, he grew increasingly weaker until he succumbed on January 19, 1889, to "general paresis." The newspapers, as previously noted, gave scant attention to his passing, but a respectable group of friends and relatives gathered in the beautiful cemetery of West Point to pay their respects as the corpse was laid to rest beside a host of other military great. At the early age of forty-eight Ranald Slidell Mackenzie had more than earned the right to rest in eternal peace. After the lapse of sufficient time to appraise his work judiciously, there are probably few, if any, who understand the nature of the nomadic Indians and the hostile geography of the Great Plains who would not agree with Sheridan, Sherman, and Grant that the accomplishments of the bold and gallant Fighting Colonel of the 4th Cavalry were among the most significant developments in the history of the Texas frontier.

FOOTNOTES — CHAPTER XI

[1] Since this chapter is merely an epilogue to the central study, documentation, except in a few unusual instances, is not used; if thoroughly done, the citations would be longer than the narrative itself. The principal sources, however, are Parker, *The Old Army*; Dorst, "Mackenzie," *20th Reunion*; "Letters Received" in AGO-RG 94, Army Commands, RG 98, and Mackenzie's ACP-AGO-RG 94 file; the printed reports of the Secretary of War and the Commissioner of Indian Affairs in *House Executive Documents*; George A. Forsyth, *Thrilling Days in Army Life* (New York, 1900); H. H. Bancroft, *History of Colorado* (San Francisco, 1870); H. H. Bancroft, *His-*

tory of Arizona and New Mexico (San Francisco, 1889); *San Antonio Light*; and *Galveston Daily News*.

² Newspaper clipping entitled "The Platform Adopted by the Republican Party in Convention on September 21st," Albuquerque, New Mexico, September 23, 1882, and Governor L. A. Shelton to Hon. Robert T. Lincoln, October 14, 1882, 6032 ACP 1882 (filed with 3877 ACP 1873), AGO, RG 94.

³ Thos. W. Hyde, late Comdg. Brigade, 6th Corps, to President, 6143 ACP 1882, filed in *ibid.* Many other letters of recommendation are in this file.

⁴ The handwriting in this particular letter is partially illegible and bears strong evidence that its author had suffered a stroke or had been adversely affected by some physical or mental handicap.

⁵ *Galveston Daily News*, October 31, November 1 and 14, 1883.

⁶ *San Antonio Light*, December 18, 20, and 27, 1883; *Galveston Daily News*, December 21, 1883. The date for the wedding is problematic. The *San Antonio Light* on December 18 reported that it would occur one week from that day — Christmas Day, two days later it announced that the wedding would take place on December 27, and on December 27 the editor stated that it was to have been "just one week ago today." Nohl states that it was to have taken place on December 19, but a careful evaluation of all the evidence indicates that December 20 was the date set.

⁷ *Santa Fe New Mexican Review*, April 3, 1884; Thomas M. Vincent, Asst. Adj. Gen., San Antonio, to Adj. Gen., Washington, and Adj. Gen., Division of the Missouri, Chicago, December 19, 1883, 6245 and 1245 ACP 1883 (filed with 3877 ACP 1873), AGO, RG 94. A copy of the report of James R. Smith, Medical Director of the Department of Texas, on Mackenzie's health was enclosed with Vincent's reports. The account hereafter of Mackenzie's illness, retirement, and death is compiled from a mass of official telegrams, correspondence, and reports filed with 3877 ACP 1873, AGO, RG 94.

⁸ The diagnosis, though logical at the time, was made many years before the medical profession discovered that general paresis was caused by syphilis infection. A careful comparison reveals that Mackenzie's condition and behavior was almost identical with the norm patterns for patients with the disease as described in recent studies.

Index

Adams and Wickes, government contracting firm, 62, 63
Adobe Walls, 72; attack on, 121
Alamogordo Creek, 71
Albee, George, 133
Amangual, Francisco, 69
Anadarko, Oklahoma, 123; battle with Indians at, 139
Anderson, Adrian N , xii, xviii
"Anderson's Fort," reason for name, 147
Anderson, Thomas M., 125, 130; commands Supply Camp, 131, 132; Mackenzie asks for, 161
An-zai-te, 142
Apache Indians, xvii, 4, 185; in Arizona, 188, in New Mexico, 189, surrender of, 188
Apache Indians: Chiricahua, flee to Mexico, 188
Apache Indians: Jicarilla, 189
Apache Indians: Lipans, 106, 110, 176; escaped, 102; location of, 97; Mackenzie ordered to attack, 176; raids in Texas, 93; village, 100
Apache Indians: Mescalero, 161, 189; escaped, 102; location of, 97; raids in Texas, 93
Appomattox, surrender at, 11
Arapaho Indians, 22, 121
Archer City, Texas, 21
Areola, steals Texas cattle, 180

Arizona, 189; Apache uprising in, 4; Mackenzie ordered to, 188; Sherman recommends Mackenzie as commander of, 189
Arkansas, Department of, Mackenzie assumes command of, 186
Army of the Potomac, 7, 8
Arthur, Chester A., 190
Aspermont, Texas, 129
Atascosa County, Texas, 93
Atkinson, Henry M., 109; distributes goods to Kickapoos, 109; negotiates with Kickapoos, 107–109; requests release of Kickapoo captives, 108
Augur, C. C., 69, 77, 92, 108, 123, 124, 125, 154, 157, 161, 165, 169; asks Mackenzie's opinion, 159; consultation with Mackenzie, 85–86; demands release of white prisoners, 87; Indian campaign organized by, 124; inspects Mackenzie's command, 88; inspects Southern Column, 126; issues orders for 1872 campaign, 64–65; issues orders for 1874 campaign, 129–130; lauds Mackenzie, 74; opposes Sheridan's plan, 159; plans for 1873 campaign, 87–88; provisions for Indian captives, 86; relative to Mackenzie moving Supply Camp, 159; replaces Reynolds, 64; requests supplies for Mackenzie, 130

197